To Paul,
Never Underestimate
follow your dreams ☺

THE **MAN** **INSIDE** THE **MACHINE**

The Approved Biography Of Steve Edwards - One Of The World's Most Successful Multi-Marathon Runners

Best Wishes

Steve Edwards

HELEN SUMMER

First published by Starpress Publishing in 2016

Cover images of Steve & Teresa extracted from photographs
taken by - Martin Campbell - Grasmere

Printed by
Dolman Scott Ltd
www.dolmanscott.co.uk

Former UK Athletics endurance coach, club and county runner, press officer and disabilities officer, Helen Summer, has been involved in running for over 40 years. Her proudest athletic moment was watching one of her former athletes win silver at the London Paralympics. Helen has written for running magazines, women's publications and the *Food & Drink Guide* and is the author of two books – *Running Crazy* – true stories from people who have run over 100 marathons, and *Are You Tough Enough?* – featuring over 70 of the world's toughest endurance events.

www.helensummer.com.

The Man Inside The Machine
The Approved Biography Of Steve Edwards
One Of The World's Most Successful Multi-Marathon Runners
Helen Summer

- *'What Steve has achieved is amazing.'* Daley Thompson CBE
- *'Who is to say that a marathon world record is better than running 500 marathons under 3 hours 30 minutes?'* David Moorcroft MBE OBE
- *'In an event [the marathon] in which excellence and eccentricity rub shoulders, he [Steve Edwards] deserves to be regarded as distinctive.'* The Daily Telegraph
- *'His misadventures are the stuff of legends.'* The Daily Telegraph
- *'Edwards is the marathon marathon man.'* The Independent
- *'What is so remarkable is not just the number of marathons, but their quality.'* Polytechnic Marathon Souvenir Programme
- *'The time standard set by Edwards has also been considerably higher.'* The Sunday Times
- *'The man who knows all there is to know about running 26.2 miles.'* Runner's World
- *'One of the most unique sportsmen in the world.'* Wilts & Gloucester Standard

Copies of this book may be purchased direct
by emailing teamedwards@hotmail.co.uk,
seasidehelen@hotmail.co.uk or through
www.helensummer.com.

CONTENTS:

ACKNOWLEDGEMENTS AND DEDICATION:

For some years now many people, inside and outside the running community, have suggested I write a book. At first I was sceptical, not imagining for one minute that anybody would really be that interested. But then, in 2011, I met author, Helen Summer. Helen was writing *Running Crazy*, a book featuring members of the 100 Marathon Club. Over time, we became good friends and discussed the idea of my biography, with Helen suggesting that I was capable of writing it myself! I wasn't so sure. However, it got me thinking more about it. I liked the idea of preserving an account of my life so far, which might perhaps help to inspire others looking to achieve something positive in their own lives.

My biography would, of course, revolve around what I've tried to achieve in the sport of multi-marathon running, but I wanted it to be more than that. I remember going through school being told by teachers that I had the 'potential' to do better, without ever being told exactly what that meant or, indeed, how to achieve it. Also, most people only know me as 'Steve the runner'. I turn up at a race, run, and then go home. Which brings me back to people suggesting I write a book. They wanted to know what motivates me, what drives me, how I keep going, and why I do what I do. They also, perhaps, wanted to know a little bit more about the person who can at times be a little shy, the closed book - who was the man behind the multi-marathon runner and how did he achieve his potential?

Having read *Running Crazy*, I thought Helen would be the perfect author for my book; but would she want to write it? By chance, Helen happened to be at a marathon in May 2014 promoting her two books, *Running Crazy* and *Mental!* (now '*Are You Tough Enough?*'), so I asked her, and she said yes. I then spent every spare minute over the next 18 months writing the 'bones' of my story, some 200,000 words! I included everybody I'd ever met, especially 100 Marathon Club members and the year they completed their 100th marathon - it was the pioneers of that club back in the 1980s, few though they were, who inspired me to join the world of multi-marathon running in the first place. However, I was advised that with the average book containing around 90,000 words, there wouldn't be room for them all. I therefore apologise to those who don't get a mention – it wasn't for lack of trying! That said, I still feel it important to thank everyone I've met who has helped forge the person I've become today.

Writing my 'bones' has made me realise how much life is like a tapestry. You look back at events that unfold and realise you go in certain directions at certain points that ultimately lead to where you are today. It could all have been so different!

Although I've tried to give an accurate account of everything that has happened to me during my life so far, some 53+ years, I apologise if I've made any mistakes or forgotten something that should perhaps have been included.

And so, to the people I wish to thank for helping me on my incredible journey:

- Dr Ron Hill MBE, one of the all-time running greats and a huge inspiration to me, for being kind enough to write the foreword to this book.
- 100 Marathon Club members, past and present, and the Brathay 10in10 family for inspiring and supporting me.
- My club mates at Alvis RC and Bourton Roadrunners for their support and inspiration.
- All the race organisers, crews and marshals. Without you, there wouldn't be any events!
- The physios, sports therapists and consultants who have helped keep me on the road, including Lucy Walmsley, Gary Edwards, Richard Rasdall, Clare Woodward, Amy Bateman, Graham Theobold, Anthony Fox, Peter Stanworth, Rod Jaques and Peter Binfield.
- My current sponsors: Mannatech (nutritional supplements); Team Nutrition (hydration and recovery drinks); and Sub Sports (compression and base layer clothing).

- My family, especially my parents, Pauline and Terry, for raising me with the right moral values and development to be the person I am today.
- Helen Summer – for not only writing the book, but also for her integrity and professionalism during the whole process. As a private person, I've found it a challenge to reveal my innermost feelings and experiences from the past to somebody else. It's something I've never really done, apart from with my wife, Teresa, and I thank Helen for making it so painless.
- All those not mentioned above who have helped me in my life or who I've shared the road with in a race. Sadly, I cannot mention you all, but you will know who you are.

This book is dedicated to my lovely wife, Teresa, best friend and soul mate. I couldn't have achieved all that I have without your love and support. I will be forever in your debt.

XXX

Steve Edwards

INTRODUCTION
BY HELEN SUMMER

When Steve first asked me to write his story in 2012, I was reticent. I explained to him that whilst his story (or what I knew of it at that time which, as it turns out, was very little), was admirable and of interest to his family and close friends, it would probably not be of much interest to the wider public – which meant the book would never get published. However, I saw no reason why he shouldn't write it himself.

Move forward two years. My first book, *Running Crazy,* is doing quite nicely and people seem to be enjoying it – which is the main thing. It's also become apparent that non-runners have been enjoying the book too – because it is essentially about human endeavours to overcome the odds through running marathons. In other words, it has the human-interest factor.

In those two years, I'd also got to know Steve and his adorable wife, Teresa, a whole lot better, and gained far more insight into just what Steve has overcome to achieve his remarkable running record. More importantly, I'd come to know him as a person and learned of his personal struggles, his inner fears, and his courage to overcome such. I also learned why

Teresa is so important to him. In other words, I learned about his whole life, not just his running life.

Just as revealing was seeing how runners and non-runners responded to Steve and how he responded to them at races. He was never too tired, self-obsessed or disinterested to listen, to offer advice if asked for, to encourage, or to give of himself. I noticed too that if I was signing books at a marathon event and Steve was nearby, people wanted him to autograph the book and to have their photo taken with him.

Such is the man's position amongst the marathon tribe.

And so I changed my mind. I'm a woman, what did you expect?

And I'm so glad I did, because writing Steve's book has been both an honour and a privilege. For me, Steve Edwards is a marathon guru, and an incredibly modest one at that. There can be nobody in the world better qualified to give advice or talk about marathons than a man who ran his first marathon aged 18, after just six weeks' training, wearing old football trainers, learned from the experience, and then, 30+ years, 700+ marathons and several world records later, reckons he's still learning. But take it from me - what he doesn't know about marathons isn't worth writing about.

Many people today take on physical challenges and set world firsts, but these are usually carried out over a finite period, and then that's it. Their challenge, great as it is, is over. They can rest. Maybe they'll even write a book about it.

But for Steve Edwards, the challenge continues, even now after 30+ years of running. He still pushes boundaries and sets new records. Above all, Steve Edwards wants always to do nothing less than his best. And, while he has breath in his body, he intends to continue doing so.

As for how great his achievements are, that may be for others to answer in the future. For perhaps the true gauge of a great achievement is whether or not it stands the test of time; only then can its greatness be measured.

My thanks go to Steve for allowing me to write his story, which was very much a joint effort, him writing his bones, me fleshing them out; to Pauline, Terry and Teresa for their input and proofreading the manuscript; and, finally, to Steph Stafford for casting her professional writer's eye upon my words. Despite all those checks, if there remain any errors or omissions, I consider myself wholly responsible and apologise unreservedly.

FOREWORD BY DR RON HILL MBE

I know something about marathon running. On October 13th, 1985, I became the first person to have run 100 marathons, having run 47 marathons that year to get there. My 100th was on the original course from Marathon to Athens (chosen because I'd won marathon gold there in the 1969 European Games). At the time of my 100th I was 47 years old and finished in 2:43:56.

In March 1992, Steve Edwards was somewhat ahead of me, running 100 marathons by age 28. At 29, he completed 87 marathons in a 12-month period. The stage was set for an incredible series of marathon achievements.

After my 100th, many more marathons were anticipated. In fact, only 15 happened, of which just three stand out. Two were London Marathons – 1988 in 2:51:47, and 1991 in 2:51:12. I could accept that these were my slowest ever times, but the last six miles of each had really hurt. I asked myself: 'Why am I doing this? What have I got to prove?' But I didn't wish to retire at 114 marathons – an odd number! I would go for 115. I targeted the 100th running of the Boston Marathon, five years ahead. In 1970, I'd been the first Brit to win the race, so it seemed a fitting stage on which to bow out. In 1996, I finished the race in 3:12:46; my slowest time ever, and my marathon career was over.

Looking at Steve's statistics, my final marathon time of 3:12:46 is identical to the second as Steve's average finish time for his fastest 500 marathons!

I have met Steve on several occasions and always found him polite and self-effacing. The last time was at the Great Langdale Marathon in 2013. This was a super-tough, hilly, two-lapper (I only ever ran the half-marathon there), and Steve must have known it would affect his average times. I think it was his 600th marathon. He accepted the challenge finishing 12th overall, and 1st in the 50+ age category, in 3:22:26. What a man! And a gentleman at that. He has now run over 700 marathons. When you look at his barely credible statistics, remember that all this has been achieved while holding down a full-time job – and I have not mentioned injuries!

Spare a thought for his wife, Teresa, too. Her support, both past and future, has been and remains vital for Steve's exploits.

Long may he continue setting records that will never be surpassed.

Dr Ron Hill MBE
Former Olympian, European & Commonwealth champion, holder of 4 world records, second man in the world to break 2:10 for the marathon, and 1st Brit to run 100 marathons. Dr Ron (77), also holds the record for the longest running streak – running every single day for the past 51 years, and counting.

PROLOGUE

1974

In a secondary school in the city of Coventry, a 12-year old boy finishes his games lesson and enters the changing rooms. As usual, he carries with him the stigma of not having been picked for a team until he was the last boy standing. But that is nothing compared to the dismay he feels when he lowers his shorts to his ankles and notices the telltale damp patch, only then becoming aware of the warm moistness still tingling hotly on his inner thighs.

He bows his head in shame, steps out of the soiled shorts before gathering them gingerly from the floor with his gnarled excuse for a hand, and waits for the taunts to begin. He doesn't have to wait long

The boy, who is known at school as, 'Spaz, Hook, Fingers, and Cripple', is Steve Edwards, and he is their fall guy.

2012

The excited crowds watch awe-struck as the tall, tautly muscled and tanned, 49-year old lead runner hones into view. He crosses the finish line, arms triumphantly aloft, before falling to his knees and bowing his head as if in supplication. His wife joins him, and gathers him lovingly into her arms.

But the intimacy of their embrace is interrupted by the surging crowds, taking photos and popping champagne corks, for this is what they've been waiting for - the first time anyone in the world has run 500 marathons under 3 hours 30 minutes. It is a record that will gain entry into the record books and is likely to outlive the man, his children and, quite possibly, his grandchildren too.

The man, who is known in marathon circles as, 'The Godfather', is Steve Edwards, and he is their hero.

Chapter 1

ABOUT THE BOY

Steven Clive Edwards was born on the 29th November, 1962 in the Gulson Road Hospital, Coventry, to Terence (Terry) Edwards (27), a former Coldstream Guardsman/aircraft fitter-turned-window cleaner, and wife, Pauline, (19), a former legal secretary/semi-professional singer.

Sadly, the joy of their first child's birth was marred by the discovery that Baby Edwards had been born with only half his left hand. The half-hand had no fingers; just three tiny nodules, referred to as 'rudimentary digits', and a twisted thumb.

With no familial history of any kind of deformities and little help from the authorities, the stunned young couple followed the only medical advice they were given and allowed the three 'digits' to be trimmed off. The hand was then stitched leaving a neat scar and the thumb. The thumb came complete with nail but no central bone and was flexible enough that it could be bent ninety degrees in any direction.

More bad news followed. Shortly after Steve's birth, self-employed Terry, broke his leg and was unable to work or continue making the damp, former rented property they were buying, habitable. As normal back then, Pauline had also stopped working to care for their baby. With sick pay and unemployment benefit non-existent, the only financial relief available was a small amount of 'National Assistance'.

It was not an auspicious start for the young Steve. However, neither he nor his parents are the sort to dwell on life's difficulties; instead, they accepted their lot and got on with their lives.

The family adopted the same attitude to Steve's disability, refusing to notice it or make allowances for him, letting him find his own way of dealing with any problems it caused as he went along. This suited Steve, whose parents describe as a very determined child; never giving up if something was difficult, sticking stubbornly to the task until he succeeded.

However, despite the setbacks and lack of material wealth in the Edwards' household, there was no lack of love and all three recall those early days with happiness, with Pauline and Terry describing the young Steve as: '...a happy, sunny child, a joy to be around.'

In fact, the only time they recall Steve being slightly less than happy was when sister, Samantha, was born.

'Didn't they have any little boys?' complained the four-year old, who'd wanted a brother to play with.

Female siblings aside, Steve's natural ebullience spilled over into all areas of his young life; he loved to dance and was quite the comic, playing up to an audience whenever possible.

Indeed, Steve stayed that way right up until he started Ravensdale Infants and Junior School in September 1967, at the age of four.

That was when the bullying started.

It came as a total shock to Steve. Up until then, he'd always been treated the same as everyone else and had never considered himself any different. Being born without fingers on one hand was the same as being born with brown hair instead of blonde. It wasn't an issue, it was just part of who he was.

But for the children of Ravensdale School, existing in an era when political correctness and disability awareness weren't even a glint in a politician's eye, a boy with no fingers was ripe for ridicule.

Soon, the happy-go-lucky Steve found himself the butt of everyone's jokes. Not only did the children delight in calling him names such as, 'Spaz, Hook, Cripple, Fingers and Thumbs', they took even greater delight in pulling on the elasticated tie (supplied by his parents to make life easier), and letting it spring back in his face.

The teachers also picked on him - the boy without fingers was easy to identify in a crowd.

It was probably hardly surprising then that as he grew a little older - apart from a few friends his own age like Darren Edwards, who, as well as sharing the same surname also shared Steve's passion for Thunderbirds and Joe 90 - Steve tended to play with younger children or girls, who were less inclined to ridicule him.

Consequently, by the age of eight, Steve's best friend was a girl called Carol. The pair spent hours playing together, acting out scenes from their favourite television programmes such as The Persuaders and The Champions, or racing down hills in the go-kart built by Steve's father from an old pram chassis and named 'Speedy Deedy' by Carol. They remained firm friends until Carol started secondary school a year ahead of Steve, when her mother told him somewhat mysteriously that, 'Carol has other things to do now'.

Away from Carol and school, Steve attended Sunday School, Cubs, and later Scouts, and embarked on the martial art of Aikido. He also loved to collect anything that had significant meaning to him, from stamps to football programmes, a trait that has stayed with him throughout his life.

Like most children in the 1960s and 1970s, Steve's days were spent outside, playing football and cricket at the local park or having conker fights – safety goggles not required! When darkness fell and his mother or inclement weather forced him inside, he'd content himself with Lego or Meccano, Dinky cars or Action Man. He also enjoyed entertaining his family with magic tricks, and played a mean game of chess, beating all his contemporaries in the junior school chess club and some adults.

And if all his parents could afford to give him was one shilling (5 pence) pocket money each week, Steve's enthusiasm in spending it on comics such as Beano or Dandy and sweets such as Black Jacks and Fruit Salads (eight for one old penny in those far off, halcyon days), knew no bounds.

Likewise, with school trips unaffordable, the family's annual summer holiday more than compensated, with Terry driving them to Devon in his work van. Steve and Sam sat in the back on a bench-seat made by Terry, which, according to Steve: '...wasn't very comfortable and we could only see out through the front and back windows, but it got us there!'

Steve fondly recalls those holidays - paddling, crabbing in rock pools and spending his holiday money in the penny arcades; his enthusiasm ensuring he always ran out of pennies before his more prudent sister.

In a nutshell, Steve was, and still is, passionate about living; a few missing fingers were no deterrent, he had life and he entered into pretty much everything it offered him with undiluted enthusiasm.

But children are cruel; they care nothing for enthusiasm. If a child is buck-toothed or wears bottle-end glasses or has no fingers on one hand, he will not be chosen for a sporting team until he is the last boy standing. And so it was for Steve. Despite demonstrating time and again that his zeal came accompanied by a good level of skill and leg speed, he was sidelined in favour of children whose physical appearance matched the majority.

At least in this instance the teachers were able to separate Steve's disability from his ability, with his final junior school reports acknowledging how well he participated in all aspects of sport, despite his handicap.

And it wasn't just teachers who recognised Steve's sporting ability. Aged about ten, Steve was invited to play cricket at his local park with some older boys – primarily because they were short of players. Perhaps unsurprisingly, they stuck 'the spaz' way out on the boundary outfield.

As the batsman struck the ball high into the air and it headed straight towards the outfield, the rest of the team were already shaking their heads in anticipation of certain failure as they watched Steve, the sun in his eyes, attempt to take the catch - only to have it bounce straight back out of his palm. The head shaking increased. What else could they expect of a boy with no fingers on one hand?

But then, unbelievably, that same boy was diving forward, grabbing at the ball a second time. Incredibly, he managed to catch it before it hit the floor.

'Well done, Fingers, I thought you'd f***** that up!' yelled the bowler, his amazement undisguised.

And cricket wasn't the only game at which Steve's single-handed catching ability was becoming legendary, the local rounders team were equally happy to have him on their side.

It was also around the age of ten that Steve had his first taste of competitive running. Ironically, he wasn't a big fan of the sport back then, preferring team games, and, whenever cross-country was scheduled at school, would pretend he'd forgotten his kit or hide in the bushes for a lap or two!

It was fortunate then, that it was only a 400-metre race he was required to run at the local summer group's athletics tournament. Less fortunate, was that having been given the inside lane and following a staggered start, Steve ran flat out over the first 250 metres to draw level with his rivals, confident he could hold on to win – until the rest of the field moved across the track into his lane, shortening their own race and effectively barging Steve out of the way. Consequently, Steve finished second to last and was robbed of what would very likely have been his first running medal!

For any child the transition from junior to senior school can be traumatic, particularly in the early 1970s when children were generally expected to get on with it without complaint. For a boy with a disability in those thankfully almost forgotten times, it was a living nightmare, with the bullies at Caludon Castle Comprehensive School in Wyken, Coventry, making Steve's life a veritable misery from the outset.

Matters weren't helped when around the age of 12, like many boys of a similar age, Steve went through a stage of minor incontinence. It lasted a couple of years and made life for the boy who was already being singled out for torments and verbal abuse, even more wretched. Even those he counted amongst his friends, few though they were, couldn't resist poking fun at him whenever he had an accident.

But in those days telling tales in or out of school was not encouraged and Steve suffered in silence, too embarrassed to tell either parents or teachers; keeping his shame to himself. A boy of his time, Steve had no choice but to tough it out.

Such bullying and self-containment had its effect; the boy whose parents once described as one who enjoyed playing to an audience, became rather more subdued. Indeed, today, Steve the man would describe himself as a fairly private person, unwilling to open up too freely to others; then worrying that this may make him appear a little unsociable. He also admits to still being quite sensitive and under-confident in large groups, happier to be doing things on his own.

But whilst the bullies may have had their effect on the man Steve has become, so too have his parents, who Steve says have remained the single biggest influence on his life, arming him with traditional beliefs and values; hard work, money self-earned, and the importance of loyalty and helping others. Certainly loyalty seems to be an Edwards' family trait - Steve's sister once chased a boy around a field after he'd made a derogatory remark about her brother's hand!

And so it was, that whilst Steve had to endure the bullies at school, his home life at least was steadfast and happy, providing enduringly fond memories of family Sunday lunches followed by afternoons in nearby Coombe

Park; watching 'Happy Days' on the family's first colour television set; hiring films from the local video store; and learning DIY skills from his father, something Terry says his son was perhaps surprisingly good at given his disability. It was an opinion shared by Steve's metalwork teacher who, one day, exasperated by one particular class, told them they were nowhere near as good as a boy he'd taught who had only one hand!

Away from school and like most teenagers, Steve's independence was growing. He'd travel by train with his friends to watch England play cricket and became the proud owner of a Coventry City season ticket. As his interest in both sports grew, so did his autograph collection. He even wrote to clubs, enclosing team photos cut from football and cricketing publications, asking players to autograph the pictures. It's an impressive collection that remains one of Steve's most treasured pieces of memorabilia.

As when younger Steve's enthusiasm for life knew no bounds, and never more so when it came to music. Like many 1970s teenagers, Steve listened to the late night John Peel show on his little transistor radio, hiding it under his pillow and keeping the volume low so his parents wouldn't hear. It was there he first encountered the likes of The Damned, The Sex Pistols, and Stiff Little Fingers, describing their music as: '... raw, blood and guts stuff, great punk music!'

However, there was an unfortunate aside to Steve's musical enthusiasm. He wanted to own the records, but didn't have the money. With the encouragement of a group of not so desirable 'mates', Steve started helping himself, whilst his so-called mates watched from the sidelines, never getting caught in the crossfire that followed. Not that Steve was bothered by this lack of fraternal loyalty - it was enough that for the first time in his school life he was accepted by a group of his peers who allowed him to hang out with them. He would do whatever it took to keep them.

Ultimately, thanks largely to his moralistic upbringing, Sunday School attendances, and love and respect for his parents, Steve's 'criminal activities' were cut short after he got caught not once, but twice, and decided his parents' wrath, shame and disappointment were not to be incurred a third time.

But it wasn't just the short period of petty crime and undesirable friends that worried Steve's mother in her son's teenage years, it was also the influence his tastes in music had on his physical appearance and dress sense. Never one to do things by halves, Steve progressed through punk (ripped clothes, safety pins and spiked hair), to skinhead (turned-up jeans with braces, Doc Marten boots and shaved head). On seeing Steve out one day when he was in his skinhead phase, Mrs Edwards crossed to the other side of the street, not wanting to acknowledge that the young, 'thug-like' creature in front of her was her own son! She was none too pleased when her son returned home blind drunk on his 17th birthday either.

But Steve has always been, and still considers himself to be: '…just an ordinary bloke', and he has lived his life as ordinary blokes do. Which is probably why he's so inspiring – with no advantages (indeed, the opposite could be said to be true), or special treatment, his achievements have come solely through his own dedication and hard work. Other people can relate to that, for surely it is only when one seemingly ordinary person reaches up and manages to touch a star, that the rest of us start to believe our own star may not be as far out of reach as we once thought.

Of course, Steve's particular star hadn't yet been discovered, but, unbeknown to him, it was already glinting in the darkness.

Chapter 2

THE BOY GROWS UP

Leaving school when unemployment was rising and inflation was at an all-time high would be hard for any 16-year old; for a 16-year old with a disability, it was even harder. But that was the situation when Steve left school in 1979 armed with six 'O' levels and reports unanimous in their verdict that he had the 'potential' to achieve more, but no indication as to how he might practically do that.

With no idea where he was heading and following his father's advice not to apply for what he called 'dead-end' factory work, Steve eventually succeeded in securing a white-collar position as an accounts administrator in the treasurer's department at Coventry council.

It wasn't the dream job; being treated like a general dogsbody and having to answer the phone as a nervous youth, had Steve quaking in his boots. But needs must, and in typical Steve fashion, he got stuck in and gave it his best shot.

As for many people entering the working world, the job Steve started off hating became one that - though he never actually fell in love with it - did bring its own rewards. In particular, the opportunity to develop that mystical potential his school reports alluded to, with weekly college attendances to study for ONC (Ordinary National Certificate) and later HNC (Higher National Certificate), in business studies.

There was also the small matter of a salary, allowing him not only to pay for his board and lodging at home, but, more importantly, allowing him to indulge more freely in his passion for music, which progressed from punk (The Stranglers, The Clash), to two tone (The Specials, Madness), to new wave and electronic (Ultravox, Human League).

Consequently, Friday nights saw Steve continue to tune in to John Peel's show to discover what new releases were coming out the following day. Saturday morning, when most teenagers were still cocooned in their beds, eager Steve would be up bright and early waiting for the doors to open at his local record store so he wouldn't miss any limited editions that might be available.

Steve's salary also facilitated his attendance at concerts where he'd watch enthralled as his favourite bands performed live. Soon his bedroom walls were covered with music memorabilia, and scrapbooks bulged with concert tickets. Although no longer adorning his bedroom walls, those items, together with his vinyl record collection, remain in Steve's possession; treasured as much today as they were back then.

However, Steve's most improbable memory of that time is being thrown out of an 'Echo and The

Bunny Men' gig – for spitting at the singer! Although spitting was common at punk concerts, it's a charge Steve absolutely refutes: '...I never spat; other people's spit would land on me, as I was usually in the pit at the front bopping and po-going around.'

Hard as it may be to imagine today's clean-living marathon man "bopping and po-going" around whilst being spat upon by strangers, the young, zealous Steve loved it: '...I'd come out at the end of the night with my clothes saturated in sweat and my ears ringing!'

As well as music, Steve also had a passion for the hit TV series, 'Kung Fu', and, duly inspired, took up the Lau Gar form of the martial art. There he discovered a love of fitness training and body conditioning, possibly inherited from his maternal grandfather, who enjoyed weight training and jogging in his younger days.

With a sensei who insisted that if the floor wasn't slippery with sweat by the end of the warm-up his students wouldn't be allowed to move on to the more interesting punches, kicks and moves, Steve was in sweat heaven.

Of course, it wasn't all about the sweat; Steve was now 17, and like most 17-year olds he was fast developing a taste for alcohol, and spent most weekend evenings crawling around the local pubs with his mates.

Ironically, it was on one of those pub-crawls that Steve noticed a fellow crawler who had particularly well-developed shoulders and upper arms. Curiosity aroused, Steve grilled the poor young man to find out exactly how this had been achieved. It was the first time he'd heard the term, 'weight training'.

Before you could say Bullworker [a small steel piece of equipment that uses isometrics to increase strength and muscle definition], Steve had invested in one and began using it every night. Next, he joined a private gym and followed a programme designed specifically for him. As well as weights, he also started using rowing machines, fixed exercise bikes and crunching benches.

Despite the twice-weekly Kung Fu sessions, numerous musical soirees and weekly pub-crawls, plus his full-time job, Steve somehow managed to fit three gym sessions a week into his busy schedule. It was an early indicator of the single-minded dedication he would later apply to his marathon running; the early rising to fit in training sessions, the self-discipline of regular exercise, and the enquiring mind wanting to know how a specific objective could be achieved.

It was also through those pub-crawls, that Steve met fellow punk fanatic, Terry Winders (who, incidentally, fitted windows for a living), and it was through Terry that Steve met his first wife, Mandy.

With her own passion for punk, and a car, Mandy travelled with Steve and Terry to gigs all over the Midlands, including Steve's ultimate favourite, The Jam, seen in Birmingham, and also U2, who they saw for the princely sum of £1.50 at the General Wolf

Pub in Coventry: '...a few years later they were filling Wembley!'

All in all, at 18, with the bullying left behind at school, there began a gradual re-emergence of the happy, sunny child his parents had described: '...I had punk, money in my pocket and I'd found what I thought was love.'

The feeling was mutual and the couple were engaged before the year was out.

Meanwhile, Steve's enthusiasm for the gym ran unabated - so when it closed down, financially astute Steve bought some free weights from Argos and built himself an exercise bench. Later, when he joined the council-run gym at his local sports centre and discovered they didn't offer personalised programmes, Steve looked to all he'd learned previously and devised his own.

Soon he was working out at the gym most lunch times and on Saturdays. As he started to develop pecs, biceps, triceps and a six-pack, his love for the gym knew no bounds. For this was a young man for whom a part of his body had been cause for ridicule from an early age and the bodily changes he was now witnessing began to affect the way he saw himself. For the first time in his life he actually began to feel confident about the way he looked. Understandably proud of his new physique, the young Steve couldn't resist showing off his well-toned torso in tight, short-sleeved tops: '...I was a bit of a poser in those days!'

But it wasn't just how to get into shape physically that interested Steve, he was also becoming interested in nutrition. It was an interest that sprang from noticing one of the gym's newer members getting really big, really quickly. A relatively naïve young man, it wasn't until some years later that Steve realised this was probably due to anabolic steroids. (One thing it certainly wasn't due to was slugs - a 'nutritional supplement' that Steve had once experimented with as a toddler, popping a large, bright orange specimen into his mouth before running down the garden and sticking out his tongue to show his horrified parents!)

Fortunately, Steve's natural integrity, coupled with his naivety, ensured steroids or any other kind of illegal drug was a route he never considered taking himself. Instead, he turned to nutritional supplements to help his athletic performance and overall health. As a child of the 1960s brought up on cod liver oil and vitamin C, the idea of using supplements to enrich his diet seemed quite natural and Steve began adding kelp, alfalfa, yeast, desiccated liver and multivitamin tablets to his normal diet; ordering them through mail order catalogues in those pre-Internet days. It's a practice he has continued, although he has replaced the yeast, kelp and alfalfa with other supplements containing the same vitamins and minerals.

By the time 1980 came to a close, Steve was in better shape physically than he'd ever been in his life. He'd embraced his new found confidence, had a job with prospects, and a fiancée. Overall, it had been a pretty good year.

Of course, Steve had no idea then that 1980 would pale into insignificance when he saw what 1981 had to offer. For this was to be the year that was to shape the man he was to become; a year that would define the rest of his life, a year when his star inched inexorably closer. For 1981 was the year that Steven Clive Edwards would run his first ever marathon.

Chapter 3

1981 – OPPORTUNITY (INNOCENCE LOST)

It started with a poster Steve had seen advertising the inaugural Coventry Marathon. 'Why not?' he asked himself, without any concern that the marathon was only six weeks away and the furthest he'd ever raced before was 400 metres. Indeed, so confident was he, that he even made a bet with his drinking buddies that he could do it.

He then started training – even though he had absolutely no idea what he was supposed to do to prepare for running 26.2 miles and even though in those days there was no Internet to advise him. But perhaps that was a good thing? What he didn't know couldn't scare him; ignorance may indeed be bliss and naivety an added bonus.

At least the lamb heading for the slaughterhouse did have a vague notion that perhaps he ought to run a bit. And so, logic firmly in place, Steve decided he would run 20 laps of his old school running track five nights a week, making a total of 25 miles a week. He would also continue his gym sessions and Kung Fu, plus, of course, living at a time when walking and cycling were the usual modes of transport for young people, he would maintain his natural base fitness.

Looking back, Steve is convinced that the combination of these different forms of exercise increased and complemented his running fitness, not just for his first marathon, but beyond. He especially believes Kung Fu provided a really good grounding in fitness and strength, improving his flexibility, core and general body strength.

He may be right, for over the ensuing weeks his running speed improved considerably, so that with one week to go he was able to run 20 laps of the track in exactly 30 minutes; equating to a fairly impressive six minute mile (mm), pace.

Despite his physical progress, the theory remained hazy and he had no idea what sort of time he should aim for on race day. Consequently, he interrogated a gym buddy who did some running and was told that if he broke three and a half hours that would be very respectable, describing it as an average standard time for a club runner, which, back then, it was. Curiously enough, today, despite every man and his dog running marathons, that standard time has slowed considerably.

However, back in the 1980s and with naivety still firmly in place, Steve was certain he'd have no problem achieving that sort of time – after all it was only eight mm pace and he'd been running at six!

And so, filled with the optimism of youth and marathon innocence, race day dawned. It was Sunday,

4th October; a dry, mild, unimpressive day weather-wise. To save Steve catching the bus, his father gave him a lift to the start at the Coventry War Memorial Park. It was then that he spotted his old junior school friend, Darren Edwards, whose father was also running the marathon. The two enjoyed a catch up and then the runners were called to the start.

Toeing the line in the trainers he wore for indoor five-a-side football – ones with no cushioning or support – Steve set off happily enough and fairly breezed along.

A little later, he became aware that a perfectly flat, cinder track does not closely replicate the hard, unforgiving surface of a road, rough rural byways or hills.

Despite that, at 15 miles he felt fine and was on course for sub 3 hours 30 minutes (3:30). As he trotted cheerily along, he pondered all he'd heard about the difficulties of marathon running and the awfulness of the ubiquitous yet mysterious wall. What, he wondered, was all the fuss about?

A mile later, he no longer wondered; his legs turned suddenly heavy, as though tonne weights had been attached to them, and he felt drained of energy. He began to labour.

With no idea as to what was happening to him, and even less idea as to what he should do about it, he forced himself to carry on running. His discomfort grew until he had no choice but to walk. Then he tried running again. The same thing happened. In the end, he simply ran until he could run no more, then walked till he felt sufficiently recovered, then started running again, and so on.

Nine miles later he entered the final 400 metres. As soon as he saw the finish line, his innate ebullience sprang to the fore and tiredness was forgotten. Overcome with a sense of almost uncontrollable excitement, he started sprinting and continued all the way to the finish.

'When I crossed the line, I felt like I'd conquered the world!'

Steve's ecstasy at crossing the line and the warm glow of satisfaction that accompanied it couldn't even be dimmed by the discovery that he'd finished eight minutes outside his hoped-for sub-3:30 time, in 3 hours 38 minutes and 41 seconds (3:38:41). Today, Steve would consider that to be miles off his target time and would be heartily disappointed. Back then, he considered it close enough, and turned his attention to further bathing in the delicious warmth of his own satisfaction. He'd never known a feeling like it.

Even when his Herculean efforts were meagrely rewarded with just a plain paper certificate from the Coventry Rotary Club, albeit with his name and time typed neatly upon it, it never crossed his mind to be disappointed not to be receiving a medal, a goody-bag or a t-shirt: '...that bit of paper meant everything to me!'

Next day was a different story. The euphoria was gone, replaced by a bone-aching weariness never previously experienced. His legs felt like gateposts and he was only able to walk down the stairs backwards. His feet were also incredibly sore, turned black and blue by his old football trainers.

'Never again!' vowed the walking wounded.

The star that still hovered in Steve's orbit merely winked.

Chapter 4

1982 – NEVER SAY NEVER

It was to be a whole year before Steve ran his second marathon. In the meantime, at the age of 19, he moved out of his parents' house into Mandy's sister's house. It was the perfect solution to the age-old problem of older teenager wanting more space, freedom and privacy with his fiancé, and older teenager's parents wanting some peace, quiet and nobody crawling home at all hours. In fact, the advantages went beyond that for Steve. As Mandy's sister charged him less for board and lodging, Steve had more money to spend on his beloved records – and saving to get married.

At around the same time, having passed his ONC, Steve embarked on the HNC course, but with love in the air and weddings on his mind, his heart really wasn't in it and he found the whole thing totally uninspiring. Maybe it was the boredom of the HNC that prompted it, or maybe it was the idea of starting a new collection, but whatever it was, Steve entered the Coventry Marathon a second time.

Only then did it occur to him that perhaps he was stretching himself a little too thinly - working, going to the gym, doing Kung Fu, attending gigs, keeping his bride-to-be happy, preparing for the wedding, and, now, training for a marathon. Something had to give – but it wasn't running that got the chop, it was Kung Fu. Clearly, something about the marathon, or at least running, had got its claws into Steve.

And so he began for a second time to train for a marathon, sort of. Gone was the wide-eyed, innocent lamb of a year ago; in its place a wide-eyed, optimistic youth. Yes, he went out for a few runs, and yes, he continued with his gym work, but he didn't do any specific marathon training. It was more a matter of turning up and then relying on his general fitness to get him round.

Perhaps the main difference this time, though, was that Steve decided not to worry about his time and just to keep running for as long as possible. Which, in the event, took him about halfway, after which he resorted to the old tried and tested walking/jogging routine, with a final 400-metre dash to the line. He finished in 4:12, and received a medal. His first running medal, it remains one of his most precious.

There was one other thing Steve did differently by way of preparation this time round – invested in a pair of proper running shoes. They may only have been Hi Tec Silver Shadows, the cheapest and, by uncanny coincidence, the most popular shoes available back then, but they were a vast improvement on the old football trainers and Steve finished the race with perfectly pink feet; not a bruise in sight.

In fact, so impressed was Steve by his super new running shoes that he kept them until they were completely worn out. The Steve of today wouldn't dream of doing such a thing, religiously changing his running shoes every 500 miles or so.

One thing that hasn't changed with time, though, is Steve's adamant resolve not to include in his total number of marathons, any in which he didn't run all the way (first marathon excepting) – and that includes the second Coventry marathon.

There are many things that the meticulous Steve considers important when it comes to the number of marathons he has run, particularly for record purposes, and this is one of the most important ones: '...it's as much about the quality of my performance, as it is about the numbers - perhaps more so. If I've walked some of the way like I did in Coventry, I don't consider I've done it properly and won't count it.'

For Steve, in line with the origins of the marathon as a competitive athletics' event, treats every marathon as a running race. Every time he steps on to a start line, no matter how he may be feeling, he sets out to run as fast as he can from start to finish. It is this self-imposed determination and self-discipline - a trait he believes he inherited from his father - that stands Steve apart from the crowd. This sense of wanting to be the best he can, never giving anything less than 100 per cent to each and every race – something he has been doing now for over 30 years in more than 700 marathons - is not only remarkable, it is unique.

Of course, back in 1982, Steve was merely quivering on the cusp of what would turn out to be a life-long challenge; he had no idea then that his whole future lay in marathon running. Why should he? Steve Edwards was not psychic, nor was he a professional athlete; he was the same as any other man, working full-time, progressing his career, getting married...

On top of which, he didn't own a telescope so he couldn't see the star that was beginning to burn ever brighter in the darkening sky.

Chapter 5

1983 – AN ORDINARY BLOKE

In January, with their wedding planned for April, and some financial assistance from Steve's father, Steve and Mandy bought their first home; a two-bedroom maisonette in Longford, Coventry. Condensation and damp were a constant problem, and although there were electric radiators in every room, the young couple couldn't afford to run them. The same applied to Mandy's car, which had fallen into expensive disrepair some time earlier.

Steve's can-do attitude and his parents' teachings about hard work and the value of money earned, saw Steve take on additional jobs to help make ends meet. The pay was penurious, but the extra pennies proved a handy buffer against unexpected expenses.

They also proved an innovative way of improving Steve's general fitness, as he ran between houses on his pools and paper rounds to save time. Walking or running the three miles to work or town rather than paying for public transport also helped. Likewise, if there was a bargain to be had, such as the odd lawnmower or kitchen unit, no matter how heavy or cumbersome, Steve would happily lug them home in his arms or wheel them through town in a shopping trolley. It was as good as a workout in the gym any day!

As for entertainment, gone were the crazy days of spitting punks and pub crawls. Instead, Steve and Mandy went to their local pub once a fortnight. At least Steve could still afford a season ticket for his beloved Coventry: '...they were good value back then.'

Steve has no regrets about having so little in those early days: '...it made it all the more exciting later on when I got a better job and earned more.'

In April, Steve and Mandy married at Coventry Registry Office, followed by a reception for around 50 in a room above a pub. They honeymooned in Blackpool, staying in a cheap B&B, and hiding from the rain in amusement arcades, with occasional forays onto the beach for romantic strolls between showers.

Settling down to married life, Steve continued to work like a Trojan while Mandy took occasional jobs and ran the home.

And then May brought the unwelcome news that Steve had failed the second year of his HNC and would have to re-sit the entire year again. He wasn't surprised. He knew he hadn't done enough revision or completed all the course work.

But while his working life may have taken a retrograde step, thanks to all that running to and fro the office and during his secondary jobs, plus the transportation of household wares by Shanks's pony,

Steve's fitness had improved considerably. After running local five and ten-mile races, Steve ran his first ever half-marathon in Coventry in 1:37, before entering the Coventry Marathon for the third successive year. He'd enjoyed the shorter distances, but it was the marathon that really tugged at his heartstrings: '...I seemed to get more out of it; it was a harder challenge and the accomplishment felt greater.'

Once more, Steve adopted the same, non-specific training and racing routine as before, completing his run/walk in 4:26; his slowest marathon to date at that time. Consistent with the standards he later set himself, it's another performance discounted from his totals. However, that performance taught Steve that whilst his casual attitude towards training was fine for shorter distances, it didn't work for 26.2 miles.

And while Steve was learning invaluable lessons about running marathons, someone else was receiving an invaluable lesson about life. It was four years since Steve left school; four years since seeing any of his old tormentors. Now, though, he read in the local paper the tragic story of a young man who'd lost his hand through an industrial accident. The victim had the same name as the biggest school bully of them all. Was it him? Or was it mere coincidence?

By some quirk of fate, soon after reading that report, Steve came face to face with his old adversary. A thick bandage ran the length of his arm and wrapped around the stump where his hand should have been. The two men looked at one another, but neither spoke.

Meanwhile, Mandy fell pregnant. It was unplanned and quite a shock. He was too young to be a father! How on earth would they manage financially? Steve didn't know, but he did know he loved Mandy and his concerns were unimportant against the idea of them becoming one small happy family.

It was perhaps fortunate that, still without a telescope, Steve wasn't able to see his star disappear momentarily behind a small black cloud.

Chapter 6

1984 – FATHER GUMP

On Saturday, 3rd March, 1984, while controversial band, 'Frankie Goes to Hollywood', were ordering everyone to 'Relax', Mandy Edwards was doing anything but. Twelve long, pain-filled hours after being induced, Mandy finally gave birth to Jason Ben Edwards, her husband beside her: '…being at the birth was very emotional and the memory of seeing your offspring born into the world stays with you forever.'

Steve was incredibly proud, and also incredibly excited. On winged feet he ran the mile from the hospital to his parents' house to share the good news. Then he ran another mile to Mandy's sister's house to share the good news with them. It was just fortunate Mandy's parents were staying there at the time, otherwise he'd probably have carried on running to their home in Grantham some 60 miles away!

It was also fortunate, according to Steve, that: '…I always wore loose-fitting trousers and t-shirts, so it was never a problem just taking off and running anywhere!'

Of course, there may have been another reason for Steve's haste to carry out his interpretation of Pheidippides relaying his very important message – Coventry were playing at home that afternoon! In his defence, it was an era when hospitals strictly adhered to the 'only two visitors at one time' rule and he had been at the hospital all morning...it would have been selfish not to give others a chance to visit Mandy and the new infant. It was just a shame that Coventry weren't able to reward such selflessness with a win.

And so the Forest Gump of new Fathers faced the challenges of parenthood. It was a daunting task for the 21-year old. Conversely, Mandy, despite being the same age, was much more relaxed about it, and some of her calmness rubbed off on Steve.

It helped that Jason was a good baby, slept well, fed easily and, like his daddy at that age, was happy most of the time. An early developer, he was soon crawling and walking and, later, just as Steve's parents had done with him, Steve taught Jason to read and, later still, taught him his multiplication tables.

Steve has no doubt that having Jason so young made him grow up very quickly. With a hitherto unknown sense of purpose, he suddenly had no trouble knuckling down to college work, resolving to improve his career and financial situation to better support his wife and son. He duly passed his HNC, with Mandy and Jason attending his hat and gown ceremony at Coventry Cathedral later that year.

It also brought him and Mandy closer as they shared the same traditional values in raising their child, including that mummy stay home with Jason. With an extra mouth to feed stretching their already straitened financial circumstances, Mandy spent Saturday afternoons at jumble sales, finding cheap clothes for them all.

Still car-less, the family took pleasure in simple things, like walking Mandy's Jack Russell, Suzie, picnicking, and feeding the ducks in the park.

Meantime, Steve's musical interests had taken a back seat. The gigs had already stopped, but once Jason arrived even the record buying was limited. Instead, the couple invested in a video recorder, recording music videos off TV. However, they stopped short of accepting the kind offer from Steve's mother to loan them her tape recordings of six-year old Steve belting out all his favourite TV soundtracks!

Whether due to his natural good grace and positive outlook, or the influence of his parents who also raised a family with little material wealth - or perhaps a little of both - Steve has no complaints about those days. Whilst acknowledging it would have been good to have more money, he doesn't recall ever feeling depressed about it. Rather, he counted his blessings – he had a secure job with Coventry council, an established home life, enough money for bills and food, and, generally, life ticked along okay: '...you could say because it was so simple back then, we didn't really have any major worries.'

Neither did they worry about getting enough exercise; every week they'd walk the three miles to Steve's parents' home with Jason in the pushchair, or to Mandy's sister, two miles away. With last year's disappointing Coventry Marathon still fresh in his mind, Steve had also started running most days, either on the road or on the local school's cinder track, incorporating tempo runs into his sessions – though he didn't know they were called that back then. He also continued working out in the gym.

It was perhaps not surprising then that when he ran the Coventry half-marathon, he took seven minutes off his previous time, finishing in 1:30.

But it was the marathon that really benefited from Steve's new regular running training. In his fourth consecutive Coventry race, Steve set a personal best (PB) of 3:16 – an improvement of 22 minutes, and 70 minutes faster than last year.

Clearly, he was doing something right. Curiously, though, he wasn't going out on mega long runs, in fact the furthest he'd run between marathons had been the few half-marathon events he'd completed. The real difference was regularity of training. That appeared to be the key he'd discovered more by good luck than good judgement: '...it wasn't a conscious decision, I just didn't know any better.'

It may have been pure chance that led to Steve realising he could improve his performances by training regularly and using quality workouts rather than piling on the miles, but unbeknown to him at the time, that chance discovery was to set the benchmark for all future training. Indeed, the furthest he's ever run in training is 20 miles – and then only when training for a multi-marathon event. It's possible that Steve's approach to training may explain why he's been able to run hundreds of quality marathons on hard, unforgiving surfaces for over three decades with very little time out for injury or ill-health.

Or maybe it's just down to his lucky star?

Chapter 7

1985 – MEDALS

By 1985 it wasn't just the running that was improving, so too was Steve's financial situation when he successfully applied for an internal training position in the Council's IT department.

Early days for computers, Steve worked first as an IBM mainframe operator, doing rotating early and late shifts between 7 am and 10 pm. Thankfully, technological progress was swift and Steve's role developed into PC and network support, installing and troubleshooting PCs and servers. The changes brought him rapid promotion, a senior position and better working hours.

With work and finances improving, Steve began browsing through running magazines in that famed high street library, WH Smiths, during lunch breaks, and discovered a whole world of marathons and races outside Coventry. But, still car-less, he remained restricted to those accessible by public transport or a lift from his father.

Consequently, in April 1985, Steve ventured to Stratford-upon-Avon for the Shakespeare Marathon. It was the first time he'd run two marathons in one year. It proved harmless; Shakespeare was run in 3:44, Coventry, six months later, in 3:31.

But it wasn't so much the times Steve interested in back then: '...the Shakespeare medal was the best yet, a Birmingham Mint issue with the event and year printed on it – and it had a nice ribbon too!'

Chapter 8

1986 – PERSONAL BESTS & PLATES

The following year, Steve stretched his marathon wings further, with races at Stratford and Wolverhampton in April, followed by Stoke ('the Potteries Marathon') in June. He'd also entered Coventry again, but the event was cancelled due to insufficient numbers. Regardless, it retained a special place in Steve's heart as the race where it all began.

But it was in July at Sandwell, West Bromwich, that Steve set a new PB of 3:09; increasing his record number of marathons run in a single year to four.

Again, it wasn't the time that mattered: '... Sandwell and Wolverhampton had nice medals, but the Potteries gave everyone a Wedgwood plate!'

Meantime, thanks to his career changes and careful financial management, Steve and his family were able to progress from their two-bedroom maisonette to a three-bedroom end-terrace.

While moving day proved a little confusing for two-year old Jason, who wanted to know when they'd be going home, Steve furnished the third bedroom with a weights bench from Argos: '...it was a lot more convenient training at home than at the sports centre' - and his beloved medals, all carefully displayed in date order on a pin board. Plates went on the lounge wall though!

Chapter 9

1987 – A LESSON LEARNED

By 1987, Steve's lounge wall displayed a second Potteries plate and a framed piece of Nottingham lace courtesy of the Robin Hood Marathon; another new race for Steve and his third that year, having already run at Stoke and Wolverhampton. His medal collection also grew, but: '…if I got a rubbish looking medal, I'd be disappointed!'

Collector Steve was in his element; as well as his football programmes, autographs and musical memorabilia, he now had the start of a whole new running collection!

Today, however, the prizes matter far less; it's all about his performance and the desire to leave a meaningful legacy through his running history and finish times: '…the medals will probably get thrown away or rot in a box somewhere when I die.'

Whilst remaining passionate about collecting, Steve also remained passionate about Coventry City. Never more so than in 1987, when, with old college friend, Chris Coyle, who'd driven Steve to numerous matches over the years, he watched Coventry beat

Spurs 3-2 at Wembley to win the FA Cup final. Soon after, Steve stopped buying a season ticket: '...I didn't want to stop supporting them, but the prices became ridiculous. I felt the clubs were taking the fans for mugs.'

Every cloud has a silver lining, though. Without the expense of a season ticket, plus his increased salary and overtime, Steve - who still caught a bus or ran the three miles to work and back - decided it was time to ignore those who'd told him he'd never be able to drive a normal car with his disability, and at least investigate the possibility, particularly as his new job involved occasionally travelling to remote offices. Currently, whenever this occurred, someone else had to take the job or drive Steve in one of the Council's pool cars. It worried him that, ultimately, this could hold him back professionally. And although his inclination may have been to simply run around Coventry with a backpack, the clothes he wore for the office were not quite so suited to the task as Father Gump's more casual attire.

Consequently, Steve approached his local driving school. They said that so long as he could demonstrate he had full control of the car, there shouldn't be a problem. Steve could; his one good right hand and super-strength left wrist were perfectly capable of holding the steering wheel and operating the gearstick safely to a standard that satisfied the driving school, and, ultimately, the test examiner. Unfortunately, pulling out in front of another vehicle to avoid a second hill start was not considered quite so satisfactory and produced a first-time test fail.

Undeterred, Steve passed second time around the following month. His success surprised everyone, including Mandy, for Steve had told nobody he was taking lessons, having them in secret during lunch breaks at work. If he'd failed, he wouldn't want anyone to know; it would have eradicated all the self-esteem he'd been building up since school. The effect of the bullies lingered.

Regardless, Steve had learned a valuable lesson: '... just because other people say you can't do something doesn't make it true.'

The star above smiled benignly down upon its developing charge.

Chapter 10

1988 – AMBITION & INSPIRATION

The year started with the purchase of Steve's first car - a brand new Mini Metro - paid for with overtime and HP.

Further excitement followed in June, with two weeks in Corfu; the first time Steve, Mandy or Jason had flown or been abroad. Steve still vividly recalls his first experience of Mediterranean heat and the cheapness of the drachma in those pre-euro days.

But perhaps the biggest excitement was the opening of a door to a world of marathons previously unavailable to a man with little cash and no personal transport. With the world now his marathon oyster, Steve set his first long-term marathon challenge – to run 12 marathons in 12 months and raise money for the Great Ormond Street Children's Hospital. Papa Gump could think of no more worthy cause.

Having decided that running an average of one marathon a month would be challenging but sensible, his first two races were actually a 'back-to-back'- two marathons, a week apart. [The term 'back-to-back' later came to mean marathons run on consecutive days, but, today, this is known as a 'double', whilst 'back-to-back' applies to two marathons run on the same day.]

Running his first marathon at Stratford in 3:27, unaware how he might feel running a second so soon, but conscious he could usually barely walk for a couple of days after just one, Steve approached Telford a week later as he'd approached his very first marathon - what he didn't know, he wouldn't worry about.

It was an attitude that worked well; his initial tiredness abated fairly quickly and only returned in the last few miles. Then it was a case of hanging on: '...that's what the marathon is about – hanging on through the rough patches, hoping you'll get through them until you feel better again. Sometimes that doesn't happen, and it's a slog right to the end.'

With a 3:28 finish it was a good start to Steve's campaign and a successful sub-3:30 'back-to-back' debut. A fortnight later, he ran Hereford in 3:21, and three weeks after that, Swindon in 3:15.

Whilst happy with his progress and improved fitness, Steve's natural thirst for knowledge nagged him. He wanted to know what training he should do between marathons, especially ones only a week apart. With nobody to ask, and pre-Internet, he considered the matter himself. Eventually, he settled on 2-3 miles, three times a week, at 'threshold' or 'tempo' pace [a comfortably hard pace that can be consistently maintained for a reasonable distance – about 6-minute miling (mm), in Steve's case]. On weekends when he wasn't racing, he'd add in a couple of 4-5 mile runs, at a similar pace.

He also continued his gym sessions: '...I didn't want to lose my hard-earned, all-over body muscle tone!'

Joking, and vanity, aside, Steve believes those gym sessions have helped maintain his overall running efficiency, strength and stability; contributing to keeping him relatively injury-free.

But the real challenge for Steve in 1988 was raising money for the Great Ormond Street Hospital (GOSH). Today, social media platforms inform the wider world of charitable challenges and sites such as 'Just Giving' assist in collecting sponsorship. Back in 1988, it wasn't so easy. Then you had to speak to individuals personally, explain your intentions, sell the cause, physically collect the money and then post it on to the charity. One thing in Steve's favour, though, was that hardly anyone ran multiple marathons in those days making his challenge unusual. People responded to that and sponsored him £1 per marathon, handing over their £1 each time he finished a race.

But if others considered Steve's challenge special, it paled into insignificance when Steve first met Richard Bird at the Gainsborough Marathon in August. Richard was attempting to break the world record for running the most marathons in a 12-month period, namely 52. He also told Steve about the 100 Club and how people were trying to run 100 marathons in their lifetime. Steve listened spellbound. Driving home, it was all he could think of. He considered more deeply his own goal.

He met Richard again later that month at the Devizes Marathon, and was introduced to Colin Greene, then 'chairman' of the 100 Club. Colin explained that the club was an unofficial one with no committee, no club vest or logo, no subscription fee and no affiliation to any athletics federation. It had been formed when several runners recognising each other at marathons decided to try and run 100 of them. It was agreed all races must be official road races with proper results and must be run within any time limit/cut-off points. [Back then, many races had strict cut-off times often between 4-5½ hours; if runners didn't reach a certain point by a certain time, they wouldn't finish by the cut-off time and were disqualified.]

Runners became eligible for 100 Club membership once they'd run 26 marathons with the intent of reaching 100. They'd then become full members and receive a medal and card paid for by a £1 contribution from all other members. Only after 100 officially measured marathon races had been run, could ultra-marathons and Long Distance Walking Association (LDWA) events be included in a runner's totals.

The performances of those early pioneers of the 100 Club tell their own story, although even they don't recognise the arduous journeys and head-scratching logistics that were often necessary to locate and attend the few races that were then available. Also, unlike today's click-of-the-mouse-and-you're-in race entry system, entering races back then required perseverance and diligence, with entries being applied for in writing, accompanied by a cheque or postal order for the entry fee, and a trip to the post office. Consequently, it took years of blood, sweat and toil to reach 100 marathons. Membership was consequently far smaller than today, although it remains true to this day that fewer people have run 100 marathons than have climbed Everest.

Probably due to the time it took for runners to become 100 Club members back then, most were aged over 40, whereas Steve was only in his mid-20s. But age didn't distil his admiration of them and they were his inspiration for running 100.

It was that inspiration that made Steve wonder whether there was a world record for the youngest person to run 100 marathons and, if not, perhaps he could set one? The idea of becoming a pioneer, like Roger Bannister breaking the four-minute mile barrier, lit a fire that still burns bright within Steve today.

Whilst that fire was kindling, Steve met Edwin Bartlett, who in 1986 became the second Brit to run over 100 marathons, following the great Dr Ron Hill MBE, in 1985. Edwin was famed for wearing two watches when running, in case one failed. Such attention to detail appealed to Steve's own meticulous nature, particularly when he heard that during a race

Edwin had announced to the runner alongside him: 'That's my millionth second of marathon running!'

Statistically-minded Steve was impressed: '...it's incredible that he knew, to the exact second, how long he'd taken to run the marathons till then and had worked out which marathon, and at what time during it, that millionth second would be!'

The quirky characters of the 100 Club, the friendship and camaraderie heightened Steve's desire to join them. It was never just about the running, but as much about the common bond that running forged between them: '...we were like a band of brothers, and about three sisters!' For a man who'd struggled to fit in all his life, such sense of belonging was understandably welcome.

As Steve's interest in his fellow runners grew, so the interest of the local press grew in Steve, with sports correspondent, John Wilkinson of the Coventry Evening Telegraph, publishing regular updates of Steve's achievements and fundraising efforts, alongside two other 100 Club Coventrians; Dave Phillips and Phil Duffy.

Almost without noticing, Steve ended the year with 20 marathons under his belt, a few more than the 12 he'd sold to his sponsors: '...some of them were a little annoyed, but they still paid up!'

In all, Steve raised £1035 for GOSH and, at the official fund raising presentation in London, met special guest, 1970s/80s rock queen, Suzi Quatro. She might not have been a hissing, spitting punk, but for music-mad Steve, it was still a thrill to meet her.

By the end of 1988, Steve had not only exceeded his goal of running 12 marathons in 12 months, he'd actually run 12 of the 20 in 12 consecutive *weeks*. During that time, he'd experimented with completely resting between marathons. However, it just didn't suit him. Instead of feeling refreshed, he felt rusty, and it took ages for his legs to start moving freely. He therefore reverted to his previous two or three threshold runs between races instead, and the experiment was never repeated.

What really surprised Steve in 1988, though, was that despite the additional marathons, all bar one of his races were sub-3:30, with an average finish time for all 20 of 3:23. Indeed, his best time was just 20 seconds short of his PB.

It may have been Edwin Bartlett's influence, or maybe Steve's own natural inclination, but it was around this time that he became what he calls: '...something of a statistics geek', entering all his marathons on to a spreadsheet, keeping a cumulative total of marathons run and average finish times. Later, he began adding totals for time barriers, such as sub-3s, sub-3:05s, sub-3:10s, down to sub-3:30s. Later still, he included number of countries, capital cities and race wins!

By the end of 1988, Steve's records showed he'd run a total of 33 marathons. His ambition to become the youngest person to run 100 was underway. He then checked the Guinness Book of Records to discover who'd run the most marathons. It was an American Indian called Sy Mah, who'd run 524 in an average time of just over 3:30. Steve's imagination was captured. It wasn't just the quantity, but the quality. Suppose he could run more with an average time below 3:30?

The amber flames of the pioneering fire lit earlier blazed skywards, kissing gold a shimmering star.

Chapter 11

1989 – THREE DAYS, FOUR MARATHONS

As soon as he heard that Coventry Hospital were trying to fund a new cancer ward, and keen to continue using running as a charitable fundraiser, Steve adopted the Coventry Cancer Ward Appeal as his charity for 1989.

Starting with a solid run at Gosport in April in 3:11, followed by Taunton a week later in 3:19, Steve returned a fortnight later to the Shakespeare Marathon setting a new PB of 3:02:25; a 7-minute improvement on his 1986 PB.

Also running that day was the inspiring Richard Bird. Having run the London Marathon in the morning, helicopter was his only means of reaching Stratford in time for the 1 pm start, which followed the carnival procession celebrating Shakespeare's birthday. Unfortunately, Richard didn't quite make it but, as this was his 71st and final marathon of his world record attempt to run the most marathons in a 12-month period, the organisers allowed him, plus a few other 100 Clubbers, to start a little later.

Interviewed afterwards, Richard expressed the hope that when his record was broken it would be by another Brit, alluding to the intense rivalry for this record between the US and GB. He needn't have worried; a young Brit called Steve was already picking up the gauntlet.

Meantime, whilst happy with his new PB, Steve questioned whether, if he'd run harder, he'd have broken the 3-hour barrier? Consequently, a week later at Telford, he set out at sub 3-hour pace, maintained it, and finished in 2:59:09. It was his second new PB in just 7 days, and his first ever sub-3 marathon – the Holy Grail for club runners.

Two weeks later at the Ramathon in Derby, hoping for an even better time, a confident Steve fearlessly elected not to run to a set pace but to simply go out even faster and hold on as long as possible. Despite slowing towards the end, his (some may say) 'foolhardy' approach paid off, as he set his third PB in 21 days with 2:56:15.

With prizes for the first 50, 40th-placed Steve won his first running award of £10: '...it paid the race entry and fuel!'

Still fairly green as a runner, Steve assumed his PB streak would continue, but, of course, it didn't. The more experienced 100 Clubbers reassured him that running didn't work that way, explaining how the body grew tired and couldn't produce faster times every week. Whilst accepting this to a degree, Steve instinctively felt that something wasn't quite right with his body. However, he didn't dwell on it and it was some years before he discovered how right that instinct was.

Meantime, no matter what anybody said, he made a promise to himself to push his body from start to finish every time he ran to achieve the best possible time he could on that particular day. It's a promise he has now kept for over 27 years.

The more marathons he ran, the more 100 Clubbers he met - Brian Goodall, Fred Stevenson, brothers Dave and Richard Tann, Phil Nutley, the now late Maurice Rhodes and Malcolm Long. Eventually, after several races ranging from 3:06 to 3:28, Steve broke the 3-hour barrier again in October at Gloucester.

A week later he was at Tilford for the Masters and Maidens Marathon. He'd just finished when he saw 100 Clubber, Harry Martin (in 1988 became third Brit to run 100 marathons), approaching the final 400 metres. To Steve's amazement, Harry suddenly stopped running, ripped off his number and marched back to his car without finishing the race. How could anyone so close to finishing just pull out like that? But, apparently, if Harry couldn't run a sub-3:30, that's what he did, so it wouldn't count in his totals.

At the time, Steve thought this slightly ridiculous. Later, however, when he starting setting his own standards, he understood it more. However, the shame of a DNF [Did Not Finish] against his name in the results would be unthinkable. To this day, Steve hasn't ever not finished a race, even though: '...I've had some real stinkers!'

His resolve to this end was severely tested when he took on his next challenge – four marathons in three days! The first, the Seven Sisters Marathon (now 'Beachy Head'), was traditionally one of just two official marathons held on a Saturday, the other being White Peak. Despite a streaming cold, Steve drove the 180 miles to Eastbourne with Mandy and Jason, and kept pace with the other 100 Clubbers undertaking the quadruple challenge - Colin Greene, Leon Moss, Mike Olivera, Maurice Rhodes and Rita Banks. Richard Bird was running 'just' three of the four.

Steve finished the hilly marathon in 4:28. Looking back, he wishes he'd run faster, but having never attempted a double before, never mind a quad, he adopted a sensibly cautious approach. Later, however, he discounted the race from his totals having walked some of it with the group.

Next came a 90-mile drive to the Bracknell home of 100 Clubber, Andrew Radgick, who was running the Midnight Marathon at Bracknell athletics track. One of the faster 100 Clubbers, and with the benefit of the race being on the night the clocks went back an hour for British wintertime, Andrew hoped to turn his usual sub-3 marathon into a sub-2!

For the others, the attraction of this race was that although ultra-marathons, 12 and 24-hour events had been run on tracks before, this would be the first time an official marathon distance race had ever been run entirely on a track in the UK, and, therefore, one for the marathon bucket list.

After a meal and a meagre two-hour sleep, the weary group began running the 106 laps. Andrew finished in 2:53 and, allowing for the loss of an hour at midnight, achieved his rather quirky world record sub 2-hour marathon! Steve was equally happy with his 3:39 finish to complete his second marathon within 15 hours.

Next, the group drove 70 miles to Harlow. Arriving at 4.30 am, they parked in a car park near the start and slept for around three hours. Steve woke feeling drained, and dragged his weary body around the Harlow course in 3:46. He didn't need the others to tell him how terrible he looked; his treacherous body told him all he needed to know. His cold, coupled with running three marathons in three different locations with 340 miles of driving within 27 hours, had taken their toll. He doubted he'd be well enough to run the fourth and final marathon the following day, an Irish Bank Holiday Monday, in Dublin.

But Steve has never been a quitter. Mandy drove him to Luton Airport where he met the others, though Leon Moss nearly missed the flight: '...he came running across the airstrip carrying his kit bag still wearing his running kit. He normally ran topless, but at least he had a top on when he boarded the plane!'

One pizza, a decent night's sleep in a cheap B&B, followed by a hearty breakfast, and Steve completed his fourth marathon in 3:51.

The challenge was complete. They'd done it: four marathons in four locations in 51 hours. It was Steve's first double, triple and quadruple; all accomplished in one go, and his first international race. Now that's what you call a long weekend! It was also the first time Steve met blind runner, Paul Watts, who was trying to join the 100 Club and was guided round the Dublin race by Richard Bird: '...I can't imagine being blind and running one marathon, never mind 100.' (Paul has now completed nearly 300.)

In the final weeks of 1989, Steve ran Harrow in 3:10, followed by the notoriously tough Cornish Marathon (the original Saltash to Lostwithiel), in 3:08, before finishing with a new PB of 2:55:27 in Majorca; his second international marathon, and his, Mandy and Jason's second foreign holiday.

It brought a very satisfactory year to a very satisfactory close. Steve had run 29 marathons in an average finish time of 3:19, increasing his cumulative total to 62. Barring anything unforeseen, and provided he could find enough races, 100 was possible the following year – ideally around his 28th birthday in November.

But it wasn't just numbers of marathons that were mounting up, so too were miles driven and places visited: '...it was like a geography lesson about the UK road network, its towns and cities.'

The other thing that mounted up that year was Steve's sponsorship money for the Coventry Cancer Ward Appeal. In all, he raised £500 and was invited to attend a formal presentation at the hospital. This time there were no rock stars, just the hospital hierarchy. They were obviously grateful for the money Steve had raised but equally obviously perplexed by what he'd done to raise it.

But they didn't have the benefit of second sight and, therefore, had no idea that in less than 20 years, thousands of seemingly ordinary people, possibly themselves and people they knew included, would view running as a social activity and be pounding the streets just like Steve. They may not run as many marathons as him, but, just like him, each would have their own reason for making running an integral part of their lives.

Chapter 12

1990 – WORLD RECORD NO. 1

Steve entered the new decade 38 marathons short of becoming the youngest person in the world to run 100 marathons. Confident he could do it, provided he stay fit and healthy, the only problem he could foresee was finding 38 events to run. Perhaps surprisingly, given the intense boom of the early 1980s, the 1990s had brought with it a substantial decrease in the popularity of running and numbers of events were falling.

As meticulously organised as ever, Steve carefully mapped out all known UK events and, as anticipated, fell short. As the UK road-running season then didn't start until March, Steve booked two international events for February.

The first was Apeldoorn, Holland, with some other 100 Clubbers, plus Mandy and Jason. Steve finished in 3:04 – and then went for a shower, where he discovered a group of naked women! Assuming he was in the wrong changing room, he was about to walk out when he noticed naked men were also present: 'I'd never seen a communal shower before, but no one seemed bothered so I just got on with it!'

The second was Malta in 3:08, again with Mandy and Jason, but this time without the communal shower!

The first race of the UK road marathon season in March saw Steve celebrate Jason's sixth birthday with Mandy at Macclesfield. The remainder of the month and April brought a race virtually every weekend, while in May Steve ran his first official pure double marathon (one on Saturday, one on Sunday) at White Peak and Telford respectively, with a cumulative time of 7 hours 1 minute.

Reasonably happy with his performances so far that year, Steve nonetheless hankered after another sub-3. At Derby, just seven days after his double debut, Steve entered the final 400 metres to see the clock turn over to 2:59:00. Fifty-nine grittily determined seconds later he crossed the line, unlike poor fellow Coventrian, Phil Duffy, who missed a sub-3 by 15 seconds thanks to a bee-sting at 20 miles! After that, Phil and Steve became regular running buddies: '...he was full of great one-liners, very entertaining; it was a real pleasure to know him.'

The next weekend in Hereford, Steve ran another sub-3 with a new PB of 2:52:18: '...it came out of the blue. I just felt really strong.'

That glorious performance was followed a week later with 3:11 at the notoriously tough Plymouth Marathon; a race started by the not then lordly, yet nonetheless great, Sebastian Coe MBE OBE!

Poole followed a week later in 2:58, with the Potteries the weekend after in 3:09 - a course record at that time for Steve and one of which he was particularly proud given its arduous nature. The Potteries had, in fact, become one of Steve's favourite marathons: '...the whole community got involved, music played outside pubs or in front gardens, there were street BBQs and spectators cheering virtually all the way. There were even camping facilities for people staying overnight.'

A few marathons later in July, Steve ran Gainsborough with Phil. A humid day, the two were covered in thunderflies by the finish, so decided to utilise the handy rugby club's bath. Unfortunately, the flies had got there first: '...the water was a mass of black; it was like stepping into liquid tar!'

The following week Steve ran the inaugural Luton Marathon, organised by Richard Bird, missing out on another sub-3 by 2 minutes.

But with the Elgin Marathon just a week away, there was no time to dwell on disappointments. Steve finished his first Scottish marathon in 3:08. A fortnight later he ran his second, the Inverclyde Marathon at Greenock. Also running was Rita Banks, a female veteran [aged over 35 in 1990], and one of only three lady 100 Clubbers at that time. Rita was aiming to run her 100th marathon before the end of 1990 and was also trying to break the women's world record for most marathons run in a 12-month period.

For Steve this was to be a good race with bad consequences - he finished in 2:58, but immediately after he stopped running his right knee started aching profusely. Steve ran again the following weekend and, although donning a precautionary knee support, finished in considerably more pain.

However, it wasn't enough to stop the keen if still slightly naïve Steve from continuing with his weekly races, ducking under 3:30 at both the Humber Bridge and Dartmoor marathons in September.

Believing the injury was easing, Steve put his foot down for the next couple of races. His body rebelled, the pain returned with a vengeance, and Steve's performances slipped beyond his 3:30 target for the next two marathons.

But, if running itself wasn't proving too much fun at this time, the travelling and Steve's travel companions were compensating. Returning from a particularly bad run in Brussels, where his knee and stomach cramps had ensured his most trying run to date and a 3:35 finish time, Steve boarded the overnight ferry with Phil Duffy, Colin Greene, and trip organiser, David Jones.

Anticipating a cheap but uncomfortable night in reclining seats, they couldn't believe their luck when they stumbled upon the kids' crèche. The four adult men promptly locked themselves inside, played about with the toys for a while, and then fell asleep on the luxuriously padded play mats!

The smile left Steve's face a week later, though, when he struggled round at Gloucester in 3:36: '...it wasn't pretty.'

It didn't return the following weekend at Rotherham either. On a cold and wet October day, the competitors were bussed out to the start in the middle of nowhere and left shivering in their race kit for an hour with no loos and just a telephone box for shelter. How many runners can you fit into a phone box?

But for all the fun and not so fun experiences, Steve never lost sight of the rather more serious business of running 100 marathons by the end of that year. Despite careful planning, he was still one short.

Looking back, Steve avers that if he hadn't been chasing the 100, he *probably* wouldn't have run at least two of those marathons when the knee pain was at its worst, although he admits he didn't listen to his body back then. Nor did he have any idea what was causing the pain, and, pre-Internet, there was no easy way to find out. Neither, in those days, did he stretch or have massages: '...I was still learning and getting away with things probably because of my young age.'

Luckily for him and the marathon world in general, and without ever knowing what had caused it initially, Steve's injury cleared up almost entirely and his times started returning to normal.

By late October, still undecided about where to run his 100th, Steve checked the events listing in *Today's Runner*, courtesy of WH Smiths. Lady luck was obviously looking over his shoulder that day (as well as the shop manager); the Black Isle Marathon in Fortrose on Saturday, 3rd November, was exactly the race he was looking for. Scribbling the details on to a scrap of paper he just happened to have in his pocket, Steve excitedly returned to work to check his diary, only to discover that the race was the day before the Harrow Marathon. Otherwise, it was perfect. So what if it meant driving 500 miles to Fortrose after work on Friday, running Black Isle on Saturday, driving 500 miles home again, and hopefully having time to grab a few hours sleep before travelling another 100 miles to Harrow?

'It had to be done. I entered the race and didn't give the logistics another thought.'

However, before Steve could ponder (or not) any potential problems of his epic journey, he had a double to run – Seven Sisters and Harlow. His cumulative time of 7 hours 3 minutes may have been slower than his previous double, but given the tough Seven Sisters course, Steve was relatively happy: '...it was good training and good experience for what lay ahead.'

By which he means that running a marathon each week used to be considered excessive, and doubles were hard to find. Doing a double (or more), also meant travelling between races, as multi-day events at the same location were then non-existent. Indeed, such was the travelling done by some of those early 100 Clubbers, they used to joke that marathons should only count if you'd driven yourself there on the morning of the race and then driven back afterwards, no matter where it was!

If that hadn't been mere banter, Steve would certainly have been able to count his foray in November for the Black Isle/Harrow double weekend, when he and Colin Greene ran two marathons in two consecutive days, and travelled 1130 miles; albeit with Mandy doing some of the driving.

Despite the travelling, Steve ran the scenic Black Isle: '...a marathon I wish they'd bring back', in 3:08, although he felt he could have run faster had he not been mindful that he had another race next day.

Tempted though they were to stay for the buffet lunch common to Scottish events, given the journey ahead the trio settled for a shower and snack, before hitting the road. With considerably less traffic than today, they were home before midnight.

A few hours sleep and one drive later, Steve crossed Harrow's finish line in 3:26, setting himself a new double PB of 6:35.

He had now run 97 marathons and was positively galloping towards his first world record.

Number 98 came two weeks later with 3:18 at the Cornish Marathon, and 99 a week later at Benidorm. Determined not to jeopardise making it to 100, Steve wore a knee support even though it had been fine, and stormed round in 2:52:07 - another new PB, followed by a holiday in the sun for him, Mandy and Jason.

Four days later, Steve celebrated his 28th birthday, and three days after that, on 2nd December 1990, he lined up for the St Albans Marathon - his 100th.

Everyone from the 100 Club was there; with a room booked in a nearby pub for the after-race party and a special t-shirt listing Steve's 100 marathons, including dates and times. Steve wore race number '100'.

Naturally, the pragmatic Steve had a plan. It was simple - he wanted his 100th to be sub-3, so he would set out at a good pace and keep it going. However, the demanding undulations of the course thwarted him and despite reaching halfway in 1:28, he couldn't maintain his form, finishing just 43 seconds outside his target: '...it was a little frustrating.'

Frustrating it may have been, but his first ever world record totally eclipsed any disappointment as he became the youngest person in the world to run 100 official marathon races at the age of 28 years and 3 days! Rita Banks also set a new world record for the most official marathon races run in a 12-month period by a woman, with 52.

Over 100 people attended the after-race party where presentations were made to Steve and Rita, as well as to Mandy, in acknowledgement of her support, and six-year old Jason, who'd become a popular little figure running the final few metres alongside his dad at races.

But despite his heartfelt gratitude, Steve was far too nervous to stand up in front of a room full of people and tell them just how much it meant to him.

The statistics leading to Steve's record, however, speak for themselves - of his 100 marathons, 9 were sub-3, 37 were sub-3:15, and 83 were sub-3:30, giving an average finish time for all 100 of 3:19. He'd run at 61 different events in different locations in 8 different countries, including Scotland and Wales.

At the end of his record-breaking year, Steve had run 38 official marathon races in an average finish time of 3:14, and had broken his PB twice.

John Wilkinson, who'd watched the race, provided a full report of Steve's world record in the Coventry Evening Telegraph, alongside a photo of Steve crossing the finish line at St Albans.

It was just the tip of the media iceberg that was about to float Steve's way.

*1964 - Aged 19 months, loved
playing outside from an early age*

*1965 - First bike, aged 2 - dressed
for the occasion!*

1969 - Aged 6 - Happy hols in Devon

1975 - Second year of comprehensive school

*1979 - Last year at school and a
sign of things to come!*

1980 - Teenage Rebellion!

***1981 - After first ever marathon,
never again!***

***1990 - Finishing the Malta
Marathon with Jason and ET!***

1990 - Second best ever finish time in Benidorm

1990 - 100 club presentation from Colin Greene after becoming the youngest person in the world to run 100 marathons

Chapter 13

1991 (Part I) – Targets

"You're only as good as your last world record" may as well have been Steve's motto at the start of 1991. The gauntlet thrown down by Richard Bird at Stratford was now firmly picked up by Steve. With barely a pause for breath following his first world record, and with the Sy Mah record effectively light years away, he needed an interim goal. Running the most marathons in a 12-month period fitted the bill perfectly.

So, in February 1991, Steve returned to the Apeldoorn Marathon. Watching the romantic film 'Ghost' during the ferry crossing from Harwich, he felt the absence of Mandy, who'd stayed home with Jason.

Following what turned out to be a one-off marathon in Langborough, and with the continued decline of UK races and non-existence of multi-day events, if Steve was to achieve his goal he had no choice but to travel to Germany and Holland for his next double; again without Mandy.

Accordingly, Steve hooked up with David Jones, an old hand at the European circuit and non-driver, whose driving girlfriend, Hayley, was delighted to have Steve along to share the load.

The load was a heavy one. Without the benefit of today's budget airlines, car ferry was the most cost-effective way of travelling around Europe, especially if you needed to reach smaller towns across different countries.

There was also a lot of pre-race organisation required in the days before Europe became one big, happy, all-inclusive, family. Every country had its own border control where a valid passport was required, and every country its own currency, so sterling had to be changed for every trip. Steve learned to keep a watchful eye on his passport expiry date and was soon on first name terms with the currency exchange teller at his local bank.

Friday evenings, he'd arrive home from work, enjoy the dinner Mandy had cooked, load up his (or Hayley's) car with a weekend's worth of sandwiches (again, courtesy of Mandy), plus cereal portions and sterilised milk - all packed neatly into his sports bag, with racing kit, running shoes, spare clothing and a towel.

That first trip with David and Hayley began with driving 180 miles to Dover, grabbing an hour's kip on the ferry, driving a further 310 miles from Calais to Steinfurt, passing through two border stops in Belgium and Germany, and then entering the race, which had to be done on the day in person, and, in this case, in a foreign language. Fortunately, David spoke fluent German, and, after handing over his deutschmarks, Steve was finally ready to race!

Given the long overnight journey and mindful of next day's marathon, Steve was content with his 3:16 finish time, though he was less content to discover there was no medal - just a nice, special edition towel and certificate. He also came away with a rather useful booklet, listing all the German marathons, with dates, locations, entry fees and contact details.

Empty tums replenished, bags neatly re-packed, it was back in the car for the 150-mile drive to Schoorl. Arriving around 10 pm, and having anticipated the use of some kind of roomed facility, Steve was somewhat perturbed to discover they would be sleeping in the car!

It was a long night. With just a jacket to keep him warm and little legroom owing to the lengthy, slightly stocky David sleeping in the seat behind, Steve spent the night freezing cold and cramped. By morning, he'd hardly slept a wink and his legs had stiffened up so much, he was barely able to exit the vehicle. Not ideal preparation for his second marathon in two days.

At least this time entry into the race was straightforward with the English-speaking Dutch and a handful of Dutch gilders.

It was not one of Steve's better runs; it took ages to get going and even then, he felt terrible, finishing in 3:30:25. Initially disappointed with his cumulative time of 6:46, once he'd allowed for this being his first international double, travelling hundreds of miles and barely sleeping, he decided it wasn't so bad after all.

One thing he couldn't find any consolation for, though, was the lack of a medal, again! This time they were given a picture: '...it was different, but I'd still rather have had a medal!'

On the plus side, Steve had learned a lot about running doubles overseas, such as the wisdom of taking extra warm clothing and/or booking overnight budget accommodation ahead of travelling. He'd also learned that, unlike British events at that time, European marathons offered a plentiful supply of fruit and sweet snacks at drink stations. It was the start of Steve's quest to find the best energy products to use during a race.

So, knowledge gained, lessons learned, and a new quest, all that remained was for Steve and his cohorts to make the return 440-mile car journey, plus ferry crossing. He arrived home at midnight. He'd travelled 1100 miles and run two marathons. He was back at his desk in work at 8.30 the following morning.

The following weekend, Steve, David and Hayley started all over again, except this time Steve was armed with an old duvet!

Leaving Steve's house at around 10 pm on Friday, they drove 180 miles to Dover, napped on the ferry, then again in a lay-by near Calais, drove 270 miles to Bensberg, near Cologne, for the Kongisforst Marathon, entered the race, ran the race (Steve in 3:15), and then received – a certificate! It would seem Germans had no interest in medals.

With no time to ponder this intriguing fact, the trio set off once more, this time to France for the Val De Marne Marathon, just outside Paris. Once more, they slept in the car, entered, and ran the race. Whether it was down to the old duvet or adapting to his nomadic weekend existence, Steve finished his second marathon in 3:17, bringing him a new double PB of 6:32, and – a medal!

The relatively short return 200-mile journey to Calais, followed by the 180 miles from Dover to Steve's house, accrued a total of 1150 miles on that weekend's marathon driving clock. Arriving home early enough to enjoy a full night's sleep, Steve returned to work fully refreshed on Monday morning.

But even Steve had his limits, turning down a third successive weekend invitation from David to run four marathons in three different countries in favour of spending the long Easter break with his family – or at least some of it. Compromise was the name of the game, with Steve settling for running two races in France, but forgoing Holland and medal-free Germany.

Mandy duly drove Steve to Dover on Saturday to meet up with David and Hayley at Calais. At least that was the plan. Unfortunately, unbeknown to Steve in those pre-mobile phone days, David and Hayley had got lost. Meantime, a concerned Steve phoned Mandy from a public phone box apprising her of the situation. When David and Hayley eventually arrived in the early hours of Sunday morning, Steve phoned Mandy again to update her.

Then the cheery trio were on their way, with Steve doing most of the driving so Hayley could sleep after her long drive to Calais from Holland.

Despite his own lack of sleep, and the 470-mile drive to southern France, Steve still managed to run 3:08 on the pretty, picturesque course of the Perigord Marathon. Refuelling themselves and the car, they then drove 420 miles north to Cherbourg, where, again, they slept in the car. But first, Steve, missing Mandy dreadfully, located a phone box so he could at least speak to her.

The following day, Steve ran 3:17, setting another double PB of 6:26: '...I was amazed how well my body was coping and adapting to the gruelling race schedule, as well as all the travelling and sleeping rough.'

They then drove 300 miles to Calais, caught the ferry to Dover, and then drove the final 180 miles back to Steve's house.

Total mileage for this trip? 1550. A very tired Steve was back at his desk the following morning at 8.30.

Something had to give.

With a full-time job, a home to run, a wife and young child to support, plus an increasingly demanding race schedule, it simply wasn't possible to keep so many balls in the air at once. Steve decided to replace his evening weight training sessions with weekend jobs, such as mowing the lawn, washing the car and DIY, although he continued his mid-week threshold runs.

With eyes firmly on the statistics, Steve, who had now run seven marathons in three weeks, was beginning to seriously believe it was possible to break Richard Bird's record of 71 marathons in 12 months. But David Jones was also gunning for it and had already run double Steve's number of marathons since the start of the current year. The race was on.

Despite his hunger for the record, Steve did allow himself the rare treat of running a single marathon the first weekend in April at Thanet, finishing in 3:13. Thanet was, in fact, only the second official road marathon to be held at home that year, confirming Steve's notion that racing overseas was the only chance he had of taking Richard's record.

A week later, David and Hayley arrived once more at Steve's house on a Friday night. Together, they made the now routine trip to Dover, caught the ferry to Calais, drove to Maassluis in Holland, and entered the Westland Marathon, which Steve finished in 3:23. They then drove to Vienna, reminding Steve of his favourite Ultravox record, although he couldn't recall anything in the song about driving 750 miles to get there!

Racing along the notoriously speedy autobahns at over 100 miles per hour to ensure they'd have time for a few hours sleep before the race, the bigger city marathon had allowed them to pre-enter by post, enclosing Austrian currency for the entry fee, involving a trip to the bank *and* the post office!

Finishing the race in 3:19, Steve happily agreed with David and Hayley's suggestion to take a different route home, driving through Czechoslovakia and taking in some famous landmarks en route. Unfortunately, though, they got lost. With road maps for most of Europe but not Czechoslovakia, which had only recently freed itself of communist rule, and with every major road junction signalling north to Prague when they needed to be heading west, things were not looking good. Night was falling and so was the fuel gauge. Although David spoke German, people were reluctant to talk to three strangers after dark, shops were closed and not a garage was in sight.

By sheer good luck they eventually stumbled across a road taking them to the German border. After mistakenly joining the queue for Czechs crossing into Germany, they rectified their mistake, had their passports stamped and went merrily on their way.

About a mile later, their merriment ran out with the fuel. The men pushed the car to a garage, which was, luckily, only half a mile away and, luckier still, open.

The instant he saw a phone box, Steve phoned Mandy to warn her of their delay, and eventually arrived home just in time for breakfast. He was beyond tired, but still went to work. Flexi-time had never been so useful.

That weekend Steve travelled 2500 miles, ran two marathons and pushed a car half a mile, but that didn't stop him being thrilled when the Stockholm Marathon race organisers invited him and David to their June marathon, offering to pay for flights, accommodation and subsistence, in response to a letter he and David had sent informing them of their attempts at the 'most in a year' record.

It was to be the first of many such offers Steve would receive from race organisers keen to use his record attempts for event publicity.

A week after Vienna, Steve recorded his first sub-3 of the year at Stratford, while fellow Coventrian, Dave Phillips, scored his century.

And then it was back to Germany with David for another double. The first race, just outside Cologne, was one Steve had found in the handy race booklet he'd acquired at Steinfurt. Unfortunately, the booklet hadn't mentioned that this was a local championship race for German athletes only! Despite David's excellent linguistic skills, the Germans wouldn't let them run, forcing them to endure the frustration of watching the race from the sidelines.

Fortunately, there were no such problems the following day. After the drive to Bremen and a good night's sleep in the car, Steve enjoyed a great run in 2:57, winning his first German medal!

It compensated a little for the previous day's disappointment, but the 1200-mile round trip for just one marathon was not good use of resources. Steve tried to be philosophical about it: '...doing what we did, we had to expect things wouldn't always go to plan.'

But the disappointment rankled. Less than a week later, spotting a mid-week marathon in Kamen, Germany, on their May Day, a Wednesday, Steve made some phone calls, arranged some flexi-time and booked a ferry ticket. With Kamen less than 300 miles from Calais, he snatched a few hours sleep before leaving home just after midnight on Tuesday and drove to Dover through the early hours of Wednesday. Five hundred miles later, he was in Kamen.

Steve's perhaps slightly desperate plan paid off; he finished 3rd, his best ever finishing position, in 2:58, his third consecutive sub-3 in an 11-day day period. With true German consistency there was no medal, but his 3rd place did earn him a set of German road maps split into all the different regions of Germany.

'It was a very thoughtful prize, and a pity I didn't have something similar for Czechoslovakia a couple of weeks earlier!'

The following three weekends, Steve managed to book doubles in the UK, which meant Mandy and Jason could go with him: '...happy days!'

First came the Neolithic Marathon at Avebury on Sunday, followed by Belfast on the Bank Holiday

Monday - which Mandy and Jason didn't go to because of the ongoing troubles at that time.

The following Saturday, the family travelled to the White Peak Marathon at Ashbourne, met up with David, drove to his house to stay overnight before travelling to Scotland early the following morning for the one and only Dundee Marathon, where Steve ran his 100th sub-3:30.

That double was followed by the Isle of Wight (IoW) Marathon, the UK's longest running marathon still in existence, second only to the famous Polytechnic Marathon, which sadly is not. In those days the IoW was held on a Saturday and was, and still is, ranked in the top five of the UK's toughest road marathons.

Back then, medals were only awarded to those finishing in under 3:10, with sub-2:50s receiving first-class medals and sub-3:10s second-class medals. Finishers outside 3:10 received a sew-on patch. Steve's 3:02 won him a second-class medal.

Next day, the family drove to Hereford. Steve finished in 3:14, for a new double PB of 6:17.

With things going so well, Steve was convinced he could amass near to 100 marathons for his record year.

The following weekend, he, David and Malcolm Long, were running in Holland and Denmark, the latter courtesy of the race organisers. Unfortunately, Hayley was unable to travel, so Steve left early on the Friday, collected David from Hull, then Malcolm from Ipswich, and was about to head to Dover, when the normally faultlessly well-organised Steve, realised he'd left his passport at home.

'Mandy was quite surprised when the three of us turned up on the doorstep just after midnight!'

Steve had driven 450 miles to get back to where he started.

Unruffled, he went on to drive the 180 miles to Dover, napped on the ferry, drove 220 miles to Rhenen and arrived 20 minutes before the start. Grabbing race numbers, getting changed, and eating a banana on the start line, he was amazed to finish in 3:12. Waiting for the others to finish, he grabbed a couple of hours much-needed sleep in the car.

He awoke to face a 360-mile drive, a ferry crossing from PuttGarden (north Germany), to Rodbyhavn (on Denmark's southern-most island), and a further 100-mile drive to Copenhagen. Thanks, perhaps, to the pre-race pasta party, a live band and a good night's sleep in a complimentary hotel room, Steve finished his second race of the weekend in 3:18. And, with tons of food left over at the end of the race, they were able to stock up for the return journey!

That was the good news. The bad news was that they now had an 850-mile drive and two ferry rides to get back home. Guessing he probably wouldn't be back in time for work on Monday, Steve had booked the day off. Which was fortunate, as they ran out of fuel, again. Despite finding a garage, it had closed early being Sunday. They had no choice but to park up and wait for it to open the following morning.

Another mishap, another phone call from another phone box to Mandy.

By the time Steve got home, he'd driven nearly 2200 miles, run two marathons in Holland and Denmark, and been on four ferry crossings.

'But, hey, I'd run 21 marathons in 11 weeks. I was beginning to get an idea of the kind of total I could amass in one year if I could maintain that kind of schedule.'

If...

To realise this potential, the following weekend Steve and David were to enjoy the rare luxury of a flight to Stockholm, courtesy of the race organisers. They would then fly home early Sunday morning and drive to England's south coast for the Poole Marathon later that day. Having learned from recent experience that things don't always go to plan, former 'Be Prepared' Boy Scout, Steve, secured the Poole race organiser's assurance that so long as they finished the race within the five-hour cut-off time, they could start whenever they liked.

With an early Friday morning flight from Heathrow, Steve took the day off work and David stayed over Thursday night. Bright and early Friday morning, Mandy donned her chauffeur's cap and drove the men to the airport.

At Stockholm, they were driven to their hotel, and given money for their evening meals, but warned not to get excited as Stockholm was very expensive: '...it just about covered one large pizza and a drink each, which cost about £50!'

On Friday afternoon, the press interviewed Steve and David, although their interest was mainly in David, who at that point had run more marathons than Steve. The media interest amazed Steve, especially as David's finish times averaged around 4½ hours. How interested would they be if he broke the record with *his* average finish times, which were over an hour quicker?

Thus inspired, Steve ran the next day's race as if he had a Guinness Book of World Records man chasing him, threatening to hit him over the head with the giant tome if he didn't run faster. He crossed the finish line in the Olympic stadium in 2:51:55. It was a new PB, and one he has never broken.

Dousing his excitement for the short flight back to Heathrow, the following morning, Steve and David met up with Mandy and Jason and were then driven approximately 100 miles by Mandy to Poole, arriving an hour after the official start. Unlike David, who decided he'd never make the cut-off time and didn't run, Steve, despite running a PB the day before, felt quietly confident that he could run sub-4 to finish in the required time.

Until that moment, such self-belief would have been unthinkable in a man whose esteem had been so badly bruised by those schoolboy bullies, but through running Steve was being enabled to slowly but surely re-build himself. The star that had silently guided him towards the running path gave a contented sigh.

His confidence was not misplaced; he caught the back markers at around 16 miles then weaved his way through the field to finish in 3:08.

'I never expected a time like that, not even in my wildest dreams!'

However, Steve acknowledges that his success that weekend was largely due to having the 'elite athlete treatment' in Stockholm and to Mandy doing the driving, allowing him to rest.

Steve's two fast times smashed his double PB to smithereens, at just below six hours.

But disappointment followed. On the return journey David was quiet and Steve sensed some tension. Initially, he blamed it on David's dissatisfaction at not running at Poole, but later it occurred to him that maybe it was down to a potential conflict of interest with them both chasing the same record. Consequently, despite becoming such good running buddies and sharing so many trips together, they could no longer continue. In following the same dream, they had, in effect, become rivals. Nothing was ever said, but from then on, as if by tacit agreement, the two men went their separate ways.

By now, Steve was completely immersed in his record attempt and was starting to plan much further ahead with his marathon schedules, making contact with race organisers in advance of events to promote his cause. It was a good move, resulting in many invitations that included complimentary race entries, occasional accommodation and, even, sometimes, a return flight in exchange for using his story for publicity. Steve the runner doubled as Steve the agent.

As Steve's reputation grew, so too did the interest of both national and international media; he began to appear regularly in newspapers and magazines, and was interviewed for radio and TV. Occasionally, he was invited to attend press conferences and, much to his surprise and delight, would find himself sitting alongside top athletes answering questions and telling his story. Even more gratifying, was that the awe Steve felt at being in such prestigious company appeared to be reciprocated; the minute he finished recounting his achievements, his athletic heroes would rush to shake his hand.

But, as they say, it's walking the walk not talking the talk, or in Steve's case, running the race, that counts, and so he planned another weekend double for June - Enschede in Holland on Saturday, the Potteries in Stoke on Sunday.

On paper this seemed relatively straightforward, with Steve planning to be back in the UK by the early hours of Sunday morning to enjoy the 'luxury' of a UK marathon later that day, after which he would be: '... back home in time for tea!'

It was the first time Mandy and Jason accompanied him on a European trip, and the three of them were excited and happy as they drove to Dover late on Friday night, boarding the ferry to Calais, grabbing some sleep and then driving on to Enschede for the race.

As Steve reached the final few metres, seven-year old Jason ran alongside him all the way to the finish. A 2:58 for Steve and a real adventure for Jason!

All too soon it seemed they were heading back to Calais.

As they neared Ghent in Belgium, Steve told Mandy he was feeling tired and would take a break at the next services. Mandy offered to take over at that point and drive the remaining 90 miles to Calais. Somehow, though, Steve missed the services. No matter, he'd stop at the next one.

But they never reached the next one. Instead, Steve fell asleep at the wheel.

The next thing he knew they'd hit the central barrier. Then they were rolling over and over. Mandy was screaming and Jason was shouting for his dad.

'I thought we were all going to die. I was just waiting for that final moment.'

Fortunately, that moment never arrived. The car came to a stop on its wheels. Steve looked across at Mandy, then behind at Jason.

'For a couple of seconds, I wondered if we'd actually died and were about to meet our maker.'

Then a driver who'd witnessed the whole thing opened Steve's door. All he could say was: 'I can't believe you're alive.'

The three of them quickly vacated the car and hurried over to the verge, all apparently unharmed and able to walk, albeit shakily. On closer inspection, though, it was apparent Steve had sustained a deep gash on his head from hitting the windscreen. By some miracle, Mandy and Jason escaped unscathed, as did ET, Jason's favourite stuffed toy, which he had safely tucked under his arm.

Seemingly minutes later, the police arrived, closing off lanes, taking statements and, with no other vehicles involved, arranging for a breakdown truck to tow Steve's wrecked Rover away. It was only then Steve realised they were on the other side of the carriageway and that they'd actually rolled over the central reservation. If a car had been coming in the other direction, it would have been a head-on collision and they almost certainly wouldn't have survived.

Still in shock, Steve now had to find a way to get himself and his family home. The police offered them a lift to the hospital for Steve's wound to be checked, but after that they'd need to get to Calais. Fortunately, the tow truck driver kindly offered them a ride to Ostende ferry port. They'd have to change their tickets, but there was no alternative. Steve gratefully accepted.

Retrieving their bags from the boot of his crumpled car, Steve was shocked afresh to see items from the glove compartment now in the boot and items from the boot liberally scattered throughout the car's interior.

How on earth had they managed to walk away from that alive? Steve shivered, and felt an unearthly presence. Looking up at the late evening sky, a star winked gently back at him. His mother had always said he was lucky, that he had a guardian angel watching over him. He knew now it was true.

Certainly, he was lucky that his car had been leased through work and because it was a complete write-off, the Belgium garage agreed to scrap it at their end, saving Steve the cost of having it shipped back to the UK.

After refusing the hospital's offer of stitches, Steve and his family arrived at Ostende and successfully changed their tickets, but would have to wait for the next day's crossing. They spent what was left of the night bunked down in the port's waiting room.

When Mandy's sister picked them up from Dover the following day to drive them home, all Steve could think about was that he was missing the start of the Potteries Marathon. Twenty-four hours later at work, it was a different story. Steve broke down in tears as he realised just how serious the accident had been.

'I could have killed us all by my own stupidity, all over an attempt to run a load of marathons.'

Realising he was still in shock, Steve's employers sent him home with two days compassionate leave: '... they were good like that.'

Over the next few days, Steve felt utterly destroyed and questioned everything he was doing. There was no way he wanted to continue running.

Logic eventually rescued him: '...I realised I'd already invested a lot of time and effort, which would all be wasted if I didn't carry on. I just needed to be more careful and take breaks when I needed them.'

He also needed a car while the company organised a replacement for the Rover. Enter Steve's line manager, who offered the use of a department pool car at weekends should Steve need it - so long as he paid for the fuel and only drove it in the UK. Steve gratefully accepted, although getting back behind the wheel presented its own problems with an anxious Steve no longer feeling able to drive for miles on end without a break, terrified he would fall asleep again, stopping every 50 or so miles to take some air and stretch his legs.

But at least the running show would continue.

Chapter 14

1991 (PART II) – PLANNING

Over the next few weeks Steve continued increasing his numbers, running UK marathons and/or ultras. Guinness rules then allowed inclusion of ultras so long as an official time was given at the marathon cut-off point.

A week after a terrible run (3:40), due to stomach cramps at the flat yet scenic Loch Rannoch Marathon, and with no marathons in sight, Steve ran his first ultra – a tough 35-mile trail event over the Malvern Hills. It took him nearly twice as long as a normal marathon, but at least he finished and got a cut-off time at the marathon distance, so it could be counted for the record. A week later, he ran the tough Pennine Marathon in 3:28.

It had been a few weeks of below-par performances and, on reflection, whilst never wanting to make excuses, Steve wonders whether he was still suffering from the trauma of the accident: '...I think, mentally, it affected me more than I realised.'

However, time waits for no man, especially not one on a record-breaking mission, and come mid-July Steve finished the Finglas Marathon in Dublin in a much-improved 3:05.

'The Irish 100 Club were always very welcoming, picking us up from the ferry port early in the morning and taking us home with them for breakfast!'

Ireland was followed by Sheffield; another 'disappointing' (3:17) run for Steve, perhaps due to a lack of drink stations in the latter stages of the race held on a hot July day.

At the end of July, and without a UK race, Steve had entered the Swiss Alpine Ultra Marathon. In recognition of his record attempt, the organisers waived his entry fee and paid for two nights' accommodation, so Steve took Mandy and Jason with him, turning the trip into a mini holiday.

Hiring a Ford Escort van which doubled as their accommodation, and reminded Steve of those happy childhood holidays in his Dad's reconfigured van, they toured the surrounding area for a couple of days prior to the race, making good use of Steve's latest marathon accoutrement - a travel kettle.

'To this day I think Switzerland is one of the most beautiful countries I've ever visited; the scenery is stunning and the air so pure.'

Pure air, however, comes at a price. Venturing out for a couple of training runs, Steve was shocked at the effect of the altitude: '...to say I was labouring would be an understatement.'

It wasn't just altitude that Steve had to contend with during the race. His short-sleeved top made no allowance for the temperature variation on a course starting 1000 metres above sea level (higher than Snowdon), with a total ascent and descent of over 2300 metres. Indeed, Steve readily admits he did no preparation for running a mountain ultra, viewing it merely as another marathon distance to add to his record list.

'Climbing the Sertig Pass, the air got colder and colder. I was freezing, and the rocky ground gradually became icy and snow-covered, which is hard to comprehend when you haven't seen that altitude transition before.'

As he descended, he went over awkwardly on his right ankle twice in quick succession; his foot cracked: '...it was excruciating.' Steve was forced to limp the final 10 miles. The good news was he had another marathon to add to his record attempt. The bad news was he may have suffered a serious injury and not be able to run again for some time.

Twenty-four hours and 750 driving miles later (shared with Mandy), Steve's ankle was x-rayed at Coventry Hospital. A small hairline fracture and severe sprain were revealed. The consultant advised Steve to rest for a month. Steve ignored him.

'Today, I would heed that advice, but then I didn't know any better. I felt I'd be letting myself down if I didn't continue. If I broke down then fair enough, at least I'd tried. I didn't want to be wondering "what if" later on.'

As a vague sort of compromise, Steve decided to run one marathon a week for those four weeks and not train in between. That way, he hoped, the ankle would still have a chance to heal.

As reality kicked in, suffering two major setbacks within such a short time of each other, it began to dawn on Steve that 100 marathons in a 12-month period was, perhaps, a little optimistic.

'I never thought to factor in any setbacks. I was young, I didn't worry about risk or danger, I did things then that I wouldn't even contemplate today!'

However, there was some good news: Sally Line Ferries had agreed to Steve's application for sponsorship, offering a 50 per cent discount on crossings during the record attempt. The company, who no longer exist, ran a ferry from Ramsgate to Dunkirk. Although it was an hour longer than the Dover to Calais crossing, Steve would benefit from an extra hour's sleep on the ferry. Plus, Dunkirk was a further 30 miles up the E40, which ran through France to Belgium, Holland and Germany.

Over the next three weeks, Steve ran three marathons with his foot heavily strapped. With each, the pain subsided a little and his times gradually improved with 3:28 in Moray, 3:21 at Romney March, and 3:13 on the Isle of Man.

With his ankle feeling stronger, Steve decided to risk a double road ultra the following weekend.

The first, Two Bridges, was a 36-mile loop starting and finishing at Rosyth, incorporating the Kinkardine and Forth Bridges. Steve's race went precisely to plan with a 3:15 marathon cut-off time, before slowing to finish in 4:39. Having pipped 100 Clubber, Ivan Field, into the final medal-winning 25th place, Steve then made the long journey home before rising early next day to drive to Blaisdon in Gloucestershire for a 50k ultra.

Tired and with throbbing foot, Steve ran steadily to finish in an almost identical time to the previous day, even though it was five miles less. For his efforts, he picked up the 3rd place trophy.

Optimistically, hoping there'd be no negative reaction from his foot and believing he was back on track, it only took the arrival of his new replacement car to see Steve preparing to run some serious doubles around Europe again.

The first was in Lille, France, minus Mandy, but with another 100 Clubber sharing the costs and driving. A boiling hot August day, Steve finished in 3:37, and then drove home.

Rising early next morning, he drove to the Norfolk Marathon. Incredibly, it was even hotter than France with temperatures in the 90s. In the sheltered, hedge-lined country lanes, not even the gentlest puffs of cooler air could be found: '...it was like running in an oven.'

Steve dragged himself round, slowing to a walk in the last few miles. He finished in 4:12, one of his slowest times ever. Although he included it for record purposes, he has since discounted it.

Regardless, it was another double and Steve's foot was okay.

A week later, another double – necessitating a long drive to southern Germany for the Bodensee Marathon, with Mandy and Jason. The two and a half hours of extra sleeping time on the ferry was a luxury, and the sponsorship itself was proving invaluable. Steve enjoyed both his 3:12 performance and the beautiful course around Lake Bodensee, which forms part of the border between Austria and Switzerland.

Happy with his run, the mental and practical stresses of the weekend faded. So what if he'd driven 700 miles to Kressbronn and now had to drive 630 miles to Slough through the night with just a couple of hours sleep on the ferry in the middle? In his uplifted state of mind, it was all very doable and indeed he reached Slough in time to grab another couple of hours sleep in the car before the race, which he finished in 3:28, before driving the meagre 100 miles home again.

Total driving mileage for this trip? 1430.

September 1991 - six months into his record attempt - Steve had run 40 marathons, including the odd ultra, averaging 3:17 for each.

But Steve refused to rest on his laurels. He knew David Jones was on for a total of 70+ and there were rumours of an American heading for a similar number. Steve would have to run in excess of 80 marathons for his efforts not to be in vain.

But it wasn't just the running that needed Steve's energies. When he'd first decided to chase the record, he hadn't appreciated the logistical element to what he was trying to achieve. Six months in, he was in no doubt that those logistics required as much, if not more effort than the run itself: '...sometimes the most difficult part was actually making it to the start line - achieving the 26.2 mile run afterwards was pretty much a given.'

Steve's ability to project manage and forward plan, once so well tested on the junior school chess board, was pushed to its limits as he organised ferry bookings, race entries, currency exchanges, travel timings, when and where to fit in sleep breaks, contacting race organisers, seeking sponsorship, and meeting his nutritional needs. Entering the second half of his record attempt year, those planning abilities were essential, with Steve scheduling five consecutive weekend doubles.

The first 'mixed' (overseas and home races in a single weekend), double was the Argentan Marathon in France, run in 3:06, followed next day by the UK's Kingston Marathon. The second was the Rheinruhr Marathon in Duisburg, Germany, where Steve was thrilled to win his second German medal, followed by the Mersey Marathon on Sunday.

There followed two weekends of UK doubles, with the fifth successive double including a Friday marathon at RAF Swinderby; a race suggested to

Steve by a serving officer, who suggested that while it was a services' personnel-only event, they might let Steve in as a guest given his record attempt. Steve duly wrote to the base and, much to his surprise, they said yes!

'It was strange turning up at an airbase, showing my passport and driving licence at the gate and being escorted to the right place, but they treated me very well and even allowed me to go to the post-race meal in the mess afterwards.'

The RAF's generosity was repaid with a 3:11 performance from Steve, followed by 3:02 at Weston-Super-Mare two days later.

But for all his consistency, Steve couldn't help feeling a little dissatisfied that he hadn't broken three hours since the day of the accident.

A week later, Steve flew to Frankfurt with 100 Clubber, John McFarland, taking advantage of a two-for-one flight offer. This rather more relaxing mode of travel, a hotel room on Saturday night courtesy of the race organisers and running just a single marathon proved the answer, with a delighted Steve coming home in 2:55:44.

As if compensating for the laxness of a single marathon, the following weekend Steve went for a triple. Traditionally, the last weekend of October offered an opportunity to run the Seven Sisters Marathon on Saturday, then either Maidstone, Harlow or Snowdon on Sunday, followed by Dublin on Monday. Steve chose

Maidstone as his middle marathon as, although it was furthest from Holyhead Ferry Port for Dublin, he wanted to support 100 Clubber, Derek Appleton, running his 100th marathon at his local race.

In return, Derek invited Steve to stay overnight at his home after the Seven Sisters, reducing his travel time to Maidstone considerably. Having not seen Mandy or Jason all weekend, Steve made a small detour home en route to Holyhead.

Another great Dublin experience, including a party for Eugene Kavanagh's 100th marathon, and Steve was back home in the early hours of Tuesday morning, having driven a total of 800 miles.

As winter approached with no UK and few European official marathon races listed, Steve realised that to maintain his record-breaking schedule, he needed to spread his wings still further, and looked to the States. Here races, including doubles, abounded year-round – provided you had the means to flight-hop between states. There was even a five-day marathon series, which David Jones had used to raise his totals, enabling him to set a new world record of 74 marathons. Meanwhile, the American suspected of chasing the same record had been confirmed as one Ed Baretto. Ed was currently on target for at least 75, thus relieving poor old David Jones of his record almost before he could say "Guinness".

As for Steve, he was on 54 after 33 weeks and had a full schedule lined up for November and early

December. But with only a couple of events booked for January, although confident of beating David's total, the American's potential was unknown. Steve could, therefore, still fail. He refused to let that happen, he'd suffered too much and worked too hard to let his dream slip through his fingers at this late stage. He needed to up his game. The precedent had been set and the goalposts shifted with the US 5-day series; if he was to have any real chance of taking the record he had to level the playing field, and there was only one way to do that.

So, when Derek Appleton offered to organise a multi-day series at Romney Marsh, Steve did nothing to discourage him, especially knowing Derek would meet all the requirements of an official marathon event. And yet, although the event would assist his record attempt, Steve never has been, and never will be, entirely happy with the designer-style set up, which is why he's always sought to go above and beyond, ensuring his records stand with or without any multi-day events he may have done.

Race-wise, the schedule would mean a quadruple just before Christmas from 21st-24th December inclusive, and another quadruple just after Christmas from 28th-31st December inclusive; so effectively 8 marathons in 11 days. There would then be a 'new year' series. Slightly less intensive, this would consist of two doubles over two consecutive weekends in the second half of January.

Meantime, with the problem of finding future marathons solved, Steve turned his attentions back to the present and his next double, the Black Isle/Harrow marathons, which involved 1130 miles of driving. Blasting round both courses, Steve recorded finish times of 3:04 and 3:14 respectively, improving his 1990 cumulative time for the same double by 18 minutes. Crossing the line at Harrow, Steve was handed one of the few remaining finisher's t-shirts, leaving his good buddy, Phil Duffy, who finished a little after Steve, sadly but vociferously without!

The following weekend, Steve ran a German/Swiss double with Colin Greene. Following the ferry crossing from Ramsgate, they stopped for a nap then drove the 240 miles to Lembeck. Steve finished the race in 3:03. Being Germany, there was no medal, but Steve did receive a complimentary entry to assist with his record attempt, plus 100 deutschmarks for finishing 3rd, some of which was spent on giant hotdogs for him and Colin!

Aware they'd be travelling into the night, Steve used more of his winnings on fuel; he didn't want to risk running out – again! The duo then began their 540-mile drive to Tenero, southern Switzerland.

All was going well until they emerged from a mountain tunnel to be confronted by a swarm of police waving at them to stop. Aware he'd been speeding, Steve jammed on the brakes and screeched to a halt just past the officers. Checking his rear-view mirror,

Steve was shocked to see four policemen armed with machine guns running towards them: '...that's when I knew we were in serious trouble.'

The officers demanded Steve and Colin get out of the car and identify themselves. Worried they might be mistaken for terrorists, Steve tried to explain they were from England, had just run a marathon in Germany, and were now on their way to run the Ticino Marathon in Switzerland. They were driving fast so they'd have time for a sleep before the race. Even to his own ears, it sounded an improbable story.

'It wasn't until they saw our kit bags and running shoes, that I think they started to believe us.'

Whether believing them or not, Steve and Colin were ordered to drive to the nearest police HQ about five miles away, under police escort.

Once in custody, their passports and car insurance documents were checked. Eventually, the officers declared they believed Steve's unlikely story, but insisted he pay a speeding fine, even though there had been no speed camera or equipment to evidence the crime. But it was pay up or spend the night in a police cell, so Steve handed over 50 deutschmarks – all that remained of his winnings: '...it was almost as if they had never been!'

The knock-on effect of this unfortunate delay was a reduction in sleeping time to a meagre two hours, and it was a weary Steve who had to work unfeasibly hard to maintain a steady 8 mm pace to finish the race in 3:27.

Another long drive home brought the total driving mileage for that weekend to 1730.

A week later, Steve, Mandy and Jason travelled to the Lipperland Marathon in Humfeld, Germany. It was another 180-mile, Friday-night drive to Ramsgate, another handful of hours sleep. They disembarked the ferry to bitter temperatures, snow, and a 350-mile onward journey.

Conditions didn't improve for the race; struggling with tiredness and fighting the freezing air, Steve was relieved to record 3:24 and stay under the 3:30 barrier.

'No medal again, but I did get a ceramic plate!'

Too cold to linger, they drove straight to Dunkirk, took the ferry back to Ramsgate, then drove to Cornwall, arriving in Saltash village hall car park in the early hours of Sunday morning in readiness for the tough Cornish Marathon later that day.

Today, Steve can't believe he expected Mandy and Jason to rough it in the car like that, even though he didn't have the finances to do anything else. At least they had duvets and pillows, kept permanently in the car specifically for the purpose. And there was the travel kettle, so they could make a hot drink any time, plus they always carried plenty of food, so they never went hungry…

Despite the driving and sleeping rough, Steve ran 3:18, culminating in another sub-7 hour double: '…I was really surprised by my time after yet another insane amount of travelling.'

For 'insane', read 1500 miles.

And then it was back to work as usual on Monday. By this time, his work colleagues were always keen to hear about Steve's latest marathon escapade, as was journalist, John Wilkinson, who continued to write about Steve's record attempt every week in his sports column.

Even Jason's teachers were taking an interest. Attending a parents' evening, Steve and Mandy were taken gently aside while a teacher expressed her concern that Jason had been making up stories about travelling to far off countries every weekend, and his dad running ridiculous numbers of marathons: '... they thought he was some kind of modern-day Walter Mitty!'

Steve acknowledges that these trips may have been physically quite tiring for his young son, but he also believes they were of immense educational benefit.

'He was the only kid in his class who knew the capital cities of most of the civilised countries in the world and all the different currencies. He experienced so much from those trips, far more than any school field trip could provide.'

And, as Steve's name became synonymous with the record attempt, so the race invites and offers of complimentary entry and accommodation increased: '...it made life much easier and I was very grateful to have those creature comforts.'

So it was, that for his next race at La Rochelle, France, Steve received the usual enticements, plus an invitation to bring along a couple of guest runners. Accordingly, Steve, plus 100 Clubbers, Colin Greene and Mike Faraday, lapped up the lavish French hospitality at the pre-race pasta party before being introduced to the crowd, with special mention of Steve's record attempt.

Steve finished the race in 3:02 and was then interviewed by a French reporter, but it wasn't until he saw the full-page spread dedicated to his story in the newspaper the following day, that he realised just how much his record attempt was starting to capture people's imaginations.

It was heady stuff, and Steve loved it! His confidence soared so high it almost collided with the stars. The boy who, pre-bullying, liked to play to an audience was back!

The only downside to the whole weekend was the announcement of Freddie Mercury's death as they were driving home: '...I immediately put Queen's greatest hits tape on, which Colin and I enjoyed, but I rather think Mike didn't!'

Steve's next trip took him, Mandy and Jason back to Germany for the Advent Wald Marathon in Arolsen. A tough course of forest trails, Steve scraped a sub-3:30 by just 30 seconds. As usual, there was no medal, just a certificate.

The family then returned to England for next day's St Albans Marathon; back then, traditionally, the last 26.2-mile race of the year on the UK marathon calendar.

It was another tough one for Steve, although a 3:23 finish meant another sub 7-hour double. However, the months of running and travelling were taking their toll: '...I was so very tired.'

During the 100 Club after-race party, Derek Appleton announced his retirement from marathon running. Previously a regular sub-3:15 marathoner, his times had lapsed to around 3:30, and he felt he'd become, 'pitifully slow'.

Another 100 Clubber Steve met at that party was Mark Pickard. Mark ran his 100th marathon in 1988 and Steve cites him as one of the Club's most talented athletes ever, having run 150 consecutive sub-3 marathons. Indeed, Mark still holds the course record of 2:20 for the Isle of Wight Marathon.

With no more races in the UK apart from the Romney Marsh multi-day event, Steve travelled to Majorca and met up with 100 Clubbers Mike Faraday, John Macdonald and Heather Stewart.

Whilst there, he also met with Barry Whitmore, director of sports travel company, Sportsman's Travel (ST), who Steve had previously travelled with and had tentatively approached about possible sponsorship. Whereas previously Barry had already been sponsoring another athlete and couldn't accommodate Steve's request, now that other athlete was retiring and leaving his sponsors, providing a handy gap for Steve.

However, businessman Barry, whilst expressing an interest in Steve, wanted to wait until he'd broken the record before making a commitment and Steve had to be content with the promise of a further meeting in January.

But Steve couldn't help feeling excited; the mere notion of being a sponsored athlete thrilled him. Why, it was almost like being a professional athlete! Such notion certainly had a positive effect on his race in Majorca, run in 2:56. Less positive was forgetting to phone his wife. Mandy was not amused.

And then the unthinkable happened - Steve found himself one weekend without a race. It was the first time since mid-March that he'd had a chance to recharge his batteries and was particularly welcome with the marathon series in Burmarsh rapidly approaching.

Meantime, the media were stirring, excited by the prospect of a world record. The Daily Mail and The Times wanted to run stories on his record-breaking attempt, while Cliff Temple, sports correspondent for The Times and notable running coach, invited Steve to Burmarsh ahead of the event for a photo shoot. Steve happily agreed, especially as the newspaper would pay his travel and time-off work expenses!

Reproduced in black and white, the photos showed Steve running along a stretch of lonely lanes across the baron marshlands that form Romney Marsh. The stark pictures epitomized the loneliness of the long distance runner.

Saturday, 21st December 1991 – Steve drove 180 miles to Burmarsh for the first of his eight marathons. He couldn't wait to get started; if everything went to plan, he'd end the calendar year on 74, equalling David's tally.

However, by shifting his record year to between 10th March 1991 and 9th March 1992, he should be able to push the record up into the mid-80s, provided he could find enough races. Steve wasn't content to merely break the record; he wanted to smash it.

Indeed, so engrossed was Steve in finding ways to increase the record, he barely considered the task immediately ahead of him: '...I should have been thinking about what effect this might have on me, would I get injured, would it break me?' Instead, just as in his earliest running days, Steve had no plan other than to turn up and run each day as best he could.

Twelve runners, including Steve, lined up at the start that first day; the wind howled and the rain fell in a steady stream. The four-loop course around flat, exposed country lanes alongside the open marsh, offered no shelter or respite from the elements. Battling the elements, Steve claimed his first ever marathon victory in 3:16.

The minute he finished, Steve was grabbed by a EuroSport reporter who interviewed him in front of a rolling camera in the presence of Cliff Temple, who was waiting to interview Steve for a Sunday Times exclusive. During the TV interview, Cliff Temple compared Steve's average times with those of previous record holders, describing them as 'phenomenal'.

Later, donning his coaching hat, Cliff suggested that while Steve's times were impressive given how often he was racing, with fewer races and the right coaching, he thought Steve had the potential to run 2:30-2:35. As delighted as Steve was to hear this, he explained that he preferred to follow the path he'd already chosen.

Staying with Derek that first night just three miles from the course, Steve enjoyed a good night's sleep before waking next day to more wind and rain. But that didn't stop him taking his second consecutive win in 3:20. He then drove home, before making the return 180-mile journey the next morning.

Fighting a build up of tiredness and gusts of wind that raged across the desolate landscape at 60 miles per hour, Steve finished day three in 3:24 in 2nd place.

Day four - Christmas Eve and, thankfully, a lessening in wind speed, as Steve positively sped round for a third victory in four days in 3:14.

With the win under his belt, Steve drove home to enjoy Christmas Day with his family and three days rest before attempting the final four marathons of the series.

Thankfully, on day five the wind decreased to a steady breeze. Steve finished 3rd to Brian 'Ladder Man' Doherty (a window cleaner who occasionally ran with his ladder for charity), who won in 2:56 – minus ladder!

On the sixth day, Steve was transported back to his schooldays when a runner made a sarcastic comment about his hand. He hadn't had to deal with that sort of thing since becoming an adult. A tired Steve saw red. He grabbed the offender by the collar and pinned him against the wall. It wasn't his normal response to being bullied. The worm had turned. With hindsight, he wishes he'd treated it as a bad joke, but he'd been taken by surprise.

Whether fuelled by his earlier ire, Steve couldn't say, but he had a great run, finishing 2nd in 3:05.

The penultimate day of the series saw an exhausted Steve, having driven 360 miles since his previous marathon, finishing joint 2nd with Ivan Field in 3:13. The two had battled all the way before agreeing to finish together. The race was won in 2:51, the fastest run of the series.

And then it was New Year's Eve, the final day, and Steve prepared to run his 8th marathon in 11 days, and his 74th and last marathon of 1991. He marked the occasion with his best time of the series, 3:02, and 2nd place, earning him the overall series winner's trophy.

Others who completed all 8 marathons were 100 Clubbers, John (Superman) Wallace, Leon Moss, Ron Martin, John Kew and John Slinn. The event proved groundbreaking for the UK marathon scene and those involved in the first multi-day marathon event series in Europe (at least as far as they knew), made history.

The calendar year drew to a close with Steve having run 74 marathons in an average time of 3:16. Ultimately, 72 of those would count towards his record year when he shifted it from March 1991 to March 1992, giving him another 11 weeks to potentially push the record out of reach of any future pretenders. For now, though, he'd equalled David Jones' tally and was just one away from equalling Ed Barretto's.

Meanwhile, his overall marathon totals had increased to 174 with an average finish time of 3:19. His dream of running 500 marathons averaging sub-3:30 looked like becoming a reality.

But for now, family man Steve was simply looking forward to returning home to celebrate the New Year with his beloved wife and son.

Chapter 15

1992 (PART I) – WORLD RECORD NO. 2

The year got off to a fine start with a complimentary trip to the Marrakech Marathon in Morocco, with Steve attending the pre-race press conference and being interviewed by media and TV. Once more the man from Coventry found himself in the surreal position of being interviewed alongside world-famous athletes.

No less surreal, but rather less enjoyable, was the trip to town after the press conference. Steve had never before witnessed such terrible poverty first-hand: '...barefoot kids were running around in rags. It was impossible not to feel sorry for them. They followed us around the market place, begging.'

Unsurprisingly, the weather was considerably warmer than the zero degrees Steve had been used to back home, but he still managed to finish in 3:09.

Post-race, it was back to surreality as Steve and the elite athletes were wined, dined, and royally entertained with a jousting contest and fireworks.

The following day, Steve had his second meeting with Barry Whitmore of ST and was somewhat surprised to be asked by Barry to remove his shoes and socks.

This turned out not to be some kind of weird ritual, but a way of checking how Steve's feet were holding up after the intensity of his marathon schedule. If he was expecting to see the hard skin, blisters, bruised toenails and other blemishes normally associated with marathon runners' feet, Barry was disappointed - Steve's feet, thanks to him having learned the value of buying running shoes a size larger than his normal shoe size, and using Vaseline (not just for armpits and groin!), were pristine.

Accordingly, Steve and his faultless feet left with the offer of a contract, allowing him free travel on a specified number of trips with ST, in return for writing articles for their magazine, chatting with and advising customers, and generally helping out on tour. He would also be expected to wear ST branded kit when racing or being interviewed by the media.

The only downside to Steve's Marrakech trip was weight loss due to the unpalatable food. Once home, though, Mandy loaded him up with calorific dishes in preparation for the second race series at Burmash.

This time, the series consisted of four marathons run over two weekends on the same Romney Marsh course as before, and, this time, Derek invited Steve, Mandy and Jason to stay Saturday night of both weekends to save driving between races.

Derek's generous hospitality paid off. Steve finished the first weekend's races in 3:13 and 3:12; both races being won by Andrew Radgick in 2:52.

More importantly, this took Steve to number one in the world for the most marathons run in a 12-month period – with two months still to go.

The media were hot on his heels. An interview with the Daily Mail followed as soon as he'd broken through Derek's specially made finish ribbon proclaiming: "Steve Edwards World Record 76 Marathons In One Year!"

EuroSport also did a second interview, which aired the following weekend, by which time Steve was back at Burmarsh for the final two marathons of the series, both of which he won in 3:00 and 3:11: '...should have broken 3 on the Saturday, though!'

The following week he was on an IT course for work, which meant driving to Southampton every day. On Thursday evening, he packed his car with running kit and supplies, so that on Friday he was able to finish the course and then drive direct from Southampton to Cheltenham to collect Colin Greene, before driving on to Ramsgate to take the ferry across to Dunkirk. By the time he reached Apeldoorn in Holland, he'd driven 620 miles. The next day, he got up, ran a marathon in freezing temperatures in 3:11, and then made the return journey to the UK.

Back in Blighty, he and Colin drove to Surrey through thick fog. Driving along the M25, Steve could barely see the bonnet of his own car and only just made out the diversion signs taking them through a chicane on to the opposite carriageway. Unfortunately, a driver coming along that carriageway in the opposite direction didn't have Steve's efficient eyesight and drove straight at them, lights on main beam. In the split second he had before hitting the other car head-on, Steve swerved out of the way into some cones. He was instantly taken back to the accident the previous June: '...my heart was going like the clappers.'

Fortunately, there was no damage to Steve, Colin, or the car, and they resumed their journey physically unscathed, but mentally somewhat stressed. It proved to be a long night with only a few hours of sleep in the car before running their second marathon, a trail ultra. Steve then drove Colin home before continuing on to Coventry alone: '...I was very relieved to get out of the car.'

Total mileage? 1080.

Thankfully, the next weekend proved a lot less stressful, with a UK double, followed the weekend after by an all expenses-paid trip to Malta. Despite extreme tiredness, Steve ran a surprisingly swift 2:57 before being lulled to sleep on a park bench by the soporific Maltese sunshine!

At the post-race party that evening, Steve was thrilled to be photographed alongside Sir Roger Bannister CBE and Dr Ron Hill MBE, two of his all-time athletic heroes, who chatted to him about his record attempt. The following morning, Steve and Barry exchanged signed contracts. Steve was now an officially sponsored athlete!

The excitement continued when he returned home to a letter from Virgin Airlines offering him a free return flight anywhere in the world to aid his record attempt. This wasn't just a lucky coincidence, but the result of Steve's diligence in contacting companies trying to obtain as much assistance as possible. With the same diligence, Steve decided to use Virgin's generous offer for the Los Angeles Marathon in March, as ST would be there to cover his hotel costs.

But first he had a double to run at Dartford Park, an event organised by 100 Clubber, Peter Sergeant. Peter and wife, Leo, had generously invited all 100 Clubbers to stay at their home on Saturday night between the two races.

The course consisted of 61 flattish laps run along the Park's footpath, with Mandy assisting Peter, Leo and members of Peter's running club, Dartford Harriers, with lap counting and timing.

Feeling good from the gun and running an even paced race until the final few laps, Steve was initially delighted to finish in 2:56; his second sub-3 in a week. Later, he worried he may have gone too fast, given next day's marathon and the fact that he didn't want to risk injury so close to the end of his record year.

His worries were unfounded. After copious amounts of home-cooked pasta and a restful night, he finished in 3:01, setting a new double PB of 5:57, which stands to this day - although he regrets missing out on a double sub-3.

February closed with Steve on 84 marathons for his record year and two weekends remaining in which to top it up.

March – LA, Steve's first trip to the States. His only regret was that Mandy and Jason couldn't join him. That disappointment later turned to relief. Finishing his race in 3:04, there was the sudden sound of gunshot followed by terrified screams. A man lay on the ground surrounded by armed police: '...the man had a gun and was threatening to shoot somebody in the crowd, so the police shot him! It was a real shock being that close to something so disturbing.'

For the final weekend of his record year, Steve had scheduled two events. The first was on Saturday, 7th March, at the Birmingham Indoor Arena; a 200-metre running track, where he was running a marathon within a 24-hour ultra event [competitors run as many laps as possible within 24 hours]. Steve would run 212 laps.

It was to be the first and only time Steve would run an indoor marathon and also, so far, the most laps he's ever run in a single marathon. Following pre-race interviews, Steve was introduced to the crowd with an explanation about what he was doing, while the other athletes were advised not to worry about how fast he was running, as he wouldn't be doing any more than 26.2 miles!

'It was strange running indoors on a carpeted track with banked bends. Every time I rounded those bends

I could feel and hear the track moving as I landed and took off again. It was also strange to be running nearly twice as fast as everyone else!'

About halfway into the race, Steve became aware of a blister developing on the sole of his right foot, caused by his foot slipping sideways in his shoe as he took each bend, and probably exacerbated by wearing fully cushioned road shoes on an indoor track. With 13 miles to go, plus a full marathon the following day, it was the last thing he needed. He therefore took the unprecedented decision to stop and apply a blister dressing. It did the trick, preventing the blister from worsening or bursting.

After two hours, the runners were turned around to run in the opposite direction; a normal precaution in this type of event to prevent one-sided injuries occurring from running in the same direction round the bends: '...it felt weird and took me a couple of laps to get properly going again, and I worried I might get a blister on the other foot.'

Fortunately, he didn't, and despite losing nearly five minutes for the dressing stop, Steve finished in 3:07. As he crossed the line, it was announced that his run was not only a course record, but also a new indoor world record, claiming that a marathon had never been run indoors before! Whether or not that was true, Steve didn't know. He was far more interested in the fact that he'd just finished his 86th marathon within 12 months and had one more record run still to go!

Sunday, 8th March 1992 – Steve Edwards awakes with the expectation of making history and setting a new world record. He doesn't need to check his kit; it has been packed the night before with the usual organisational precision of a royal emissary packing for an overseas tour. His wife drives him to Windsor Castle for the start of the Polytechnic Marathon. Held annually since 1909, the Polytechnic Marathon was, at that time, the longest running marathon in the UK.

Just over three hours' later, Steve enters the Polytechnic athletics track at Chiswick for the final 400 metres.

'I couldn't believe it was nearly over, just one lap of the track to go. Suddenly, I was 10 years old again and running the 400 metres at the Coventry summer club tournament where I'd been cheated out of my gold medal!'

Spurred on by the memory, Steve sprinted: '... at least it felt like sprinting'; just as he had on that inglorious day 19 years earlier.

'As the finish line drew nearer, I could feel the hairs standing up on the back of my neck. I was very aware that this was it, the moment I'd been working for all year; the hard work, the thousands of miles of driving, the planning and the actual races themselves. It was all about this one final moment.

'Then I crossed the line and it was all over.'

Except it wasn't; Steve had 'sprinted' so fast round that final 400 metres that 100 Clubber, Derek, hadn't had time to position the finishing tape he'd made specially, proclaiming: 'Steve Edwards World Record 87 Marathons In One Year!' Amidst the cheering, and all but on his knees, Steve was forced to re-run the final few metres so the press could get their pictures of him actually breaking the tape!

Re-takes and interviews done, it was time to celebrate, right? Wrong. Instead, Steve cheered his fellow 100 Clubbers across the line, handing each a personal card thanking them for their support throughout the year. Only then was it time to celebrate in the Stadium's clubhouse with a cake made by Mandy, and, of course, some bubbly!

A stunning trophy was then presented to Steve on behalf of the 100 Club. It still holds a special place in his huge trophy collection and his heart. Colin then made a speech suggesting Richard Bird's record was like Sir Roger Bannister's 4-minute mile - once one person breaks through what was previously considered an unbreakable barrier, others follow.

Steve knew he should respond, but the man with the confidence to run nearly 100 marathons in record times in a year was terrified. This was different to media interviews, which were carried out on a one-to-one basis; this was standing up and talking to a crowd, who would surely laugh at him and mock him, just like his tormentors had at school. But he had no choice; they were waiting. Dry-mouthed and jelly-legged, he stood to face them; family, friends, press, including the notable Cliff Temple, not to mention some fairly elite athletes.

He started speaking, trying to explain about the travelling, the planning and logistics, as well as the actual running itself; he thanked his wife and family and all those who'd played key roles in his quest, and supported him along the way. He spoke the only way he knew - from the heart. By the end of it, he was as exhausted as when he'd run his hardest, fastest marathon. It was a gutsy performance by a man with no experience of public speaking and a fear of crowds.

But at last, it was over; not just his speech but also his mission. He had run 87 marathons - the most official marathons ever run in a 12-month period. Of those 87, 33 had been run abroad and 64 were run as doubles, ie: two marathons completed on consecutive days on 32 occasions.

Unlike today, where most doubles are run at the same location, allowing runners to stay in nearby accommodation and enjoy a full night's rest and recovery, Steve had travelled hundreds of miles, sometimes overseas and countries apart, between races, snatching sleep when and where he could. Indeed, on one occasion, he drove 2500 miles to complete a double. In the 12-month period of his record, he'd organised 46 ferry crossings, 14 flights, and had driven over 40,000 miles, taking in 13 different countries along the way. It was no mean feat.

Of his 87 marathons, 9 were sub-3, 44 were sub-3:15, and 71 were sub-3:30, giving an overall average finish time of 3:14, while 75 had been run in totally unique locations.

It was to be seven years before Steve's record was broken. It has been broken many times since in quantity, but Steve's average time of 3:14 has never been bettered and still stands at the time of writing this book 23 years later.

Running shoe companies may also be interested to know that all Steve's record running was done wearing the same pair of Asics trainers! Admittedly, they were torn to shreds, but Steve was determined to keep them going to the bitter end - a rather drastic bid on his part to get some sponsorship from Asics! It was worth the effort, for although Asics couldn't offer full sponsorship, they did kit Steve out with their latest range of clothing as a one-off, including a new pair of running shoes!

These days, by the way, the rather more experienced Steve, wouldn't dream of using just one pair of running shoes for that number of marathons.

And so, with the record safely packed away in his kit bag, it was time for Steve to consider the future and his longer-term goal to break Sy Mah's record. At least, it would have been, had Barry at ST not requested that Steve move the dates between which he'd run his record number of marathons to incorporate the Barcelona Marathon in a week's time, making that the grand finale event of his record year. It wouldn't change the number of marathons run, as the first one in his current record year would simply be discounted and replaced with the final one at Barcelona.

The reason for Barry's request was, unsurprisingly, a business one. Barcelona were hosting the Olympic Games that year and the marathon was being run on the Olympic course finishing in the Olympic stadium. As such, the event was being covered by a leading running magazine, which had expressed an interest in using Steve's story as part of the Games build up. With Steve's connection, ST would receive some welcome publicity. In line with his contract, and despite already celebrating at Chiswick, Steve agreed to Barry's request.

Travelling with ST at least meant there was no additional cost and, although disappointed that his tiredness from the previous weekend's efforts only gave him a 3:11 finish time, Steve allowed himself to feel slightly appeased at having run in the same stadium as the Olympians.

Interestingly, as soon as Steve claimed his world record, having had his application to run the London Marathon rejected on three previous occasions, he was suddenly inundated with offers of a guaranteed entry. He eventually elected to run for Tuskforce, who help protect rhinos and elephants from extinction. As one of the charity's ambassadors, Steve would attend the London Marathon press conference on their behalf, allow them to use his story for promotional purposes, and be a guest of honour at one of their fundraising events. It was a double thrill for Steve to at last be able to run London and, at the same time, promote a worthy cause.

But it wasn't just charities who wanted Steve's help at London, ST also wanted him on their stand at the expo for two days prior to the race.

Steve Edwards was becoming a commodity; everyone wanted a piece of him, especially the media, as invitations for interviews poured in from press, radio and TV.

One such invitation came from the BBC's Manchester studios for an appearance on "People Today", a BBC1 programme that went out live every weekday morning. 'Ordinary guy', Steve, was tickled by their offer to not only pay travel and subsidiary expenses, but also an appearance fee!

The following day, Steve took the first train to Manchester: '...they wanted me there early to explain how it all worked and to powder my face!'

Feeling extremely nervous, but assuming the interview would be recorded and edited before being aired, Steve allowed himself to be further comforted by the fact that his interviewer would be the experienced Adrian Mills (co-presenter at that time with Esther Rantzan on the popular 'That's Life' programme), who the producers assured Steve would put him at his ease and only ask straightforward questions.

Mindful of his contract with ST, Steve duly arrived at the BBC studios wearing the company's top. It didn't occur to him that this was the BBC, where advertising was taboo. When they insisted he must wear something else, even offering to find him another top from their wardrobe department, Steve explained that the terms of his sponsorship stated he had to wear the company clothing for any media functions and if he couldn't wear it, he couldn't do the interview! Bold as this may appear, not being aware that this was a live interview, Steve didn't realise the BBC had no choice but to go ahead with him, as there wasn't time to find a replacement. Consequently, the interview proceeded with Steve wearing his company top and ST enjoyed probably the most expensive few minutes of advertising they'd ever had - for free!

Sitting nervously on the edge of his seat while footage of the London Marathon was played, Steve was eventually introduced to the viewers by Adrian. As promised, under Adrian's skilful questioning, Steve started to relax – a little too much as it turned out. Having been asked to bring along the running shoes he'd worn for all 87 of his world record marathons, Steve had elected to wear them instead, so Adrian asked him to put his feet up on the coffee table in front of him so the camera could zoom in allowing viewers to see the state they were in: '...but I forgot to remove them and did the rest of the interview with my feet up on the coffee table, as if I was lounging about in my own front room!'

Back in his actual own front room, and with two weeks before his next race in Paris, Steve used his free time to gather all the documentation he needed to send to Guinness as evidence of his record performances. These would be verified, and then, hopefully, accepted as a Guinness World Record. It is testament to his methodical mind and organisational ability that within just a few days, all the paperwork was presented in a neat package to the post office. Steve's diligence in obtaining results, taking photocopies of them as well as his race numbers, had paid off. He'd also taken photographs and: '...of course I had a very concise spreadsheet detailing my schedule over the record year period.'

Assuming everyone to be as organised as himself, he then naively anticipated confirmation and a certificate in time for the London Marathon Expo in two weeks, which he could then display on ST's stand. Dream on! Despite phoning Guinness every couple of days and making a thorough nuisance of himself, Guinness proceeded at their own speed, following their usual protocol and doing all their checks to verify Steve's claim. Frustrating as this was, Steve accepts they were doing their job and appreciates the necessity.

Consequently, it wasn't until June that Steve finally received the confirmation and certificate - duly signed by Norris McWhirter, co-founder of the Guinness Book of Records - that he'd been waiting for, for so long. The certificate was duly framed and, to this day, remains proudly displayed at home.

Meantime, Steve travelled to Paris with ST, recorded a 2:56 finish time, then a week later ran 3:02 at the Bungay Marathon in Suffolk; another new race for Steve.

And then, after years of patiently waiting, it was time for London. First, though, he did his duty at ST's stand for two days: '...I hadn't appreciated just how tiring it is standing around talking to people all day.'

He also attended the pre-race press conference for Tuskforce. Surrounded by a horde of reporters and officials, Steve was interviewed by former Arsenal and England goalkeeper, Bob Wilson. It was another nerve-racking experience and probably just as well that he wasn't aware at the time that London's race organisers had attached a health warning to him and his achievements, cautioning others against emulating him, stating: '...it would take a unique constitution and character'. Steve didn't know whether to feel flattered or insulted!

It was a similar dilemma to that experienced in a lift at the Strand Hotel the evening before the race. Returning from a short run, Steve entered the lift with another man, who immediately started looking him up and down: '...I was wearing my running shorts and he complimented me on my muscular legs. I ignored him thinking he was drunk or not quite right mentally.'

But as the lift started to ascend, Steve was grabbed in the crotch and propositioned: '...he said I was playing hard to get!'

Poor, innocent Steve was totally shocked. Torn between whether to hit the man or just politely tell him he wasn't that way inclined, he opted for the latter and, fortunately, the man backed off and apologised.

It was the first time Steve had faced anything like that and it shook him up: '...I'm in no way homophobic, but the incident left a sour taste for some time afterwards.'

Today, however, he views the incident as comical: '...it's just another story for the book!' But not one, perhaps, to be shared with Jason or his teachers!

It certainly made Mandy's arrival on race day extra welcome, though by the time they'd strolled around the capital that evening, Steve realised just how weary he was. The excitement of all the media attention, standing about at the expo, running 26.2 miles in 2:55 (which still stands as Steve's best London time ever), had taken its toll, and it was with a huge sigh of relief that he tumbled into bed that night.

Despite his weariness, over the next fortnight Steve ran a couple of UK marathons before venturing to the Belgrade Marathon in Yugoslavia, a country seldom visited back then due to political unrest prior to the final splitting of the country into Croatia and Slovenia.

It was another invitation event and, this time, Mandy and Jason went too: '...it was always a real treat to have them with me.'

As was becoming the norm, Steve was interviewed for live TV immediately prior to the race, and then trotted around the sweltering course in 3:08.

As the weeks and marathons passed inexorably by, Steve once more considered his future. He had Sy Mah's record to aim for as a long-term goal, but what of the shorter term? Just as when he'd become the youngest person to run 100 marathons, so too he now needed something to keep him motivated in the interim.

And then it hit him, it was obvious really; he would become the youngest person in the world to run 200 marathons! Unbelievably it wasn't that far off, as while he'd been totting up his single year totals, his overall total had shot up to 198. And so, two races later at the White Peak Marathon in Derbyshire, Steve Edwards became the youngest person ever to run 200 marathons, aged 29 years, 161 days.

More publicity followed, but by now Steve was beginning to handle it with a certain amount of aplomb, and despite racing, training, working full-time and caring for his wife and young son, he still managed to find the time to meticulously file each newspaper cutting and magazine article, whether written in English or a foreign language, into a scrapbook, as well as maintaining his spreadsheet of races, places and performances for every race he entered.

With the onset of June, Steve found himself yet another challenge - to run the furthest apart official marathon double within the UK! The first marathon on Saturday, 6th June, was in the Outer Hebrides on the Isle of Benbecula, the second was on Sunday, 7th June, at Poole, on the south coast of England.

On Friday, 5th June, Steve, Mandy and Jason drove to Kyle of Lochalsh, crossed the water on the flatbed car ferry, drove to Uig and then took the foot ferry to Lochmaddy on the Isle of North Uist. A volunteer from the Army (who were assisting with the race), then drove them to barracks in Ballivanich on the Isle of Benbecula where they ate pasta in the mess hall. They were then driven to their B&B, where, despite the near 24 hours of daylight, they all fell promptly and soundly asleep.

To ensure they'd have time to catch the day's last ferry from Lochmaddy back to the mainland, Steve had calculated he needed to run 3:15 or under. This would give him 15 minutes to shower and change before an Army volunteer drove them the 20 miles back to Lochmaddy. With his mind full of logistics, Steve barely remembers the course other than it consisted of two fairly flat laps and some beautiful white sandy beaches. In fact, he won the race in 3:10, but didn't have time to wait for his prize!

A long drive and a little sleep later, leaving his family at home to recover, Steve drove in the early hours of Sunday morning to Poole. Despite his exhaustion, he finished his second marathon of the weekend in 3:28, and then drove home again.

Total driving miles for this trip? 1400. Potentially, this mileage between two consecutive marathons will never be beaten in the UK, as neither marathon exists any more.

Another three weeks, another three UK marathons, and then the family headed off on another complimentary overseas adventure - this time to Tromso, Norway, for the Midnight Sun Marathon. With stand-by tickets to Oslo, they had to wait for the very last flight for seats to become available. From Oslo they flew in a small, very noisy, propeller-driven aircraft to Tromso, and were then driven to their hotel.

The following day, they enjoyed a stunning boat trip around the Island's many fjords: '...the views and scenery were breathtaking.' Much to young Jason's delight, they were even able to do some fishing off the deck.

It was a thoroughly relaxing day, but Steve couldn't forget that come 10 pm he had a race to run, as indeed had young Jason and his mum, who were taking part in a two-mile fun run being held just before the main marathon. Suddenly, Jason was in his element; he was doing just what his dad did! Poor Mandy spent most of the two miles reining in her young son, whose excitement kept pushing him to sprint!

And then it was Steve's turn to run in the midnight sun: '...the scenery was stunning, but it felt very strange running at a time when my body clock was telling me I should be in bed.'

Despite running well, Steve's performance dipped in the final mile and he finished in 3 hours 16 seconds, just missing out on his hoped for sub-3. He wasn't disappointed, though: '...it was such an enjoyable course and I felt extremely privileged just to be there at the grace of the organisers.'

By the time Steve finished his race, it was nearly 2 am, the sun was shining in a cerulean sky, the pubs were open and people were partying. Instead of retiring to bed, the family joined the party, soaking up the atmosphere and revelling in the fun.

And then it was time to say goodbye, but the magic of the weekend lingered as, at the airport, stand-by tickets in hand and economy class full, they were upgraded to business class. It was the perfect end to a fabulous trip, with champagne, snacks and a better choice of meal!

Jason was already writing his weekend story for school in his head - they'd never believe this one!

Chapter 16

1992 (PART II) – CHANGES

The weekend after the family's magical trip to Norway, Steve was brought firmly back down to earth with the Finglas Marathon in Dublin.

Travelling through the night to catch the 2 am ferry from Holyhead, Steve hitched a lift with 100 Clubber, Brent Iddles. At that time, Brent drove an imported, souped-up, left-hand drive, Golf hatchback, built for rally driving. As they followed the A5 through Wales, they came across a white van being driven rapidly along the winding, twisting part of the road approaching the popular, pretty town of Betws-y-coed. Brent recognised a challenge when he saw one! Speeding up, he was right on the tail of the van. The van driver went faster. Brent responded in kind. Meanwhile, his petrified passenger clung on to his seat for dear life, certain that any second they would roll or veer off the road. Brent's assertions that there was nothing to worry about: '...this is a rally car, it's been built to corner at speed', did absolutely nothing to allay Steve's fears. The car may be built for rallying, but Brent had not been trained to rally!

The faster they went, the harder Steve clung on. Brent made a further futile attempt to reassure him: '...he'll roll before we do!'

Steve looked towards the sky and, in desperation, offered up a silent prayer to the guardian angel his mother was always mentioning. Not long afterwards, the van turned off and Steve breathed a grateful sigh of relief, glancing skywards in acknowledgement.

The rest of the journey passed in relative calm. The two men made it safely on to the ferry and Steve ran his race in 3:15.

But the corners of life are not always as visible as the corners of a road, and with Steve's enthusiasm for his sport burning ever brighter with notions of replicating the kind of schedule he was currently following for several years to come so that he could break Sy Mah's record by the time he was 40, Steve's vision may have become slightly blurred in respect of other areas of his life.

However, for the time being, life allowed him to follow his dream uninterrupted as he set off on yet another complimentary trip in business class to run the Paavo Nurmi Marathon in Turku, Finland.

Arriving on the Friday, Steve was met at the airport by a race representative and the famous Finnish multi-marathon runner, Kalevi Saukkonen, who offered to take Steve to another marathon the day before Sunday's Paavo Nurmi race, so they could get a double in. It was too good an opportunity to refuse.

Accordingly, in the early hours of Saturday morning, Kalevi collected Steve from his hotel and they drove the 260 miles north to Jacobstad. Arriving at the race, Kalevi was practically mobbed – everyone knew the man who featured in the world's top 10 for running the most marathons and was number one in Finland. He too was chasing Sy Mah's record and was getting close, but his times were nowhere near as fast as Steve's. [Kalevi subsequently broke Sy Mah's record and as at July 2014, aged 70, had completed over 1700 marathons, although it's unknown whether all were official races.]

The race at Jacobstad was not a good one for Steve; his 3:17 finish time reflected the uncomfortable humidity and undulating course. It briefly crossed his mind that maybe all the travelling, living out of a suitcase, being away from home, trying to juggle work, home and running lives didn't really help, but there was that niggling feeling that he'd had before that something wasn't quite right with his body. He couldn't put his finger on it, but it was there just the same. It felt as though he had absolutely no energy. Maybe it was because he hadn't had a proper break since his 100th marathon at the end of 1990 and it was now 1992? Of course that's what it was! Satisfied, Steve pushed the matter to the back of his mind.

The drive back to Turku with Kalevi was a fairly quiet one with neither Kalevi nor Steve enjoying a great command of the other's language. However,

Steve did understand Kalevi's response to his question about being married. 'No,' replied Kalevi, he was not married, '...although, maybe yes – to the marathon!'

They arrived back in Turku just in time for the pasta party. But there was no time to eat, as Steve was immediately hauled up on stage for a live radio interview. Luckily, the interview was relatively short, and Steve managed to grab a morsel of leftover pasta just as everyone else was leaving.

The following day, the sun shone and the temperature was in the eighties. Despite a good night's sleep, Steve still felt tired. Even so, he was looking forward to running a marathon named after the greatest Finnish runner of all time. As he made his weary way to the start line, though, he couldn't have felt less like Paavo Nurmi: '...I was so tired and already hot. I just needed to get the job done.'

And get it done he did, relieved to record 3:23 in such conditions. He returned home with: '...two large medals of unique beauty', which still number among his favourites today.

Another relaxing flight in business class, and Steve was back where he longed to be, in the bosom of his beloved family.

The following weekend, Steve set off from home to run the Moray Marathon in Scotland and bid a fond farewell as usual to Mandy and Jason. He'd only gone a short distance when he had an overwhelming urge to return home, pick up his family and take them with him: '...I'd never felt like that before, I don't know why on that particular occasion I felt it, I just did.'

Steve followed his instincts and returned home to collect his somewhat bemused wife and child before setting off once more on the 1000-mile trip to Elgin and back. Whether or not it was having his family close, he doesn't know, but Steve felt much better than he had in Finland and finished in 3:11.

A week later, he was off again, this time to the Monchau Marathon in Germany. Rallying Brent was once again driving, but the 200-mile drive from Dunkirk to Konzen, passed without mishap. Given that he hadn't done any of the driving, Steve couldn't believe how tired he felt, sleeping both in the car and on the ferry. He didn't feel much better when it came to the race; a hilly course on a hot day, which he ran in a disappointing 3:44.

He bucked up a bit when he saw German hot dogs and beer at the finish, but when he returned to the car he instantly fell asleep again waiting for Brent. It was that same feeling he'd had in Finland, a complete lack of energy. He just couldn't understand it, he'd only travelled 800 miles and hadn't driven - it was nothing compared to some of his other trips.

A week later, he was still feeling below par when he ran the Isle of Man Marathon in 3:21.

The drop in his times began to bother him; he was used to running close to three hours, he just couldn't understand what had gone wrong.

However, a week later he ran the Reykjavik Marathon, courtesy of the race organisers, and enjoyed a return to form with 3:02 and a top-ten finish.

Believing he'd turned the corner, Steve relaxed and enjoyed the rest of the complimentary treats laid on by the organisers, including a visit to the Blue Lagoon, an outdoor pool where troubles are soothed away by volcanically heated, piping hot, chalky soft water: '...a wonderful way to recover from running 26.2 miles,' and, later, a nightclub, where, in 1992, Steve's £6 allowance covered just one pint of beer.

Content and rejuvenated, Steve returned home from Iceland to discover not one, but two more race invitations awaiting him; one for the Auckland Marathon in New Zealand, the other for the Lake Kawaguchi Marathon (now better known as the Fujisan Marathon), in Japan. Both would pay flights, hotel and race entry. Steve's joyous cup runneth over. Never had he imagined he would be so privileged as to receive race invites from all over the world; perhaps the long tiring weekends driving all over Europe and running back-to-back marathons had been worth it after all!

In such chirpy manner did Steve's marathon tour continue with Guernsey, a week after Reykjavik. Travelling on the overnight ferry with Brent, who was now also packing in marathons every weekend to reach his 100th, Steve finished in 3:07, increasingly confident that full fitness had returned with two solid performances within seven days.

His belief was undimmed when his form remained consistent for the next two domestic marathons, and his happiness unbounded at thus being able to spend more time with Mandy and Jason.

And so he continued hammering out a marathon every weekend, his focus firmly fixed on his long-term goal and on continually upping his totals from 200 to 300, from 300 to 400, and onwards to the golden 500, and beyond.

Another trip to the Rheinruhr Marathon in Duisburg, Germany followed. Still desperate to get back under 3 hours, Steve had to content himself with 3 hours 48 seconds. So close; surely it was only a matter of time, the right race on the right day?

Next was Amsterdam, a flat, fast course. Doubtless this would be the one. Alas, once more, it wasn't to be, with Steve finishing in 3:12.

It wasn't to be at the complimentary Humber Bridge Marathon a week later either, with Steve finishing in 3:03, his 100th sub-3:15 marathon.

Steve's dissatisfaction grew; no matter how hard he tried, he just couldn't maintain his speed over the full distance any more. Mentally, he knew he was strong, but physically, something was wrong. Should he rest, or was it something else? He was still running solid times every weekend and, even if they didn't quite meet the high expectations he had of himself, they were at least in line with his original goal of keeping all his times below 3:30. If there was a problem, it couldn't be serious. Once more he pushed any concerns to the back of his mind.

Another domestic marathon followed a week later, this time without Mandy, who decided she and Jason needed a day at home. Unquestioning, Steve marched on, meeting up with 100 Clubbers at the Kingston Marathon. He finished in 3:12 and returned home.

The following weekend Steve was at the Lisbon Marathon in Portugal, again by invitation; another new marathon, another new country and another new capital city to run in. Did life get any better? Well, there was one way it would for Steve, cracking that blessed 3-hour barrier again. But again, Lisbon didn't yield up the key to that particular gate with Steve finishing just outside in 3:01. It was becoming a popular theme, so close but no cigar!

However, the pragmatic side of Steve told the rest of him not to worry and so, heeding this advice, Steve instead looked forward to his trip with Mandy to Auckland in five days time. Unfortunately, Jason wouldn't be joining them as the organisers had only paid for Steve's trip and it had been struggle enough finding the money for Mandy's ticket. Jason, therefore, would have to put up with being thoroughly spoilt by his grandparents for the week.

A few days before embarking on the 23-hour flight, Steve had been interviewed over the phone by the New Zealand press. By now, this had become pretty standard with invitational international races.

Even so, when he boarded Air New Zealand's 747, he hadn't anticipated coming face to face with an article about himself, complete with photo, in the in-flight magazine!

'It felt very strange!'

Strange it may have been, but it didn't stop Steve removing the magazine from the aircraft and adding it to his growing collection of similar publications which he still has today - all filed and neatly stored in date order, naturally.

Flight over, Steve and Mandy were welcomed to Auckland by bright sunshine and a marathon representative, who wanted Steve to partake in the 'breakfast run', in a couple of hours' time. Aware they were footing his bill and appreciating it would be good publicity for them, Steve felt honour-bound to agree. At least they let him check in and freshen up at his hotel first!

Twenty-three hours of flying, one shower, and one banana later, Steve was running in the four-mile breakfast run through the streets of Auckland. His reward? Brunch with the Mayor of Auckland! The Mayor was interested in what Steve did for a living besides running. When Steve told him running was just a hobby and he worked in IT, the Mayor suggested he move to New Zealand as they were keen to get young professional people over there with his skills. It was an invitation that after seeing how beautiful New Zealand was, Steve did consider, although, ultimately, didn't pursue.

However, at that precise moment, Steve had other things on his mind, such as an imminent radio interview when he would be taking questions from listeners. Although hoping Mandy would accompany him, he accepted her assertions that she was too tired and needed to rest at the hotel instead, pushing away a vague sense of unease; of course she would be tired after such a journey.

The interview and questions went well. Steve returned to the hotel, then he and Mandy enjoyed a wander round town, followed by dinner.

Marathon day dawned. It was a big day for the organisers as it would be the first time the race had passed over the Auckland Harbour Bridge. The bridge had been plagued with problems since its construction and with some 4000 runners pounding across its 1.02km stretch, there was concern in certain quarters that it may be unsafe! As a precaution, engineers would monitor the bridge throughout the run, checking for signs of stress and weakness. Fortunately, the bridge didn't fall down and Steve enjoyed another good run until those final few miles, when he just couldn't hang on to his pace, eventually finishing in 3:01.

The same old feelings of frustration returned. Steve questioned his training methods; maybe he needed to make some changes? Since setting the record of 87, he'd continued with the same two or three mid-week tempo runs, but maybe the absence of regular double marathons meant he wasn't doing enough weekly mileage? Maybe that, plus not taking a proper rest after setting the record, was the reason behind his slightly diminished form? Yes, decided Steve, that was it, and really, he thought, when you take both those factors into account, his times weren't bad at all!

Thus reassured, Steve turned to enjoying his last two days in New Zealand with Mandy. Together they visited Rotorua - famed for its geothermal activity, geysers and hot mud pools, explored the city, and dined at the home of a race volunteer, who couldn't believe they'd travelled so far for a few days just to run a marathon!

They arrived home in the early hours of Thursday morning and slept till Thursday afternoon. On Friday, Steve returned to work for an IT course. On Saturday, he was back at the airport, heading to Crete to run the Vardinoyiannios Marathon, which involved two flights via Athens, all courtesy of the race organisers.

On arrival, Steve met up with former Olympic marathoner, Bill Adcocks, of Coventry's famous Godiva Harriers. Every year, Bill took a small contingent of elite GB runners to the race, and the organisers had suggested Steve ask Bill if he could be added to his group. Bill had kindly agreed.

Following so soon after his exhausting New Zealand trip, it was no wonder Steve didn't feel like getting up the next morning, never mind running 26.2 miles. Forcing himself to open the curtains, he was nearly blinded by the sun's brightness. It was going to be a hot, hard run. Why couldn't he just be heading for the beach instead? By the time he stood on the start line, he'd never felt less like running; the temperatures were already in the 80s, and he was sweating profusely.

His plan to get to the halfway point in just over 1:30, instead of just below as usual, in an attempt to break the 3-hour jinx, went completely awry, with the heat seriously starting to affect him by 10 miles. Passing halfway in just under 1:36 and aiming to maintain his 8 mm pace so he'd be in with a chance of recording a half-respectable time, Steve plodded wearily on. But he'd set himself an impossible task. As the temperature climbed higher, Steve's pace slowed further. There was nothing he could do about it. He was just too tired. With the course passing through narrow vineyard lanes sheltered from any breeze, the heat was killing him. Gritting his teeth, he ploughed inexorably on and somehow managed to keep running, albeit very slowly, finishing in a disheartening 3:36. He was wrecked and embarrassed not to have performed to his best in front of the other GB runners, and especially Bill.

Following the presentations and lunch, Steve went to his room and lay down on his bed. He was asleep within seconds and didn't wake up again until he'd missed dinner by two hours! But he was too tired to care. Closing his eyes once more, he returned almost instantly to the lovely, la-la land of nod.

Finally fully refreshed, Steve rose early next day and prepared for the journey home. By now, all the travelling and running was becoming something of a blur. Looking back, Steve is surprised he can remember as much as he does, because he believes, by that stage, he was no longer able to take in very much about where he was or what he was doing.

It was hardly surprising. Since 10th March, 1991, Steve had run 126 marathons in 86 weeks at 100 different locations, averaging just under 3:14 per race. He hadn't had a proper break since then, and it was now November 1992. Consequently, he decided that after the last marathon on the UK calendar, he would take a proper break and spend some precious time with his wife and son. With just another couple of domestic marathons to come over the intervening two weekends, and his much-anticipated complimentary trip to Japan for the Lake Kawaguchi Marathon, it seemed like the perfect plan.

But, as the saying goes, life happens while we are making plans. Less than a week after he returned home from Crete, Mandy announced that she was leaving him.

Steve was stunned; it was a complete bolt from the blue. There had been no warning signs, no arguments, no waning of passion or affection. Mandy had never complained about the marathons, neither had she ever indicated she was less than happy with their marriage. Steve's world shook on its axis.

For her part, Mandy was apologetic, clearly unhappy about upsetting and hurting Steve, but refusing to discuss the matter; her mind was made up. She was going. For Jason's sake she would wait until after Christmas and New Year, but after that, she was off.

The couple went to their last marathon together in December - St Albans, where two years earlier Steve had celebrated running his 100th marathon and Mandy had made a special cake. This time, there would be no celebration.

Running with Colin, Steve confided in his long-time running buddy who said this was partly why he intended leaving the sport or at least cutting down on the number of marathons he ran. Steve's news confirmed his worst fears. Following so soon after Malcolm Long's untimely death in his early thirties after the leg pain he'd complained of for so long turned out to be caused by a deep vein thrombosis, which had moved up to his brain causing a cerebral embolism, Colin felt it was time for him to bow out and spend more time with his family.

With a heavy heart, Steve crossed the finish line in 3:26.

He returned home thoroughly depressed and immediately started looking back on his and Mandy's life together, trying to see where it had all gone wrong, searching for signs; anything that would help him understand what had made her suddenly stop loving him. He blamed himself. He'd been selfish running all those marathons; trotting around the world, while Mandy mostly stayed home alone looking after Jason.

He recalled their trip to New Zealand and how he'd had that vague sense of unease. He asked her if she'd been feeling that way then. She confirmed she had. In fact, she'd felt that way for quite some time.

Steve's world rocked some more. The guilt lay heavy in his soul. He had let his wife down so badly.

He'd already cancelled his trip to Japan, but now he decided not to run any more marathons.

Whatever it took to change Mandy's mind and save his marriage, he would do. He even contacted ST to end his sponsorship so that Mandy would realise she came first and he was prepared to give it all up if it meant they could stay together.

But it was too late. Despite agreeing to try counselling, it was apparent Mandy had already made her decision and, for her, there was no turning back.

Steve was bereft: '...my world was crashing down around me and there was nothing I could do to stop it.'

A distraught Steve was left reeling from shock and unable to grasp that his marriage could possibly be over, especially when he hadn't seen it coming.

He wasn't the only one; none of their friends or family had seen it coming either, and were equally shocked. It seemed Mandy had done a very good job of pretending to be happy and had fooled everyone.

Except, perhaps, the star...

Chapter 17

1993 – PICKING UP THE PIECES

On Monday, 4th January, 1993, Mandy left the matrimonial home. She went on her own, leaving her son behind with his dad. The details of that day remain firmly locked away in Steve's mind and are too painful to share even after all this time. Suffice to say, he was a broken man.

Broken man he may have been, but he was also a dad with a young son to look after. For Jason's sake, he had to somehow find a way to keep going. Ignoring the desire to simply lay down and cry, Steve forced himself to think only of his son and his needs. A child needed routine and stability; it was up to him to provide them and find a way to keep Jason's life as normal as possible. And that meant getting him to and from school, feeding him proper meals, doing all the domestic chores to keep the house clean and the garden tidy. But what would he do with him in the school holidays? Who would look after him then? And what about those hours between Jason finishing school and Steve getting home from work?

These were just the first things to enter Steve's mind, there were a million other things he'd have to deal with that he hadn't even thought of yet. Panic overwhelmed him. He couldn't think straight and his emotions were in turmoil. How would he cope on his own with a full time job and an eight-year old son? Not to mention a broken heart. As for running, well, that was clearly over. There was no way he'd have time to run as well as do everything else. Steve couldn't have cared less.

Thank goodness then for Steve's parents, who, in their usual pragmatic manner, entered the bombsite and immediately began clearing the debris. They reassured Steve that everything would work out eventually; yes, it would take time and no, it wouldn't be easy, but if he just dealt with one thing at a time, it would all come good in the end. They also made him look at the positives - his secure job and the fact that he and Jason had a roof over their heads. They anticipated Steve would find time to run again once he'd got a routine organised.

Steve wanted to believe what they were telling him, but it was hard, especially when the almost physical pain of his hurt remained. It abated fractionally while he was busy, but never went completely; constant and sure as his heartbeat. The worst times were the evenings after Jason had gone to bed and Steve had finished his chores. Then he'd sit down, switch on the television, and feel so lonely: '...it was like a piece of me had been ripped away and my heart ached so much I could have screamed.'

At night he cried himself to sleep.

But however much we hurt inside, life has a habit of marching on regardless, dragging us along with it, kicking and screaming in its wake perhaps, but moving forward just the same. And so it was for Steve. Little by little, slowly but surely, he began to pick up the pieces of his broken life.

A neighbour whose children attended the same school as Jason agreed to look after him while Steve was at work in return for a nominal sum. At weekends Jason stayed with Mandy, who was now living with a friend. This gave Steve a chance to run the odd Sunday marathon, so long as it wasn't too far from home and he'd be back in time to collect Jason again.

Thus encouraged, Steve contacted ST to ask if they'd consider sponsoring him again if he returned to racing. ST agreed, provided he raced regularly with the aim of beating Sy Mah's record - Steve's ultimate goal anyway. Steve considered the matter carefully. He wouldn't do anything that might compromise the new life he was in the process of setting up with his young son and wouldn't want to enter into something he couldn't fully commit to. Equally, he recognised that running gave him something much more than just physical fitness - it gave him immense psychological well being, and had single-handedly restored his confidence and self-esteem after all the years of bullying. Both were currently in short supply and it would be wonderful to once more experience the euphoria that came with running a good race.

Decision made, he visited ST's offices in late January to seal the deal. Any doubts about whether it was the right decision in his current circumstances were dissipated when he noticed the company were doing another Los Angeles tour in March. A holiday in LA was just what he and Jason needed, giving them both something to look forward to. Steve didn't hesitate - if the company agreed to let him take that trip with Jason, they had a deal. Business relations resumed, Steve returned home with a lighter step and a sense of purpose. He had two months to get fit for LA.

As soon as he got home, Steve broke the good news to Jason. He would be nine by the time they travelled, the perfect age for Disney and Universal Studios. Jason was thrilled, leaping up and down, grinning from ear to ear! A tiny piece of Steve's heart flipped; it took him a while to recognise the corresponding emotion, and by the time he did it had already passed. He may have got it wrong, but it had felt strangely like happiness.

A less fleeting emotion now Steve had something to look forward to and work towards, was his resolve to get himself into a better routine. Gradually, life began to settle. Steve adapted to working, caring for Jason, running the home. He also started weight training again, fitting in a half-hour session at home every other night.

And then he returned to his beloved running, squeezing in a few miles during his lunch break at work; taking pleasure in the joy of running and the discovery of new routes. He couldn't believe he hadn't made use of his lunchtime in this way before. Then again, previously, he'd have been busy planning the logistics for his next overseas trip. Now he wasn't travelling so far, his time could be better utilised running instead. It was really quite freeing. It was fortunate too that his workplace had a shower so he didn't offend any of his colleagues when he returned to his desk!

As the weeks passed, the combination of regular weight training and running began to pay off and Steve felt the first welcome stirrings of a return to some kind of fitness. Undoubtedly, it was nowhere near the level he was at previously, but it was a start. He was moving forwards.

Emotionally, though, the forward movement was less noticeable. He was still desperately lonely and unhappy. Even so, something had started to shift - survival instinct perhaps? For it slowly dawned on him that seeing Mandy every time she had Jason was not helping; reminding him what he'd lost, opening up old wounds. If he was to have any chance of making a full recovery, he must accept reconciliation was never going to happen and make a clean break of things. With a heavy heart, Steve took steps to begin divorce proceedings.

Meantime, he kept himself busy with his new life and its routines, completed some decorating, focussed on work, running, and Jason.

Then, one day, out of the blue, the fragile foundations he'd been so painstakingly rebuilding, collapsed.

'It hit me like a steam train. I came home from work one day feeling unwell and really tired. After doing the chores, I went to bed soon after Jason. When I woke the next day, my mouth and throat were extremely sore, swallowing was almost unbearable.'

Steve phoned in work sick and visited his GP. The GP's examination revealed a mouth full of tiny ulcers, an indicator of oral thrush and being badly run down. He was signed off work for two weeks and advised to rest completely. Such a physiological reaction was hardly surprising. Steve's whole world had been turned upside down and had affected him emotionally far more than he could ever have imagined. Add to that two years of running an average of three marathons every two weeks in average times of 3:14, and something was bound to give.

'It seemed strange that it happened when I wasn't actually running marathons. I suppose I was under the illusion that my body was physically being rested.'

Steve stayed in bed the whole of the following week, dosing himself with antibiotics, while his parents helped out with Jason. Still unable to swallow properly, his mouth too sore even to eat liquidised food, he ingested only liquids, such as shakes, soups and yoghurts. Hot drinks were also a no-no, the heated liquid searing his tender mouth. With nothing tasting as it should, it would have been easy to give up trying to eat and just sleep instead. But a man who has run 87 marathons in a 12-month period is not a man who gives up easily and Steve understood that his body needed nutrition to help it recover, so he persevered.

After two weeks, his perseverance paid off and he began to feel a little better, although the weight he'd lost through not eating meant his energy levels were still low. But he was desperate to get running, and so, the minute he started eating solids again, he tested himself out with a few exercises like press-ups and sit-ups, followed by a very steady, very short, run. It came as a huge relief to find he felt absolutely fine.

Which was just as well, as his trip to LA with Jason was now just three short weeks away. Despite his heart still being in pieces, the rest of his body at least seemed to have recovered enough that he was able to start building up his training runs again and do weights every other day.

Although Steve was looking forward to his trip with Jason, it was tempered by the knowledge that Mandy wouldn't be with them. He needn't have worried, Jason's enthusiasm was enough for them both and it was impossible not to have a good time. Even the marathon went well, all things considered, with Steve finishing in 3:27.

After LA, Steve's marathons were largely confined to the British Isles due to his domestic commitments, but he and Jason did get to enjoy one further little foray into foreign climes with a week's holiday in Gran Canaria in May. Again, Steve felt the loneliness of being on holiday without a partner, especially when people asked Jason where his mum was and he'd tell them she was at home: '...they probably thought I was an absent parent taking a holiday with my son. I don't suppose it ever occurred to them I was the main carer.'

The evenings were the worst though. Every night he and Jason would go to dinner in some romantic, candle-lit restaurant overlooking the sea and Steve would suffer extreme envy surrounded by loving couples and jolly families. How he wished his little family were still together: '...I really missed that. It upset me terribly.'

During those early days Steve struggled to come to terms with doing everything for the first time without Mandy by his side or knowing he'd see her when he got home. Keen as he was to return to running, revisiting marathon locations he'd been to with her, was very upsetting, even though he knew it had to be done.

When the Decree Absolute arrived from the divorce courts in July pronouncing the final dissolution of his marriage, Steve felt even worse. The truth was he was finding it incredibly hard to motivate himself to continue running marathons at all at that time: '...

somehow it didn't seem worthwhile any more, nothing really did. There didn't seem any point to it.'

It wasn't just marathons that seemed pointless, there were other things too, such as having a nice meal, keeping the house looking tidy, buying new clothes: '...I'd been used to sharing those things with somebody I loved. Then, suddenly, I wasn't any more. That made me very sad.'

Such sadness heightened Steve's awareness of just what was most important to him in life, aside from his son. Sharing his life with somebody special was top of the list. Like many before him, losing someone had made him realise how important the little things are, things too easily taken for granted, such as sharing a meal, shopping, or simply being together. He longed to have all that back in his life again. However, for now, he just had to focus on getting through each day, caring for Jason, and, of course, running marathons.

In early September he did just that in Norfolk, enjoying a return to form with 3:16. This turned out to be Steve's 200th sub-3:30 marathon, but such was the state of his mind at the time, he was oblivious.

In November, Steve ran the Telford Marathon, and met Jim Maine and wife, Liz, who have since become good friends. Jim was then running for Alvis Running Club in Coventry, as was Phil Duffy. Phil had tried for some time to persuade Steve to join the club but, without really knowing why, Steve had never been keen. Maybe it was the thought of having to commit to a rigid training night or having to turn up to regular races that might not fit in with his marathon schedule? Plus, he was used to training alone. It was the way it had always been and he thought he was happy with that. However, when Jim also asked him if he'd be interested in joining Alvis, Steve decided to give it a go, and has never looked back.

'It introduced me to another aspect of running that I hadn't experienced before. Running for a team at cross-country races in the winter league and at other shorter distances, which I hadn't done in a long time, gave me new impetus and motivation that went some way to helping me enjoy my running again.'

The small club really suited Steve; its numbers having dwindled since the factory from which it derived its name had closed its doors. Once a week, Steve would meet other club members at the Alvis Sports Ground and set off for a longish run accompanied by good-natured banter and friendly rivalry. It was the perfect foil for his loneliness. Plus, the longer runs, together with the cross-country and shorter races, helped restore some of the fitness and speed that had inevitably been lost since cutting down on marathon races.

The cutback had been pretty severe, with Steve running just 18 races throughout the whole of 1993. All bar one of those races had taken place in the UK, including London, for which he'd managed to get his second consecutive entry.

Despite training with the Alvis Club, Steve describes his training at that time as being: '...at best sporadic', and this was reflected in his performances. Although he continued training over shorter, faster miles rather than doing long, steady runs, without running a marathon most weekends, it was proving less effective. There was nothing he could do about it - his current domestic situation didn't allow enough time for him to run more than three to five miles at once.

Consequently, Steve's performances throughout 1993 ranged from 3:09 to 3:37. Of the 18 races run, 16 were sub-3:30 and his average time for the year was 3:20. Not a bad set of results, all things considered. Certainly, whilst Steve wasn't deliriously happy with his times, he was at least still well within his target of keeping his average finish times for all marathons well inside 3:30. Meanwhile, his overall total had increased to 246 marathons with an average finish time of 3:17:31.

Even with everything that had happened, Steve was still carefully recording every performance on his spreadsheet: '...the stats are one of the things that have driven me on over the years and helped me achieve my goals.'

However, despite faithfully logging every race, Steve was oblivious to the fact that he was now almost halfway to Sy Mah's total; such was the effect of his emotional trauma.

And then, six months after receiving his Decree Absolute, Steve went on a blind date.

They met in a local pub, the man with one hand and a fractured heart, and the woman with her candyfloss auburn hair and gentle blue eyes. He bought them both a drink and they sat down at a table next to a Christmas tree decked out in a tasteless clash of colourful baubles. In the background, Mr Blobby sang his blobby Christmas hit. All this they noticed, but she didn't notice his lack of a hand and he didn't notice anything but her smile. And then they started to talk. They didn't stop talking till they left the pub several hours later. She recalled with satisfaction that he'd only drunk one pint of beer, after which he'd switched to non-alcoholic drinks. An alcoholic father had left its mark on her. He recalled the ease with which they'd conversed and how she'd made him laugh. It was a long time since he'd laughed. They swapped phone numbers. Steve held off for three long days before he rang her. She was in the middle of making mince pies. By the time they'd finished talking, the pies were burnt.

A week later, the couple went to see the romcom, 'Sleepless in Seattle' – her choice not his, not that he minded. Pizza followed; they made up for their enforced silence in the cinema and she made him laugh again when she confessed that she'd lied about her age and, instead of being three years younger than him as she'd led him to believe on their first date, she was, in fact, six months older.

If it was time for confessions, Steve decided he should come clean too. Not that he'd told any lies, more omitted to mention certain things, like his recent divorce and his son. Just as she'd been afraid her age might put him off, so too Steve had thought the idea of dating a single parent with a young son in situ, might put her off.

They were both wrong. Neither was deterred from following their hearts.

Steve went home from that second date aware that he'd met someone special: '...we just got on so well. There was never a moment's awkwardness between us.'

Throughout December, they saw each other regularly, enjoying evenings out or staying in listening to Steve's immense record collection. By some wonderful quirk of fate, she actually shared his musical taste - even some of the punk stuff!

On Christmas Eve, Steve cooked dinner for her and, on Christmas Day, they met at her sister's house, where Steve was introduced to some of her family. As she was the eldest of seven, it was just scratching the surface, but it confirmed the status of the relationship on both sides. This was no casual attachment.

Even so, Steve was very aware that it was less than a year since his marriage had ended. His ex-wife had been his only serious girlfriend, and now here he was meeting the family of another woman he'd known for less than a month. He should tread warily. But even as his head harboured the sensible thought, his heart seemed to have developed a mind of its own, for it flipped, just as it had earlier in the year. This time Steve was much quicker to identify the emotion that went with it.

He wasn't the only one; high up above, a star, which wasn't the North Star, shone just a little bit brighter than usual. Happiness does that to stars.

Chapter 18

1994 – NEW BEGINNINGS

Her name was Teresa and she was a staff nurse working at the private Nuffield Hospital near Leamington Spa. A former NHS staff nurse and midwife, Teresa had grown tired of the rotating night shifts which were affecting her health and had moved to the private sector a couple of years earlier. She'd had a few casual relationships but unlike her two sisters who'd married young, Teresa was applying patience and waiting for Mr Right. By the time she met Steve she was 31; for a woman who wanted a family, the clock was ticking. However, she had no intention of rushing into anything she didn't feel was 100 per cent right; her parents had divorced when she was 14, memories of their unhappy marriage remained sharp, etched forever in her mind. She'd rather have no family at all, than marry the wrong man.

In Steve, Teresa recognised someone with the same values as herself; loyal, hard-working, caring, kind, responsible, a family man, a sober man. They enjoyed the same music and films, and shared the same quiet sense of humour. He was the sort of man she'd been looking for; a man with whom she could see a future.

By February, Teresa felt committed enough to the relationship to hand over the spare key to her flat. She also let Steve drive her car. Steve repaid her by driving into the back of another vehicle at a traffic island: 'I felt such an idiot!' His defence? 'The pedals were so close together that when I put my foot on the brake I also pressed the accelerator!'

Teresa didn't judge. In fact, she was grateful, as the insurance settlement enabled her to purchase a brand new Peugeot 106 – which she also let Steve drive.

As for the running, she didn't really get it: '...the only thing I knew about marathons were the bars we used to eat before they were called Snickers!' However, it seemed a harmless enough activity and she was definitely pro people keeping fit. In fact, she owned a Jane Fonda workout video that she used occasionally at home, and she had, in the past, actually run round the block a couple of times with her sister: '...but only in the dark so nobody would see me.' Of course this wasn't foolproof, other people did go out after dark: '...if I saw anyone coming, I'd stop.' Also, once, when she was a teenager, someone bet her she couldn't run ten times round the cricket field and she was determined to show them that she jolly well could – and did!

'I didn't even know how far a marathon was back then!'

Things then were about to change quite significantly for the guile-less marathon virgin...

Steve, meanwhile, was feeling pretty darn chipper. There was a definite spring in his step and he was experiencing a renewed zest for running and life in general. He kicked off his marathon season in traditional fashion in March with the Suffolk and Essex Border Marathon.

It was Teresa's first marathon and Steve wanted her to enjoy it. He needn't have worried. Teresa quickly forged friendships with Phil and Jim's wives, Mary and Liz, and later Chuck Pope's wife, Maureen. Steve also enjoyed his first time racing as a club member, revelling in the camaraderie, finishing in 3:08. The time restored his faith in his ability to still run reasonable times, and he and Teresa returned home happy.

Unfortunately, their happiness was slightly marred when two hours after arriving home the doorbell rang. Shivering on Steve's doorstep was Harry Smedt (a prolific multi-marathon runner from Belgium), wearing just shorts and a t-shirt. Only then did Steve remember that he had Harry's kit stored in his car boot! In his and Teresa's happy bubble, they'd both completely forgotten about it. Fortunately for Harry, rallying Brent had driven him to Steve's house; rather less fortunate, Harry had now missed his return flight. So ashamed were Steve and Teresa by their unintentional misdemeanour that after dropping a bewildered but none-the-less excited Jason off at his grandparents' home (he never knew what would happen when his dad ran a marathon, roll on Monday!), they drove Harry to Heathrow where he caught a later flight. If Harry hadn't been employed and sponsored by Sabina Airlines, guilt-ridden Steve would have paid for his additional flight too!

It wasn't quite the ending to the day Steve had imagined, but it did show Teresa that this marathon lark wasn't all about the running!

In April, Teresa accompanied Steve to her second race, the Bungay Marathon in Suffolk. It was all rather tame, with no abandoned runners or crazy dashes to Heathrow Airport in the middle of the night. But she saw the happy satisfaction on Steve's face as he crossed the line and understood just how much it meant to him.

Then she went with him to London.

Having previously only watched the London Marathon on TV, Teresa was excited at the prospect of actually being there and soaking up its famed atmosphere. Steve, meanwhile, was again helping out at the expo manning the stand for ST, who had paid his travel and hotel expenses.

Duties complete, the couple checked into their room at The Strand Palace Hotel, before venturing out to take in some of the capital's sights and find a suitable place to meet after Steve's race the next day.

'It was great being there with Teresa, but it did feel a little strange doing all the same things I'd done with Mandy two years earlier.'

Strange it may have been, but those were mere memories, this was the here and now. It was also the future, and Steve was slowly but surely moving into it.

Come race day, feeling healthy, happy and much fitter from all the training and racing he'd been doing with Alvis, Steve set out to run a sub-3, which, if successful, would be his first since London in 1992.

The race began well enough with Steve crossing the start line in less than a minute and starting his watch. As he approached the final mile he knew it would be close but was still confident he could do it. However, as he neared the finish, he realised he hadn't taken into account that the gun time wouldn't reflect his time from the actual start line (in those days London didn't use any form of chip timing). As he ran the final 150 metres, Steve could only watch in agony as the clock moved past the 3-hour mark, giving him a time of 3 hours 24 seconds! His own watch showed 2:59:40. But Steve is renowned for his fastidiousness for good reason. The strict standards he'd elected to aspire to for all his races meant that in the absence of a chip time, the clock time was his official time, as this was what would be recorded in the official results. No arguments.

For Teresa it was a real eye-opener. Until then she hadn't realised just how pedantic Steve was when it came to his running. But it didn't put her off, quite the opposite in fact; she respected his attention to detail, admired it even. A man who cared so much about the truth, even if it was only being truthful to himself, was a trustworthy man indeed. Cheating probably wasn't even in his vocabulary.

As for Steve, any disappointment he may have felt about his failure to dip officially under 3 hours, couldn't dispel the joyous anticipation he felt as he went to meet Teresa at their designated post-race meeting place. But when he got there, she was nowhere to be seen. His heart sank; he couldn't believe how much more disappointing her non-appearance was to him than his non sub-3. His disappointment was then replaced by concern for her welfare. Perhaps she'd caught the wrong train back from Blackheath and was wandering around some random station in the suburbs of London? Or perhaps she'd got lost after getting off at Charing Cross? Steve roamed anxiously and in vain around the vicinity looking for her. After half an hour he gave up and made his way back to the hotel. At some point, that was surely what she would do too?

It was. Just as Steve was walking into The Strand, he saw her up ahead of him walking in the same direction towards the hotel, her beautiful auburn hair bouncing playfully around her shoulders. His heart flipped. Running to catch up with her, the relieved smiles they gave each other said everything. Although Teresa hadn't, in fact, been lost. She'd just been waiting at a different statue some 30 metres away from the statue Steve had been waiting at and the crowds had prevented them being able to see each other! Just like

Steve, she'd decided to wait half an hour and then walk back to the hotel. They may not have known each other long, but they certainly seemed to know each other well. Whatever this thing was between them, it appeared to be more than just a meeting of hearts.

Hand in hand, the couple returned to their room and, as Steve showered, Teresa decided to be helpful and do some tidying up. This included removing Steve's race number from his vest and disposing of it in the bin. It wasn't until they arrived home and Steve unpacked his bag that he found his race vest minus number. Teresa proudly explained how she'd disposed of it at the hotel for him. Steve breathed deeply before explaining to her that he always kept his race numbers as part of his record of races run and racing memorabilia. Teresa was mortified. If she could, she'd have driven straight back to London and gone through every single piece of rubbish at the hotel. Steve could see her distress was real and sought to reassure her. Upset though he was to have lost his number (to this day it remains the only one he doesn't have), he was also secretly pleased that Teresa shared his tendency to be tidy.

In terms of marathon running, 1994 was a fairly quiet year, as Steve continued to adapt to his new life with Jason. He was also spending an increasing amount of time with Teresa. They got on remarkably well; she possessed all the qualities he admired and they shared the same life values.

However, when Teresa declared herself in love with him, Steve panicked. He was certain he felt the same way, but how could he know for sure? It still wasn't that long since he and Mandy had parted ways, he'd loved her completely and for a long time. Suppose this was just a rebound relationship? The last thing he wanted was to let Teresa down or hurt her in any way. There was also Jason to consider. He and Teresa seemed to get on well enough, and Teresa had already said she'd never try to fulfil a mother role and wouldn't interfere with parental issues, but how would they fare if they all lived together under the same roof? There was only one way to find out; a holiday to Turkey for the three of them was duly booked.

Steve's concerns melted away with the sunshine. This was no rebound thing, he loved her heart and soul, and Jason was clearly happy and relaxed in her presence. Whilst there was no rush from his perspective, he knew she wanted to get married and start a family of her own. Time wasn't on her side and she wouldn't wait around for him forever. So, when Teresa started looking at rings on what Steve took to be a pretext of wanting to buy one as a souvenir, he was happy to take the hint and popped the question. Teresa was equally happy to accept. The only person who wasn't so accepting was the jeweller, who insisted they take the ring without paying for it so Teresa could wear it for a few days and make absolutely sure it was the right one! That evening after dinner, as the sun set over Fethiye Bay and with Jason otherwise occupied, Steve dropped down on one knee and proposed properly to Teresa, before slipping the ring on her finger. He spent the next three days looking nervously over his shoulder, certain he was about to be arrested for theft and locked up in a Turkish jail!

Fortunately, that didn't happen and, three days later, Steve returned to the shop to pay for the ring, first bartering the shopkeeper down to a lower price, the old romantic: '...it was Turkey, they'd have been insulted if I'd just paid the original price!'

Once back in England, Teresa agreed to move in with Steve and Jason, so they could start planning their future together. In the meantime, she'd rent out her flat, which, in the then current economic climate, had unfortunately fallen into negative equity making a sale pointless. However, it was important to Teresa that they should buy a place chosen by the two of them together; a place where they could start afresh with no lingering memories of a former life. As soon as they'd saved enough money, Steve's house would be put on the market and they'd start looking for its replacement.

While Steve was happy to accommodate Teresa's wishes in this regard, he was once more struck by the speed at which everything was happening, even though it had been at his instigation. He'd been with Mandy for 13 years, almost half his life at that point. Just 18 months after she'd walked out, he was setting up home and his future with another woman. The whole thing was so at odds with his inherent loyalty as a one-woman man, that Steve suffered acute bouts of guilt at being able to move on to someone else so quickly.

He never told Teresa what was going through his mind at the time, as he didn't want her to doubt his love for her. He instinctively knew it was nothing to do with that. In fact, just the opposite - he loved her so much it was exacerbating his guilty feelings. In the end it was that wonderful healer, time, that cured him. As their love strengthened, so his guilt weakened, until it disappeared completely.

But whilst Steve managed to erase one lot of guilt, another stronger one lingered; guilt about how his running might have affected his first marriage and been partially responsible for its ultimate breakdown. Determined not to make the same mistake (if mistake it was), second time around, he asked Teresa if she would like to try the sport he loved so much. He wasn't suggesting she run a marathon, he simply thought that if she tried it, she might enjoy it and it would also help her understand why it had become a way of life for him.

Despite having hated sport at school, her earlier start-stop experiences with her sister, and her total lack of running confidence, Teresa accepted Steve's invitation, so long as he would go with her. Steve had never considered doing anything else.

And so they began. Every other evening, Steve would take Teresa round the one-mile block, running for 30 seconds, walking for one minute, until they were back at the start. Gradually, the running element increased, while the walking decreased. Initially, Teresa found it hard, but Steve was alongside her every step of the way, reassuring her that this was normal and that with perseverance she'd get used to it and find her own rhythm.

Teresa wasn't so sure. Even when about a month later she was able to run the full mile round the block, she found it really tough and uncomfortable. She'd never be a runner! Steve, however, dug in his heels and refused to let her give up, insisting it was just a matter of time before her body became so attuned to running it would feel totally natural to her. He told her to have faith; that, in time, she would be justly rewarded, not only with an improved body shape (not that Steve had any complaints), and increased fitness, but also with better mental well-being. Teresa loved the new man in her life, really she did, but seriously, how long would all this take?

And then, little by little, she realised he was right. Benefits did begin to appear, usually after a stressful shift at work when she would take herself off for a run and return feeling much more relaxed and able to sleep - two things that had eluded her previously in the same circumstances. And while she couldn't honestly say she was enjoying the running, the benefits were starting to outweigh the discomfort, and eventually she was running two to three miles quite comfortably without stopping. She couldn't believe it - she wasn't a runner, yet here she was running! Confidence brimming, she started going to the Alvis Club with Steve, running with one of the other wives. Teresa shook her head, she was a member of a running club, how had that happened?

For Steve, though, Teresa's involvement in his beloved sport was an absolute blessing. Not only did they get to spend more time with one another and share their common running experiences, Steve no longer had to fear that his sport would come between them. Instead, it bound them closer together. It also meant that Teresa understood better where Steve was coming from and she became fully committed to supporting him in his marathon quest. Even so, Steve was determined not to let his running distract him from what he considered the more important aspect of his life – his future with Teresa. With his relationship now taking priority, Steve was happy to put all his energy into saving for the new home they both wanted in one of the smaller, more expensive, surrounding villages. If that meant cutting back on marathons and saving on associated expenses, so be it.

Indeed, such was the extent of Steve's shift in priorities that when he got bored after running the first lap of a two-lap course at his final marathon of the year at Stevenage, a race held only once every ten years, he decided he couldn't be bothered to continue and returned to the car where Teresa was waiting for him with a Mars bar and coffee. Only then did it hit him that if he didn't continue, he'd face the ignominy of having the dreaded 'DNF' letters alongside his name in the results. He couldn't do it. He returned to the race and, despite his mid-race snack, finished in 3:27.

By the end of 1994, as if by way of testament to his shift in focus from running to relationship, Steve had run just 15 marathons with an average finish time of 3:21. Meanwhile, his total number had risen to 261, while his overall average finish time had slipped to 3:17:44. Not only had he run fewer races, but it was also the first year since 1988 that he hadn't raced abroad.

He was no longer interested in chasing world records either, at least not on an immediate basis. First, he wanted to move house, get married and start a family with Teresa. Sy Mah's record could wait. Provided he was able to maintain an average finish time of around 3:15 to 3:20 and stay inside 3:30, he'd beat the old record by a considerable margin, whether he was in his early thirties as originally planned, or in his fifties.

In fact, breaking Sy Mah's record in his 50th birthday year in 2012 had rather a nice ring to it.

Chapter 19

1995 – BALANCE

Steve entered 1995 brimming with confidence. His relationship with Teresa was going from strength to strength and his training likewise, as he discovered the benefit of good, old-fashioned, cross-country running, splashing through rivers, wading through mud, crawling on hands and knees up impossibly steep hills with his clubmates, revelling in being part of a team and winning a few team prizes along the way. He also returned to running half-marathons, and was reminded how much he enjoyed the shorter distance occasionally. Perhaps most important, though, was the effect that cross-country and half-marathons had on his speed when it came to marathons.

First came London in 3:11 – this time retaining his race number! There then followed Rotterdam, courtesy of ST, and a new race for Steve, in 3:13, followed by a handful of domestic marathons including his favourite Potteries.

Steve's next three marathons, with Teresa and Jason, were all overseas thanks to the continued decline in UK marathons largely due to a change in Sunday trading laws in 1994. This had created an increase in Sunday traffic leading to more road closures on race day, requiring more police presence, and spiralling costs. Fortunately, Steve had built up some credit with ST, which he now took advantage of.

First came Amsterdam, where Steve surprised himself by running his fastest marathon for 18 months in 3:03.

A few weeks later, he stormed round the Reims Marathon in 2:59:05, his first sub-3 since London in 1992. Relief flooded through him as he rediscovered the form he thought had gone forever.

Another two weeks and Steve, Teresa and Jason were in Athens. As if Steve didn't have enough on his mind with his new love, his son and the race, he also had the responsibility of managing the trip on behalf of ST for the first time. Whilst Steve enjoyed it, the responsibility of looking after everyone on the trip was incredibly tiring and ensured he could never relax. Consequently, he was relatively satisfied with his time of 3:11, run on what was considered to be the original marathon course starting at Mount Olympus and finishing at the ancient Olympic stadium in Athens.

Just days after returning home, with ST no longer running a trip to NY and thanks to a good deal from Chequers Travel (sports travel company run by former international, Mike Gratton, who Steve had met at London's expo), Steve, Teresa, and a very excited 11-year old Jason, were off to the Big Apple!

Tired as they were on arrival, this was New York on a Friday night, and no sooner had they checked in to their hotel than they were back out on the streets of the city that never sleeps: '...it was buzzing, especially around Times Square!'

The following morning all three took part in the New York Breakfast Run, a 5k fun run finishing in Central Park followed by continental breakfast. Unfortunately for Teresa, her first official running event taught her that large crowds can be perilous as she tripped and went head over heels about a mile into the run. Luckily, Steve and Jason were on hand to help her back on to her feet before she was completely trampled!

After breakfast, they joined the rest of their travel group on a coach trip around the marathon course. The diverse course passed through all five boroughs of the City. Steve decided he'd just have to take his camera with him on race day – it was a photo opportunity too good to miss! Of course, if he hadn't been so snap-happy, it's possible that his 3:04 time that day may have been another sub-3.

After the race, it was off to Macy's for a baseball-themed jacket for Jason, a trip up the Empire State building and an ascent to the very top of the World Trade Centre: '...people below looked like ants and fluffy bits of clouds floated beneath us!'

But perhaps of most interest to a man who'd just started dabbling in penny shares [stocks buyable for under a pound], was a visit to Wall Street's stock exchange. Just as Steve had enjoyed the thrill of gambling with his holiday money in the penny arcades as a boy, so he'd started to enjoy following the stock market – his initial interest coinciding with the start of the 'dot com' era; not a bad time to discover a liking for stocks and shares!

That trip to New York remains one of his fondest memories: '...one of the best races I've run and one of the most exciting places I've ever visited.'

In running terms, the end of 1995 brought with it six half-marathons with a best time for the year of 1:24, and 14 marathons in an average time of 3:13. This increased Steve's total marathons run to 275 (including ultras), and improved his overall average finish time to 3:17:29.

Despite the progression towards Sy Mah's record having slowed, Steve felt that running a marathon once every three or four weeks with the occasional half-marathon, made his life-running balance about right, as he and Teresa continued to save for their new home and Jason started secondary school.

It was something that had worried Steve considerably, not just because of his own unhappy experience of secondary school, which, not having any of Steve's difficulties Jason would hopefully avoid, but more because of the many changes that Jason's life had undergone in recent years; from the break up of his family and witnessing his dad's unhappiness, to the introduction of a new woman in their lives. Conscious that his son was now heading towards an important part of his life in terms of studying and taking exams,

Steve was extremely relieved to see Jason apparently settling happily into his new school.

He was also pleased to see the developing relationship between Jason and Teresa, as the two were forced to spend hours alone together while Steve romped around the streets, with Teresa ensuring Jason was safe at all times and Jason, who'd always had a good sense of direction, ensuring Teresa didn't get too lost!

There was really only one thing casting a slight shadow over Steve's overall contentment at this time. A work initiative was being introduced whereby a number of council departments were being considered for possible outsourcing to third party companies as part of a competitive tendering process in a bid to cut costs; Steve's computing department was among them.

Chapter 20

1996 – INTERNET INVASION

Back on the running circuit, as calendars flicked over to 1996, Steve enjoyed another good winter's training, once more combining cross-country and half-marathons prior to his first marathon of the year in March at the Suffolk & Essex Border Marathon, run in 3:08.

This was followed by the Antwerp Marathon with an invitational package of complimentary entry and two nights' accommodation. Deciding to drive and take the opportunity to try the new Channel Tunnel which opened in 1994, the round trip was a 'mere' 610 car miles, a far cry from some of the trips he'd done a few years earlier and certainly more relaxed with two whole nights in a nice hotel, offering Steve and Teresa an opportunity to take in some of the sights both before and after race day.

Starting the race confident that he could run close to 3 hours, Steve went through 10k in a brisk 41:30. Feeling particularly good, he decided to continue at that pace for as long as possible and see what happened. What happened was that this time his legs and body didn't fail him and although he tired a little in the final 5k, he finished the race in 2:55.

'It was one of those days when my legs flowed like a gazelle and my body glided like a well-oiled machine. I haven't had many days like that.'

A week later Steve was in London, having been fortunate enough to gain entry for the fifth successive year through the race's ballot system, hoping for a repeat of Antwerp. Sadly, it wasn't to be. After reaching halfway in 1:34 and feeling pretty tired, he finished in 3:12. It was the slowest London he'd run at that time and, despite knowing it was a solid performance, he was disappointed after Antwerp's euphoria.

By this time, Steve's sponsorship with ST was ending and London was his last engagement with them. It was a mutual parting of ways and a sign of things to come, as numbers of ST customers fell thanks to the Internet making it possible for them to organise everything for themselves more cheaply.

In May, Steve, Teresa and Jason travelled to Cyprus – not to run but to take a week's holiday. For once, Steve did no running at all while away. Instead he lavished all his attention on his future wife and his son, enjoying the sunshine and rest.

Despite the battery recharge, the remainder of the year was full of inconsistent performances ranging from 2:55 to 3:28. By the end of it, Steve had run 14 marathons with an average finish time of 3:15, taking his lifetime total to 275 (excluding ultras), and his average lifetime finish time to 3:17:23. The exclusion of ultras, despite achieving marathon cut-off times, was testament to Steve's determination to break Sy Mah's record properly: to be able to state categorically that he'd run 500+ pure official marathon races in an average finish time below 3:30, with no room for doubt or debate.

Steve had also run eight half-marathons during 1996, including the re-introduced Coventry event, organised by the Massey Ferguson Running Club. The route incorporated six laps of Coventry's city centre ring road: '...it was surreal running on what is normally a very busy dual carriageway with no cars, just runners.'

Meanwhile, back at the working ranch, Steve's fears had been realised when the Council decided to privatise the IT department offering no clarity about the future of their employees. Consequently, Steve took matters into his own hands and began looking elsewhere for alternative employment, eventually accepting a job offer as an IT manager with private company, 'Exploration Associates'. Having worked for Coventry Council for 18 years since leaving school, Steve was both nervous and excited at the prospect of joining a new company in such a niche role. Certainly, the first couple of months were difficult, with the transition from public to private sector proving quite a culture shock: '...I wasn't afraid of hard work or extra hours, but I soon realised this wasn't a choice like it had been with the Council where I would be paid overtime for anything over my normal hours.'

No indeed, the private sector didn't recognise the term 'overtime', it simply expected Steve to work for however long was necessary to get the job done, without additional payment. Accordingly, he often worked until 6 pm or later and almost every other Saturday. On the plus side, the job brought a higher salary, a company BMW, private medical insurance, pension, disability insurance, death benefit for his family, and end of year bonus: '...but, boy, did I have to work for it!'

It also brought an opportunity for Steve to start a lottery syndicate with his new work colleagues, his father and Teresa; 20 people in all. Steve asked everyone to pick just one number, rather than a random line. He then paired up the numbers and created a perm over the 20 lines, effectively duplicating the paired numbers over several lines. His mathematical mind reckoned that if a few of their numbers were drawn, they'd match up on several lines, enhancing their winnings! Two months later, they nearly hit the jackpot, with one line of five numbers and several lines of four and three numbers, winning them around £2000 - about £100 each. If only their sixth number had been 24, not 44!

With offices all over the UK, Steve's new job also involved a lot of driving. Whilst not a problem in itself for such an intrepid, well-travelled runner, there was a potentially catastrophic side effect: '...some days I couldn't fit in any training at all.'

The lunchtime runs Steve enjoyed when working for the Council had completely ceased, leaving just the evenings for training, but even these were curtailed if he'd been working away and returned home late. Then he was just too tired to run. Consequently, there were days when he missed sessions completely or only ran two or three miles. The result was inevitable - his fitness levels started to decrease.

Steve may have got his job sorted, but at what price?

Chapter 21

1997 – ENJOYMENT

Preferring to concentrate on what he could do rather than what he couldn't, Steve continued training as hard as circumstances allowed, starting the year as usual with cross-country and running his fastest ever half-marathon of 1:22:49 at the Four Villages event in January.

He then persuaded Alvis clubmate, Jim, to travel to Holland with him to partake in what would be Jim's first overseas event. Attempting to replicate Steve's 1991 expedition, they left Coventry late on Friday night, drove to Dover, catnapped on the ferry, and then drove to Apeldoorn. Reaching the start line in temperatures of around minus ten and donning several layers and leggings, neither felt like running 26.2 miles. Unsurprisingly, they both ran slower than normal, never really warming up. Steve was just glad to finish in what felt like an incredibly long 3:28.

After the race, however, things improved when they bumped into Steve's old mucker, Phil, and some other 100 Clubbers, Brian Mills (who later became the first Brit to complete 1000 marathons), Pete Morris and Martin Bush, who'd driven the 450 miles there in an old van. The minute Phil spotted Steve's brand new

BMW, he jumped ship and made the return journey home with Steve and Jim: '...Phil's wit and humour kept us amused all the way home and made the journey pass much more quickly!'

Steve eventually arrived home in the early hours of Sunday morning, having driven some 850 miles. He was shattered. If it had been a baptism of fire for Jim, it had been a sharp reminder to Steve just how tiring those trips were. It was the last time he was to do a trip like that.

More or less recovered, Steve's next race was the Crossmichael Marathon, a new event at Castle Douglas in March. He and Teresa went with Jim and Liz, and Phil and Mary. It was a fun weekend, staying in a decrepit B&B managed by a be-wigged gentleman so ancient and ashen he could have been a resident ghost, and meeting a couple of equally elderly and ashen ladies in a nearby restaurant, whose men folk, presumably their husbands, were also running the marathon, despite their well advanced years and walking sticks!

Steve finished the race in 3:09, with Jim and Phil also running sub-3:15, so it was three contented runners who returned to the B&B to collect their luggage and make the return journey home. However, before they could say 'wig', the unfairly maligned wearer of such generously offered them a warm bath, even though they'd already checked out of his establishment. The offer was gratefully accepted: '...the water was a weird yellow colour but incredibly soft compared to the water back home; it felt very luxurious.'

It was the first of many similarly enjoyable trips: '... they were great fun, the banter was always good and we had a lot of laughs!'

And then flaming June arrived and with it a new landmark for Steve, as he ran his 300th marathon (including ultras), at the Potteries race. Afterwards, his Alvis clubmates presented him with a pewter tankard, which he's used ever since for his favourite tipple, Guinness. Less happily, it was the last race Steve saw his old mucker, Colin Greene run, as, true to his earlier promise, Colin retired from racing: '...I still miss him and his bright red VW camper van.'

Further acknowledgement of Steve's achievements came a few weeks later at the Snowdonia Marathon where he was presented with the 'Personal Achiever Award' by then sponsors of the event, First Hydro, in recognition of the consistency and quality of his 300 marathons and for his most in a year record. The award, an incredibly weighty, giant chunk of slate, remains proudly displayed in Steve's study/trophy room today.

Sadness followed, not of the personal kind but national, with the sudden death of Princess Diana on the 31st August; the very day Steve ran the Norfolk Marathon on a warm day in a below par 3:37.

That year, Steve also ran nine half-marathons, including the Great Scottish Run - an event that had previously been a full marathon - after which he and

Teresa continued on to the Highlands for a holiday. It was as they were driving along a particularly winding road with breathtaking views, that they were overtaken by a group of bikers. As soon as they'd passed, the apparent leader of the gang, who was at the rear of the group, began waving his arms, urging his posse to pass the next vehicle. However, the posse appeared less keen to risk life and limb on the road's tight-twisting blind blends and stayed where they were. Their reluctance clearly agitated their leader who started shaking his head and waving his arms ever more frantically in a bid to get them to pass the vehicle. The longer the posse procrastinated, the wilder the leader's head shaking and arm waving became. Eventually, he gave up and went for it himself, passing the entire posse *and* the vehicle in front. The others then followed like disgraced sheep: '...it was so funny; we were in tears!'

But the most enduring memory Steve has of 1997 is of Teresa running her first proper race, a 4.5 miler in Allesley, Coventry. Having trained hard for the event and with Steve accompanying her to check her pacing, she finished a fraction over 34 minutes having run just under 8 mm all the way. Later that year, she also ran a 5k Race for Life event with some of her nursing colleagues: '...I was dead proud of her. This was the person who maintained she'd never be a runner – and then became one!'

As 1997 drew to a close, Steve had run a further 18 marathons, including 3:01 at London; 16 of the 18 were sub-3:30, giving an average finish time for the year of 3:18. His overall total now stood at 293 official marathon races with an overall average finish time of 3:17:30. Sy Mah's record was slowly but surely being chipped away.

Meanwhile, Teresa had run a 4.5-mile race and a 5k.

They were becoming quite a team.

Chapter 22

1998 – MOVING ON

At long last, after 12 months of searching, Steve and Teresa found a house they liked. It was a pretty, four-bed semi in the tiny rural village of Ansty; there were no shops, just one pub, a phone box and a post box. However, it was only a couple of miles from Coventry, so they could easily stay in touch with friends and family.

Although the house needed some work doing to it, thanks to his father's excellent DIY instruction during his son's formative years, it was nothing Steve couldn't handle. The couple's offer was accepted and Steve's house placed on the market. An ecstatic Teresa allowed herself to start dreaming of weddings and babies.

Whilst the buying and selling process ground its wearisome way along, Steve busied himself with another good winter's training and cross-country racing and tucked another three half-marathons under his belt. Marathon-wise, moving house and planning a wedding meant it would be a quiet year, but he still managed a few.

The first was a return to the Crossmichael Marathon, again with Teresa, Jim and Liz. Staying in different accommodation but dining at the same restaurant, they were delighted to come across the same two elderly ladies they'd met there last year, seated at the exact same table. It would have been deja vu if it hadn't been that the two sweet, apple-cheeked Miss Marples were in the presence of two very different, marathon-running, gentlemen!

'They were the oldest marathon groupies I've ever seen!'

Still tickled by the idea of the aged groupies, Steve enjoyed a good run the next day in 3:05. This was followed by London in April in 3:02.

He then chose to run his 300th official marathon race at Manchester. Having missed out on the original, subsequently disbanded, Manchester Piccadilly Marathon during the 1980s, Steve was looking forward to running its replacement, introduced after the city won its bid to host the Commonwealth Games, assuming the race would finish in the brand new stadium. He was disappointed. Not only was the bus taking the runners to the start so late they only just made it in time, but when Steve crossed the line in 3:24, it was in a completely unknown part of the city and he didn't get to see the stadium at all!

By the end of 1998, Steve had run 5 half-marathons and just 8 full marathons, one of his quietest years ever. However, all but one of those marathons had been under 3:30 and his average finish time for the year was 3:17, so although his total hadn't increased much, his overall average finish time for his lifetime total of 301 marathons remained a shade under 3:17:30, and he was still very much on track.

Meanwhile, in the autumn, the conveyancing wheels ground to a satisfying halt right outside Steve and Teresa's new home, together with a hired van. With the assistance of Teresa's brother-in-law, also named Steve, the trio worked like Trojans, driving back and forth between old and new homes, loading and unloading furniture and boxes.

The new house didn't stand a chance. The lethal combination of Steve's impeccable logistical skills learned from running marathons all over the world and Teresa's natural flair for order, saw the place licked into shape within weeks. Before you could say 'screwdriver', Steve had made a tour of the entire property and garden, jotted down all the DIY jobs that needed doing, worked out the order they needed doing in, and then took himself off to B&Q armed with a long list and a bulging wallet.

As for Jason, this time he was old enough to understand this was not a temporary home and, as Steve had anticipated, was thrilled by his new bedroom in an extended part of the house overlooking the back garden. Very private, it was perfect for a young lad growing up. Although Jason's room may not have been quite as neat and organised as his dad may have liked, the important thing was that his son was happy and, even though they were now a little further out of town, he soon made friends locally, whilst keeping in touch with his old ones. He didn't seem to mind the longer journey to school either - possibly because he often enjoyed the luxury of being driven there by Steve or Teresa on their way to work!

It seemed the move fulfilled everyone's needs, and for the ever-patient Teresa, now aged 37, it meant she could finally start looking forward to getting married and starting the family she longed for.

Chapter 23

1999 – THE WEDDING

The wedding was exactly what Teresa had wanted, a quiet affair in Cumbria. To be accurate, it was the quiet not the Cumbria that she'd been dreaming of all those years, but when she'd told Steve she wanted to go away to be married and Steve had discovered a gorgeous little hotel called the Lovelady Shield on the outskirts of a village called Alston, which happened to be in Cumbria, Teresa decided it was the perfect place.

They were married at the hotel on Sunday, 14th February, a date no man was likely to forget on future anniversaries, and one on which there were no marathons that year: '...I'd checked'. He is joking, or so he says! The couple actually chose Valentine's Day simply because they thought it would be a nice day to get married: '...and might give us lots of good luck on our journey through life as man and wife.'

As they both desired, it was a very quiet ceremony - just Teresa, Steve and the registrar, with the hotel proprietor and barmaid acting as witnesses. After repeating their vows to one another, Steve placed the ring on Teresa's finger. There had been no build-up, no glitz, no big do: '...to me and Teresa, it seemed the most perfect way to seal our love and commitment to one another.'

On that bright, cold, perfect wedding day, the newly-weds made one other vow to each other away from the formality of the actual ceremony, and that was to never spend a night apart. They then took a leisurely drive through the gloriously verdant countryside of the Lake District, falling in love with its majestic hillsides, cosy villages and sparkling lakes, before enjoying a late lunch at a restaurant overlooking Lake Windermere. Neither of them had ever been there before so had no idea that they were now sitting at the 25-mile point of a race Steve had yet to run, which was to become one of the most important marathon events of his life. It was almost as if some guiding star had led them on their wedding day to the very place where so much of their lives together would be spent and where so many incredible memories would be forged. But for now they knew nothing of that. All they knew was that they were married, and it felt good. Mr and Mrs Edwards enjoying their wedding day lunch beside Lake Windermere.

Altogether, they enjoyed three wonderful carefree days in the Lakes, exploring by day, indulging in sumptuous meals cooked by the hotel's Michelin-starred chef by night. They returned home full, happy and refreshed, collected Jason from his mum's house and then returned home to begin life as a proper family.

Or at least a proper family with plans to extend; Teresa came off the pill and, knowing the effects would take time to wear off and given her age, the contented couple patiently filled their days with decorating their home and sorting out the garden, so when the patter of tiny feet did finally arrive, they would be well and truly ready for it.

Following another good cross-country season and a couple of solid half-marathons, Steve's first marathon of the year was at Le Touqet, France. Steve and Teresa travelled with Jim and Liz, plus Patrick; another Alvis Clubber who wasn't running but wanted to visit his parents who lived nearby. In return for their son's transportation, Patrick's parents were accommodating the four friends over the weekend. They also provided a seven-course French-style meal the evening prior to the race – with a glass of wine between each course!

Despite that, or maybe because of it, Steve finished the race in 3:08; a pleasing start to his marathon season.

Another good run came with 3:06 at London via another successful ballot entry and his eighth consecutive race in the capital.

After that, though, Steve's form became somewhat more erratic as he struggled round the Potteries in June and Blackpool in August. It was that same old feeling of lethargy, but whereas previously it had only really hit him in the latter stages of a race, at both the Potteries and Blackpool, he'd lacked energy the whole way round. He just couldn't understand it. Maybe it was time to see his GP?

A few blood tests later and it was revealed that Steve had a low haemoglobin count. [Haemoglobin is the protein in the red blood cells that carries oxygen. Oxygen is vital for muscles to work efficiently, without it they go into a lactic state, which is painful and debilitating. Haemoglobin is therefore essential to any sportsman, but especially a marathon runner.] The average haemoglobin count in younger males is around 14 to 18; in older males it drops to around 12 to 14. At the time, Steve was in his 30s, so his reading of 9.5 was exceptionally low. No wonder he felt tired.

The GP concluded that Steve was suffering from anaemia caused by the destruction of red blood cells through his feet due to the pounding effect of all that running – the GP had read an article about Army personnel having the same problem caused by marching. Iron tablets were duly prescribed and further blood tests to check his progress would follow.

A month later, there was a slight increase in Steve's haemoglobin count and although he felt a little better, he wasn't completely convinced by the GP's diagnosis. He therefore sought the opinion of a consultant through his employer's private medical insurance.

The consultant first checked that Steve wasn't losing blood somewhere in his system and set up some investigative tests, including an endoscopy and colonoscopy. The colonoscopy took place on the

11th August, a date Steve is able to recall with such accuracy as, by some uncanny twist of fate, it was the last full solar eclipse until the one that is happening on the very day he is writing his notes about the last one - romantically witnessed by himself and his lovely new wife from the hospital car park!

The consultant's tests revealed nothing, so a barium meal scan was arranged, which would show anything abnormal happening inside his body.

Again nothing.

The consultant scratched his head. There was no blood loss and normal levels of key minerals in the blood, including iron. So why was his patient giving every appearance of someone suffering from anaemia?

The consultant consulted a haematologist.

The haematologist scratched his head.

He peered closer at the data in front of him. And it was then he noticed that the patient's red blood cells were smaller than usual and slightly misshapen. He'd got it! The patient was suffering from beta thalassaemia minor (btm) – a blood disorder usually inherited from maternal genes and more often found in people living in high-risk malaria areas, such as the Mediterranean, Africa and the Middle East - an ancestral throwback perhaps?

Steve was relieved at finally finding a reason for his long-standing lethargy and the shortness of breath he often suffered, particularly in the summer months when his breathing could be laboured right from the start and he'd run 26.2 miles feeling like he was in oxygen debt. Not being able to get enough air into his lungs had often frightened him, creating fears of imminent death!

Btm also explained why he'd never been able to run faster in shorter races or maintain a fast pace over longer distances, no matter what sort of training he did. Thank goodness he hadn't taken up Cliff Temple's suggestion to change tack and aim for fewer faster marathons, sticking instead to his original plan to be a multi-marathon runner! It was almost as though some sixth sense had led him to choose the right path without knowing why.

Certainly, if he hadn't been a multi-marathon runner pushing his body to its limits on a regular basis, Steve might never have known he was affected by the blood condition. Many people don't, and that included Steve's mum and sister. Following Steve's diagnosis they too were tested – both were positive.

As a sufferer of btm, Steve will always have a low haemoglobin count no matter how much extra iron he may take. In fact, extra iron could prove harmful as, if unutilised, the iron would remain in the body, resulting in serious, possibly fatal, consequences. That low haemoglobin count means that Steve's energy levels will always be around 20 percent below normal. Which makes his achievements all the more astonishing and begs the question: what might he have done with normal energy levels?

No less astonishing, is that none of this caused Steve to consider giving up on his dreams of one day taking that record from Sy Mah, or even just lowering the high standards he'd set for himself time-wise. If anything, his determination to succeed became stronger. Equally strong was his resolve to keep the condition to himself – he wouldn't want anyone to think he was making excuses if he had an off day.

All he had to do was find a way to manage his condition. In typical Steve fashion, he immediately set about seeking the necessary information that would allow him to do just that, particularly with regard to hydration and nutrition. This led to him introducing more fresh green vegetables, fruit and naturally iron-rich foods into his diet, plus high-quality nutritional supplements, giving his system the best possible chance of coping with the condition alongside the marathon running. Perhaps one of the most important things he learned was that a healthy diet relied on the correct *combination* of food types. For example, iron-rich foods eaten with tea or coffee would be of little benefit, as the tannins in those drinks inhibit the body's ability to absorb iron, whereas consuming vitamin C would aid the process. Cookery lessons used to be termed 'domestic *science*' for good reason!

Undeterred, Steve booked to run again at Manchester. Unbelievably, the bus taking the runners to the start was late again, so late, in fact, that Steve and Jim decided they'd be better off trying to get there under their own steam. But how? Incredibly, whilst debating this, a lady driver (who wasn't an elderly marathon groupie or any kind of marathon groupie come to that, just a kind stranger), offered them a lift, dropping them off about a mile short of the start. Uncertain of where exactly they were in relation to the start line, they decided the wisest course of action would be to follow the road. Common sense was rewarded as soon they saw runners coming towards them. Honesty dictated that they shouldn't just join the race at that point, but should run back to the official start line, only then turning round and setting off some distance behind the back markers. Not an ideal start to a marathon and the only one that year that Steve failed to finish under 3:30.

As 1999 drew to a close, and despite his health issues, Steve had run another 11 marathons with an average finish time for the year of 3:20. This saw his overall total rise to 312 official marathon races, but his average finish time slip to 3:17:35.

By the end of the year, Steve learned that his 'most in a year' record set in 1992 had been broken by a Dane, with just over 100 marathons. He was happy to think he'd inspired someone else to attempt his record. Even so, the Dane's times were considerably slower than Steve's. It reaffirmed his belief that even though his attempt to break Sy Mah's record was taking longer than originally envisaged, it would be worth it - plenty of people would undoubtedly overtake the number of marathons Sy Mah had run, but nobody would run them faster. That was for him to do.

The star that had faded just fractionally during the eclipse grew bright again.

Chapter 24

2000 – REAL LIFE

Steve waved a fond farewell to the millennium and welcomed in the new century from the comfort of his own back garden accompanied by his wife, son and parents as they enjoyed a deafening display of fireworks exploding in a kaleidoscope of colour over the Coventry skyline: '...it was exciting being part of a generation that experienced a new millennium!'

Steve was also excited by the prospect of the possibility of a baby, completing work on the house – and, of course, trying to run as many marathons as possible in the hope that the medals might be extra special for the year 2000!

Kicking off with the one-off Millennium Marathon in Leyland on the 2nd January, Steve's spirits took a bit of a dive when he struggled round in just over 3:30, although he accepted it was hardly surprising given his lack of training due to work commitments, domestic chores, and generally feeling a little under par.

Without another marathon until London in April, Steve entered three half-marathons, again with disappointing results.

And then it all came to a crashing halt. Or at least Steve did. Just a few weeks prior to London he fell out of the loft door, his coccyx taking full brunt on the ball part of the newel post: '...it was excruciating, tears flooded my eyes!'

He was six years old all over again, falling headlong down the stairs at his parents' home, all because a policeman had knocked on the front door to take a statement from his parents about stolen milk tokens. In his excited haste to meet a real live policeman in his own home, Steve had tripped and tumbled from top to bottom landing in an untidy heap at the policeman's feet. He'd then had to be rushed to hospital by ambulance and receive stitches for a nose that had narrowly missed being broken but retained a substantial scar. Still, as his mother had said of her accident-prone son at the time: '...it made him look less like a girl!'

This time he received rather more sympathy from his medically qualified wife, who after checking her husband over and given that he'd been able to get up straight away and walk, reckoned no major harm had been done to his spine or pelvis. He was, however, in considerable pain and his lower back colourfully bruised. Training was compromised once more and Steve's fitness reduced even further.

But Steve didn't get to where he is today by waiting for things to get better. Despite the lack of training and residual soreness in his back, he decided to risk running London. Nobody but Steve could be surprised that he endured an exceedingly uncomfortable run and struggled all the way round to record his slowest ever London time of 3:21.

Then, just as he was recovering from the loft fall, he suffered a slipped disc at work when he bent forward from his chair to pick up some papers from the floor. This exacerbated his back pain, so it hurt whether he was standing, walking, running or even sitting.

Although Steve was in no shape physically or mentally to tackle running 26.2 miles, having already missed several races, he was unable to resist the lure of his old favourite; the Potteries Marathon in June. All he could do was give it his best shot. Unfortunately, his best shot turned out to be nothing more than a jog/walk almost from start to finish. Needless to say, the race has since been discounted from Steve's totals – but at least he got another plate for the wall!

Sadly, it wasn't just the running that wasn't going so well in a year that had seemed so full of promise. After 18 months of trying, there was still no sign of a baby. Teresa tried to be philosophical; she was, after all, just two years shy of 40. It was bound to take time, but every month, filled with tremulous hope, she suffered the same agonising disappointment of all women in that position.

Meanwhile, the son Steve already had, now in his 16th year and acting every inch in accordance with the law of that age, was causing Steve a whole raft of problems and heartache. Eventually, the old bull and the young pretender clashed to such an extent that the tension broke in one almighty row, culminating in Jason walking out and going to stay with his mum.

Steve was upset and worried in equal measure. This was a vital time in his son's education, a time when he should be revising for his exams, concerned with nothing other than passing them and thinking about his future. It was no time for emotional trauma and sweeping changes. But Jason was a typically stubborn teenager; his mind was made up, and nothing his dad said or did could dissuade him.

And then there was Steve's back, which was still giving him considerable pain. When he could stand it no more, he made further use of his employer's medical insurance: '...it was turning out to be a crucial part of my remuneration package!'

Steve saw consultant neurosurgeon, Mr Peter Stanworth. After examination, Mr Stanworth advised that surgery was one option, but ideally, he'd prefer to try a less evasive option first. This would involve Steve attending a three-week, back therapy course at Sketchley Grange, a rehab clinic in Hinckley. A non-residential, group course, it would involve doing numerous back exercises in both gym and pool. Alongside the physical aspects, there would also be a considerable amount of theory, during which they would learn all about the back, how it worked, what was good and bad for it, and how to look after it in the future – information heaven for knowledge-thirsty Steve! It would mean being signed off work for three weeks, but if it meant avoiding the knife, Steve was more than happy to go along with it.

It was one of the best things he ever did; being taught specific exercises to strengthen back and core muscles to help stabilise the discs and enable the entire body to work more efficiently during everyday activities.

By the end of the course, he felt like a new man. Now that he understood the benefits of having stronger back and core muscles, particularly as a sportsman, he commenced implementing a new set of exercises into his training regime. They are exercises he has since added to and continues using today.

After what felt like an eternity, Steve was finally able to return to weight training and running again without any back pain.

Steve considers that consultation with Mr Stanworth and his advice to be one of the key moments of his life, defining its future direction: '...I may have seen a different consultant who may not have given me any option other than surgery. It may or may not have worked, but one thing's for sure - I wouldn't have learned anything. I can't thank Mr Stanworth enough.'

All Steve had to do now was regain his running fitness and then test it all out.

He did just that a couple of months later at the Moray Marathon in Elgin, Scotland, relieved to finish in 3:27; his first sub-3:30 since the previous October. The only remaining niggle was that his energy levels still didn't feel 100 per cent and he was finding it almost impossible to put the btm out of his mind.

He knew he had to make a conscious effort to change that, otherwise he was in danger of letting the mere thought of it have a negative psychological effect on his running performance. He needed to find a way of accepting that he would never be able to run like he would if he didn't have any health issues, without using it as an excuse. In the end, he told himself that a bad run was just that, a bad run, everyone had off days, they just didn't necessarily know why. The self-counselling worked, and aside from having random blood tests to check nothing has changed, Steve has been able to put it to the back of his mind ever since.

Thankfully this new mindset allowed him to enjoy the Chicago Marathon in October, although he was disappointed with a hard-earned 3:36 on what was reputed to be a fast course. Given that he'd taken his camera with him and snapped away at the city's most famous landmarks throughout the race, his disappointment in himself was perhaps a little harsh.

Chicago was followed by the last ever Harrow marathon and then the Cornish Marathon, which had moved from Saltash to Rilla Mill. The exposed Bodmin Moor offered no respite from the freezing conditions and Steve fought to hold back tears as a barrage of hailstones painfully battered his bald pate and ears. Hat-less, he ran with his arms covering his head until it stopped.

His final race of the year at Luton was less painful, with another sub-3:30.

After harbouring such high hopes at the start of the year, 2000 turned out to be the worst year for Steve's marathon running since he'd embarked on the Sy Mah record in 1988, with 6 half-marathons and a paltry (by his standards) 8 marathons to add to his totals, giving him an average marathon finish time for the year of 3:37, and just 3 sub-3:30s. In turn, his overall average time for 320 official marathon races slipped to 3:18:04.

Where once Steve had felt invincible, he now felt very averagely human, and with that came a certain frailty and loss of confidence.

Looking back today, Steve kicks himself for not running more marathons during this period, although he accepts he didn't have the inclination – his priorities had shifted from running to his wife and home. And maybe that was a good thing? Maybe if he'd run more then, his body would have broken and he may not have enjoyed such longevity or achieved all that he has?

And maybe that's why the star shone on undimmed?

Chapter 25

2001 – LOSS

With his loss of confidence and demands of his job, Steve's training and racing continued its downward spiral. As did his relationship with his son. Up till now the two had kept in touch and would even meet up occasionally. Invariably, though, these meetings ended with an argument. So far, so normal. The situation went beyond normal, however, when one day a massive falling out ended all communication between them.

It was hard for Steve to equate the angry young man his son had become with the little boy who'd run alongside him at so many races and who'd even shown signs of wanting to become an athlete like his dad - although as a sprinter rather than a marathoner - when the two had gone together to Coventry Godiva Harriers, after Jason won bronze in a Coventry Schools tournament 100 metres. It was just a shame he'd been put off by his one and only training session at the club and refused to return. Maybe if that hadn't happened, he'd have stayed on track both literally and metaphorically?

Either way, it was still a cherished memory of when his son and he had been close, when they'd enjoyed each other's company, when they'd talked and laughed and had fun. The memories made Steve sadder still, more so because he knew there was nothing he could do to change the present situation. For now at least, he had to accept that he was persona non grata to Jason, and, if he was honest, however much it upset him to feel that way, vice versa.

Thank God for Teresa then; with his running down the pan, the stresses of his job and the loss of contact with his son, his wife was the one constant he still had in his life and with every passing day he loved her more. The pleasure he took in her company and the happiness he felt, helped take the edge off everything else. And if he needed to justify taking some downtime from running, it came with the realisation that he could run the required number of marathons in slower times beyond 3:30 and still beat Sy Mah's record with a sub-3:30 average.

So it was that as their second wedding anniversary approached, the devoted couple headed for Las Vegas, somewhere they'd both wanted to visit for some time and where, by some freakish coincidence, a marathon was being held that very week!

They stayed on the world-famous Vegas strip in the Stratosphere Hotel; a hotel that boasted the tallest freestanding observation tower in the USA *and* a mini roller coaster rooftop ride that threw daredevils around the outside edge of a building over 1000 feet in the sky. Even hardened roller coaster rider, Teresa, wasn't tempted!

As one might expect of a man who grew up in penny arcades and dabbled in stocks and shares, the casinos were another matter! It was lucky then that his sensible upbringing ensured he limited his gambling to 25 dollars worth of one-dollar chips, betting just one or two at a time at the cheapest blackjack table. That first night, he was thrilled to double his money from 25 to 50 dollars. The next night he lost all 50 dollars, proving there is only ever one real winner in the casinos.

Turning his attention away from the gaming tables to the marathon, Steve was somewhat surprised, given the general buzz of the city, to discover it was a fairly low key event with runners being bussed into the Nevada Desert to run all the way back to the finish in a park somewhere on the outskirts of town. Not quite the Vegas Strip finish he'd envisaged. His finish time of 3:37 was nothing to write home about either, although, of course, it was hardly unexpected given the lack of training and everything else.

And life wasn't about to deal them a compensatory royal flush at that stage either, for when they arrived home it was to the devastating news that Teresa's 67-year old father had died. Even though he'd been a heavy smoker and drinker all his life, he hadn't been ill and his death at a relatively early age was a shock for his daughter and son-in-law. It also acted as a catalyst for Steve's sudden realisation that tomorrow didn't always come and that maybe it was time he bucked up his ideas and started upping the ante with regard to the number of marathons he'd been planning to run.

Following a 3:32 at Bungay and having been unsuccessful in his bid to obtain a tenth successive ballot entry into London, Steve decided to run the Tresco Marathon on the Scilly Isles instead. On the same day as London, the race was held in aid of cystic fibrosis and runners had to raise money for the charity to enter. Steve duly wrote a letter to his employers (by now Mowlem, who'd bought-out Exploration Associates), and they agreed to sponsor him.

In the early hours of Saturday, 21st April, Steve and Teresa drove to Penzance and took the ferry to the main island of St Mary's and their B&B.

The following morning, a specially designated boat ferried runners and supporters across to the smaller island of Tresco: '...it was so beautiful. We'd never seen anything like it. It was like being on a tropical island.'

The race itself had 77 runners and consisted of 7 laps of the tiny (approximately 1 mile x 2), island. Behind its natural beauty, though, lay an intensely tough, challenging course along concrete tracks with numerous bends and changes of camber, and four hills per lap. Steve was never more appreciative of nature's stunning coastal panoramic distraction.

It wasn't just nature that disarmed Steve and Teresa that weekend, though. The post-race hospitality of the islanders was the best Steve had ever experienced, and included showers and changing facilities in a five star hotel followed by a buffet lunch in the village hall. Finishing medals were then presented individually to every runner by modern pentathletes, Stephanie Cook and Kate Allenby, who'd won gold and bronze medals respectively at the Sydney Olympics in 2000.

Although Steve missed being at London, it was a complete contrast to the electric, high-octane atmosphere of a big city event: '...all those intimate touches made us runners feel that little bit special'.

They also ensured that this marathon, despite being disbanded in 2009, remains one of Steve's all-time favourites.

As the tired, contented couple made their return journey back home across Cornwall and Devon, their recent pleasant memories were suddenly clouded by dense, choking smoke rising from the funeral pyres of thousands of cattle that had been slaughtered to try and contain the spread of the dreadful foot and mouth disease, which had hit the UK in February that year. By the end of the year, over 10 million sheep and cattle had been slaughtered, costing the country around £8 billion.

The effect of such catastrophe not only hit the farming and tourism industry, with many of the country's most popular footpaths and open countryside being closed to hikers and pleasure seekers for almost a year, it also hit the marathon industry, with races across farmland and rural areas being cancelled.

Finding marathons that weren't affected became increasingly difficult, but Steve did locate some, including the Isle of Wight. Despite finishing just outside his 3:30 target in 3:33, Steve pushed aside concerns that he may never repeat such times again, and reminded himself of the toughness of the course instead.

Just a few weeks later any lingering concerns were totally forgotten as he churned out 3:29 in Blackpool, 3:28 at the Potteries and 3:23 at the inaugural Lake Vyrnwy Marathon in North Wales. Staying on in North Wales for a short break, Steve felt his spirits lift. The tide seemed to be turning and although his running confidence remained shaky, his previous good form appeared to be returning.

As did his sense of humour. Seeing 100 Clubber, Martin Bush (who has now completed over 700 marathons), at the Moray Marathon in September, which Steve finished in 3:28, he jokingly told Martin that the event didn't award medals, just coasters. Medal-mad Martin was incensed: 'You mean I've come all this way for a coaster!' Steve couldn't wait to see Martin's face when he realised it was just a joke. But the joke backfired. For the first time ever there really were no medals – just coasters!

At the close of 2001, Steve had added another 16 marathons to his total with an average finish time of 3:29. Although his overall average finish time for his total of 336 official marathon races had slipped a little further to 3:18:37, he was pleased to have averaged under 3:30 for the year and also to record a couple of sub-3:20s – something he hadn't done for two years.

And so another year passed, but still no baby. Steve and Teresa had eventually consulted their GP and throughout the year underwent a number of tests to check everything was working properly. It was. They were now faced with deciding whether to continue trying and hoping it would happen naturally in its own time, or trudging down the emotionally traumatic and often heartbreaking road of IVF.

Teresa thought about it long and hard. As a nurse she knew exactly what IVF would mean. The procedure was invasive and unpleasant. It could still be years before anything happened or nothing might happen at all. She was now 39 years old. By the time a baby was born she would be at least 40. So would Steve. Did they really want to have a baby so late in life, whether naturally or via IVF? If she did go for IVF, how would her not-so-youthful body cope and how would she and Steve cope with the emotional roller coaster that would inevitably accompany the raising and dashing of hopes month in month out?

In the end, after much soul searching and discussion with Steve, Teresa decided IVF wasn't for her. Instead, she and Steve agreed to give it one more year of trying naturally. If it hadn't happened by then, they must just accept it wasn't meant to be.

Chapter 26

2002 - ACCEPTANCE

Given his lack of training, Steve was relatively satisfied with his 3:24 finish at his first race of the year in sunny Seville in February. This was followed by three domestic marathons, including a return to Tresco, and then he was back on Spanish soil. Somewhat to his surprise and regardless of his own opinion of his lack of form, the race organisers of the Madrid Marathon were more than happy to foot his hotel and race entry costs to have Steve grace their race with his presence.

Just like Seville, it was a new race and a new city to explore with Teresa, but unlike Seville, about eight miles in, Steve was hit with severe cramp in his hamstring. It stayed with him for the remainder of the race, which he finished in 3:28.

Worse was to come at the Potteries Marathon. Steve reached the 17-mile point on an exceptionally hot June day feeling so dizzy he was forced to stop and sit down beneath a shady oak tree for fear of collapsing: '...the whole world was whizzing round in circles.'

But it wasn't the fear of collapsing he was worried about so much as the sickening thought of a 'DNF' next to his name in the results.

Luckily for him, Alvis Clubmate, Chuck Pope, saw Steve sprawled beneath the tree, and immediately stopped, helping Steve back up on to his feet and walking with him till the dizziness subsided. They then broke into a tentative jog-walk routine, which they continued all the way to the finish. Steve couldn't have been more grateful. The race has since been scratched from his totals, but at least he avoided the dreaded DNF. More importantly, perhaps, he realised that now he had less hair, he should wear a cap in warmer weather and has done so ever since.

Before the year was out, Steve had run the new Loch Ness Marathon; a scenic point-to-point race along the east side of the Loch, finishing in Inverness ('...I didn't see the monster though!'), and recorded his 300th sub-3:30 at Manchester. Actually getting to the start without difficulty for the first time thanks to a new course that didn't require the use of a late-running bus, meant he stormed round in 3:18. A week later, at Abingdon, he ran his first sub-3:15 for three years.

Steve put his improved form down to the four half-marathons he'd run in the latter part of the year, all in around 1:31, and continuing his usual three-mile runs after work and the longer seven-mile runs with Alvis once a week. However, he still felt he wasn't as race fit as he should be and blamed it on the reduction of marathons he was then running, which he believed had previously maintained his endurance.

At the close of 2002, Steve had added a further 16 marathons to his totals, 11 were sub-3:30, and his average finish time for the year was 3:32. This brought his overall average finish time for all 352 official marathon races to 3:19:15, still well inside his average 3:30 target.

Now aged 40, Steve needed another 148 marathons to reach his record-breaking goal of 500. If he was to do this by his 50th birthday, he needed to run 15 marathons a year for the next 10 years. The numbers seemed doable, but would he be able to maintain the times? He, like everyone else, would be growing older and would naturally slow down. Not even Steve Edwards could beat the ravages of time.

Certainly, the ravages of time had conspired against Steve and Teresa's desire for a baby. By the time 2002 came to an end and they'd both hit the big 40, there was still no sign of any offspring: '...obviously we couldn't get the recipe right!'

Burying their disappointment behind such light-hearted words, the couple stuck to their decision made a year earlier and closed the door on hope. Then they went out and bought themselves: '...a rather obscene 40th birthday present!'

Inspired by the James Bond film, 'Goldeneye', featuring a shameless show-off BMW Z3 convertible sports car, Steve and Teresa were first in line at the showrooms.

And, really, who could blame them?

Chapter 27

2003 –
Building Bridges

2003 was a quiet year running-wise for Steve with just 12 races, his fastest being 3:17 at Abingdon. Whilst his annual average stood at 3:24 - his best since 1999 - his overall average finish time of 3:19:26 for all 364 official marathon races continued to drift downwards. He also ran five half-marathons throughout the year.

Of those 12 marathons, his most memorable were sunny Valencia, another first for Steve, with a finish time of 3:18, followed by his beloved Tresco: '...you can't have too much of Paradise!'

However, whilst it was a quiet year for Steve, the same could not be said for Teresa, who completed her first marathon in July: '...I'd always wondered what it was like to try and run 26 miles.'

Following Steve's advice to go for an LDWA event so there'd be no time pressure and all she'd have to do would be to get round, Teresa bravely entered the Windmill Marathon, run over the heartlessly hilly South Downs. Having run two to three miles most days, plus once a week with Alvis, Teresa ran and walked her way to the finish line in 6 hours 25 minutes, with Steve beside her every step.

For Teresa it had been a carefully planned, relatively gentle introduction to Steve's marathon world and with glorious weather, plenty of snacks provided by the LDWA all the way round and a hot meal at the end, it was a reasonably enjoyable experience. However, it wasn't one that was going to be repeated any time soon!

2003 was also a notable year in another very important way for Steve. Nearly a year had passed since he'd seen his son, but he was never far from Steve's thoughts. Having discussed the situation with his brother-in-law, Mick, Steve decided Mick was right – the longer he left it the worse it would be, and if he didn't at least try to make contact, he would always regret it. Besides, the estrangement hadn't just affected him, it had affected his parents' relationship with their grandson, and that just couldn't be right. It was time to act.

No longer in contact with Mandy, Steve traced his son's whereabouts through his friends. All he had to do then was give Jason a call: '...I was terrified he'd reject me.'

Deep breaths and sweaty palms resulted in a meeting with Jason a few days later. Over a drink, the two men cleared the air and caught up. Steve was delighted to learn that Jason had a job in retail, lived with his girlfriend, Christine, and appeared happy and well. He also seemed genuinely pleased to see his dad – something Steve had been deeply concerned might not be the case. He returned home with Jason's address tucked carefully inside his wallet.

From then on, bridges continued to be built and, slowly, over time, the relationship between father and son, and the rest of the family, blossomed and grew, until it was fully restored.

Steve's son was back in his life and the hurt and pain he'd been carrying around with him ever since the break up, began to ease.

Chapter 28

2004 – THE RETURN: TAKE 1

Although Steve was still travelling round the country working long hours, with work now finished on the house, he decided he had time to up his training miles, especially as his first race of the year was a 35-mile ultra, which he planned to run at 8 mm pace for a 4:40 finish time. As usual, Steve's precise planning paid off as he finished the seven 5-mile laps in 4:39.

Meantime, Steve's training partner, Jim, reminded him that as a MV40 (male veteran runner aged 40-45), Steve could qualify for London with a 'good for age' place. In 2004, this meant running sub-3:15 and applied to anyone aged 40-59. This would guarantee him a place independent of the ballot. As a senior runner (aged 18-39), this hadn't been an option for Steve, with a 'good for age' qualifying time then being 2:45, compared to today's qualifying time of 3:05.

Too late to apply for that year's London, and having not entered Tresco either, Steve convinced himself he would be perfectly happy watching London from the comfort of his own home. He was wrong: '...I hated it!'

He vowed 'never again' and beat himself up for not having tried harder to run below 3:15 and qualify for a good for age time the very first year he had the chance.

London aside, Steve ran seven domestic marathons in the first half of the year, but none below 3:20. He wasn't worried, there was still time (back then, October was the cut-off date for qualifying for London), and added an interval session to his weekly training sessions to try and improve his speed.

Disappointment followed in August with 3:23 at a tough new marathon at Weymouth - despite a 1:37 first-half split. Undeterred, he tried again at Wolverhampton a fortnight later. Another first-half split of 1:37 resulted in a finish time of 3:29.

Time was running out. Maybe he wouldn't qualify? Maybe he'd never run sub-3:15 ever again?

But then, a week after Wolverhampton, at the Robin Hood Marathon in Nottingham, he ran another faster first half than second, but this time finished in a decisive 3:11. He'd gone from 3:29 to 3:11 in a week! Job done. He would be running London in 2005.

Robin Hood was followed by the inaugural Cardiff Marathon in 3:08 – his fastest race in over five years and equally memorable for meeting future good friend, Rush Yadevi, who was working towards his 100 marathons and had followed Steve's progress for many years.

Steve's confidence rocketed – a week later he ran the inaugural Anglesey Marathon in 3:07 and Abingdon the week after that in 3:09.

Steve Edwards was back!

Meanwhile, away from racing, Steve and Teresa decided to move to the Cotswolds, a place they knew well from driving around it in their convertible; hood down, hair blowing (in Teresa's case), in the gentle breeze of a summer's day. Here, life seemed less frantic; it was a place they'd like to put down roots.

Eventually, they settled on a new-build in Moreton-in-Marsh in the north of the Cotswolds, less than an hour's drive from family and friends in Coventry.

Following a part-exchange with the builder to reduce stress and Teresa's successful application for a staff nurse post at the local cottage hospital, Steve set about organising the move with his usual military precision. Once again, the couple hired a Luton box van and did the move themselves. They also took cuttings from their old garden and transplanted them into the new; Steve having first drawn up plans as to where everything should go, as well as putting up trellises and laying slabs. The large loft was then boarded and filled with Steve's cricketing, football and musical memorabilia. All that was left was for him to unpack and re-organise his medal boards – a painstaking task that for perfectionist Steve entailed re-hanging every single medal individually on to boards in the correct order in which they'd been won. It took weeks.

To the misfortune of the builders who were still on site, Steve applied the same stringent standards to snagging as he did to his medal boards!

Snags sorted, medals finally hung, Steve drew breath. It was time to concentrate on running. There followed a 3:11 at Leicester and 3:09 at Luton two weeks later, bringing his average time for the previous six marathons to 3:09 – something he'd not experienced since the end of 1995.

By the end of the year Steve had run 15 marathons in an average finish time of 3:19, lowering his overall average finish time for 379 official marathon races to 3:19:25. It may only have been an improvement of one second per marathon, but it was a huge relief for Steve after several years of seeing his times drifting away.

Also by the end of the year, Steve's employers had moved to Southam, near Leamington Spa. Despite still being a 50-mile round trip, the quieter roads meant a quicker, virtually stress-free commute, following the scenic Fosse Way - an old Roman road, virtually all the way to Southam - and offered Steve more time at either end of the day. With the new offices housing showers and being opposite football fields, Steve was able to start training at lunchtime again. Even if the fields were wet, there were some lovely quiet, country lanes to run along instead.

Things were definitely looking up – apart from the star of course.

Chapter 29

2005 – ON A ROLL

Steve entered 2005 with a renewed zest for running. Life was good. He and Teresa were now happily ensconced in their lovely new home in the Cotswolds, Teresa was enjoying her new job, and the company Steve worked for had been acquired by a larger, support services company, called Carillion. This reduced the need for him to drive to remote offices so often and renewed his enthusiasm for travelling to races.

Not having run cross-country with Alvis since moving and looking to get in a solid run before the start of the road marathon season in March, Steve's first race of the year was a new 30-mile event at Oldbury in January. It went well. The extra lunchtime miles had maintained his winter fitness and he went through the marathon point in 3:13, before crossing the line at 30 miles in 3:40. The only 30-miler Steve has ever done, it remains his personal best.

Oldbury was followed by a half-marathon at Bristol University in 1:24, his fastest since Bath in 1998.

It was clear Steve's rediscovered confidence was not misplaced. Next came a 3:12 at the Duchy Marathon (starting and finishing at Redruth rather than Land's End this time), followed by an identical time at Taunton.

Then it was back to London where he hadn't run since 2000 and the first time he'd be running as a MV40 from the good for age start line. What a difference! There was no jostling for position; everything was more relaxed. There was even time to use the loo and grab a coffee.

All that was irrelevant, though, as the legendary London crowds pushed him all the way to a 3:01 finish. Even with his recently improving form, it was way beyond expectation, his fastest London since 1997 when he'd finished in precisely the same time: '...after eight years, I was back to somewhere near my best.'

Steve was on a roll and didn't miss a beat, following through with 3:13 at the Shakespeare Marathon - his 400th including ultras. This coincided with fellow Coventrian, Dave Phillips' 300th and a double celebration covered by the Coventry press.

A 3:14 at Halstead and 3:09 at the White Peak Marathon ensued. It seemed he'd killed his demons as he strung together a remarkable consecutive series of 13 sub-3:15s; something not done since 1992, when he'd set the most in a year record.

And then it was over...or at least that's how Steve felt when he ran 3:18 at the Dartmoor Vale Marathon at Newton Abbot. It was a warm day and a two-lap course with a nasty steep hill on each lap that really took the sting out of the tail second time around: '...runners are fickle; not so long before I would have been thrilled to run that time on that sort of course!'

The rest of the year proved a mixed bag, with a few more sub-3:15s and a few just over. Overall, Steve ran 14 marathons, a couple of ultras and a couple of halves. All his marathons were sub-3:30, with 10 sub-3:15, giving an average finish time for the year of 3:13 – his best since 1995. With a total of 393 official marathon races now completed, Steve's average finish time improved for the second successive year to 3:19:13 – but this time the improvement was a massive 12 seconds per marathon.

A light glimmered at the far end of a very long, very dark tunnel. The tunnel led to Sy Mah's record. Steve was now close to running 400 official marathons, his average time was well below 3:30. If he could maintain his form he may make it sub-3:20. The target remained for 2012; his 50th birthday year. When London was chosen to host the 2012 Olympic Games in the very year he planned to break Sy Mah's record, Steve took it as a positive sign.

All he had to do was maintain his schedule of running 15-16 sub-3:30 marathons a year for the next seven years, and the record would be his.

How difficult could it be?

Chapter 30

2006 – LIFE'S RICH TAPESTRY

It was just over a year since they'd moved, and life in the Cotswolds was proving pretty peachy for Steve and Teresa. The regret they'd feared they might feel at leaving their birthplace and families hadn't materialised. Whenever they went away, they couldn't wait to return to the peace and sanctuary of their lovely home.

Building a good foundation for the forthcoming marathon season, Steve set out his stall with two early sub-1:30 halves in Watford and Wokingham, enabling him to look forward to his first marathon of the year with happy optimism.

Sadly, though, before that first race arrived, Steve received some devastating news – his good friend and long-time running buddy, Phil Duffy, runner of over 300 marathons, had died. The loss of a man who everyone loved for his sociability, sense of fun and witty banter was hard enough to swallow, but the tragic circumstances, which remain private out of respect for Phil and his family, made the loss even harder.

Meanwhile, the t-shirt Steve won ahead of Phil at the Harrow Marathon in 1991, was posthumously awarded to Phil when Steve left it on his old friend's headstone with his eulogy, ending with the words: '...I'm sorry I didn't give this to you before...you will always be in my thoughts whenever and wherever I run.'

Not surprisingly, it was an emotional Steve who ran his first few marathons of the year - the Duchy at Redruth in 3:15, followed a week later by Dumfries in 3:08. All he could think of was Phil. He felt so lucky to be alive, to be able to still run marathons in reasonable times, despite the number of races and years he'd now been running and despite his blood disorder. He was filled with an overwhelming sense of gratitude. It is a gratitude that remains with him to this day.

After Dumfries, there followed five more sub-3:15s, including a 3:03 at London with Steve having again qualified with a good for age place.

Steve's 400th official marathon race fell at White Peak – where he'd run his 200th in 1992. This was pure coincidence, though, and nothing to do with Steve's usual precise planning. With focus firmly fixed on the ultimate goal, his 400th was merely another rung to be passed on his climb up to the magical 500th at the very top of the ladder.

Indeed, so intent was Steve on his ultimate goal, that he broke the promise made to himself 14 years earlier not to run any more doubles. For the day after his 400th he skipped across to the Isle of Wight for the 50th anniversary of their notoriously tough marathon:

'...when I realised it was the 50th, I just had to run it, despite having already entered White Peak on the Saturday.'

Reminiscent of his earlier years, Steve and Teresa drove home from Derbyshire on Saturday evening, before driving to Portsmouth early Sunday morning for the ferry to Ryde.

Two miles in, Steve's body let him know exactly what it thought about his broken promise. It was an unpleasant and untimely reminder of why he'd made the promise initially. Steve eventually finished in 3:25, meeting his weekend goals of a sub-3:15 on Saturday and a sub-3:30 on Sunday. But, seriously - never again!

With Phil clearly still on his mind, the start of June saw Steve and Teresa head off to the Edinburgh Marathon; a race Phil had enthused about but one Steve had never previously run. Phil was right, it was a great race, even if the course had changed to include a long out and back section offering no protection from the strong headwind that blew in one direction that day, making the going incredibly tough. Steve could well imagine Phil looking down and laughing as he battled his way against the wind just because he'd recommend the race to him! He may laugh, but Steve was more than happy with his 3:12 finish time.

Then one day, about a month later, Teresa was at work and Steve was painting the trellis in the garden, enjoying the July sunshine, when the phone rang. Answering it, Steve listened in disbelief. Teresa's brother-in-law, removal man Steve, had collapsed at home and was now in hospital in a coma.

Steve and Teresa headed at once to Coventry Hospital. Apparently, Steve had suffered a cerebral aneurysm and was in theatre undergoing an emergency procedure. He was then moved to the intensive care unit; his life hanging by a thread.

All the family could do was wait.

They waited three agonisingly long days. Their waiting was in vain. The hospital could do no more and Steve's life support machine was switched off. He was 44 years old, the same age as Steve and Teresa at that time.

If losing an older friend in Phil Duffy had an effect on Steve and Teresa, the death of a contemporary had an even greater one. Life suddenly seemed so much more precious and frighteningly fragile. They clung to each other and shared many tears, while Anne turned naturally to older sister, Teresa, for support.

The funeral was heart-rending. It seemed inconceivable that just five months earlier the four of them, Steve and Teresa, Steve and Anne, had attended Phil's funeral together. Now they were attending one of their own.

Apart from time, there was only one thing Steve and Teresa knew of that could help ease their pain, and that was running. Searching to make sense of it all and in need of a positive focus, Teresa began training religiously under Steve's guidance for the Milton

Keynes half-marathon, while Steve, with just a couple of half-marathons planned for July and August, was able to give her his full support, both emotionally and practically.

As race day approached, Teresa's main concern was the heat. The summer had turned into an unlikely scorcher and she worried this would compromise her ability to run all the way. And run all the way was what she was determined to do. Walking was not an option. Was she turning into her husband?

Come the day of reckoning, the Gods smiled down upon Teresa and delivered a perfect running day; still bright, but considerably cooler. Both Steve and Teresa held her late brother-in-law fully responsible: '...he always had a soft spot for Teresa.'

And with such good care from above, plus the more earthly care of her husband who ran alongside her, pacing her, and reining her in at the start when she seemed in danger of being swept along with the momentum created by the other runners, Teresa crossed the line in 2:12, having run every single step of the way. It was hard to say of Steve and Teresa who was the more proud.

And then, as they sat on the grass near the finish sipping recovery drinks, the most unlikely thing happened. The brightest of smiles lit Teresa's face and her eyes sparkled as if a million stars had just exploded within. She smiled because she was utterly, completely, exhausted. In fact, she couldn't remember ever feeling quite so tired. At the same time, she felt supremely happy, euphoric even. For the first time in her life, Mrs Teresa Edwards was experiencing the runner's high. Go, Mrs Edwards!

In fact, there was only one negative thought in Teresa's mind at that time – there was no way she could do what she'd just done all over again and actually run a full marathon, that would be impossible!

It was only the middle of the afternoon, but somewhere in the universe a star could be heard laughing.

There was laughter of a more human kind when soon afterwards Steve bumped into old junior school friend, Darren Edwards, who'd taken up running a few years earlier and was doing a 10k in Gloucestershire, and, again, when Jason announced that Christine was expecting their first child in January. Steve would be a granddad at 44!

Meanwhile, the future Grandpa Gump had been slightly disappointed not to break the 1:30 barrier for his own couple of half-marathons, even though it was only by seconds. He was also disappointed that whilst eight of his nine marathons run in the second half of the year were sub-3:30, he'd only managed to break 3:15 once. It never occurred to him till much later that losing two people he was close to within a few months of one another could have had something to do with it.

By the end of a difficult year, Steve had added another 18 marathons to his totals with an average finish time of 3:16; a slight drop compared to the previous year but solid nevertheless. This brought his total official marathon races up to 411 and his average finish time to 3:19:06 – an improvement for the third consecutive year, this time by a further 7 seconds per marathon.

And while the rich tapestry of life was being woven in all its many guises in the Edwards' household, so unbeknown to them was an email being writ that would define their future in a way they couldn't possibly imagine or predict.

The writer of said email was Scott Umpleby who worked for the Brathay Trust, a charity established in 1946 to improve life for children and young people in the UK by helping them develop confidence, motivation and skills to enable them to unlock their potential and make positive changes in their lives.

Scott's email was addressed to the 100 Marathon Club and appealed to anyone interested in running a '10 marathons in 10 days' challenge around Lake Windermere in May 2007 (to be held in conjunction with the return of the Windermere Marathon), to get in touch. The challenge was to serve as a fundraiser for the Brathay Trust and had been dreamt up by one of the Trust's fellows, Sir Christopher Ball.

Sir Christopher had been so inspired by the achievement of Sir Rannulph Fiennes in running seven marathons in seven days on different continents, that he'd decided to try it for himself – except he ran seven marathons in seven days along the Thames from its source to Tower Bridge. Sir Christopher, then aged 69, was confident he could increase this to 10 marathons in 10 days and was looking for an opportunity to undertake the challenge with like-minded enthusiasts. In the summer of 2006, he duly approached Brathay. Brathay picked up his idea and ran with it.

It took Steve less than a day to reply in the affirmative, with Teresa's blessing. He may have turned his back on doubles, but he hadn't made any promises to himself about 'decathons', had he? Besides, he'd managed to run 8 marathons in 11 days and his body had adapted remarkably well to that, hadn't it? Sure, he may have been 29 years old at the time and he was now 44, but still...

The whole idea was thrilling! There had never been such an event before anywhere in the world, certainly not one run on an officially measured and recognised marathon course or one consisting of that number of marathons in the same number of days. The pioneering fire that simmered within Steve's soul was instantly rekindled. This was just what he needed - something different, something exciting, something between now and the Sy Mah record to aim for. It couldn't have come at a better time!

There would also be the potential of a new world record category being forged. Who would be the first person to run an official 10-in-10 and what would be the fastest consecutive and average finish times over the 10 days?

Before the year was out, Steve and Scott were in direct communication. Brathay decided that in return for runners raising funds for their charity, they would open the doors to their rather magnificent Brathay Hall, providing accommodation and meals for the 10 days. It looked like the game was on.

Steve's excitement grew, as did his nerves. How exactly should he prepare for such an event? With no precedent to guide him, he was on his own. Although he'd had experience of a few multi-marathons, he hadn't really trained specifically for them, just relied on his residual fitness. The 10-in-10 deserved better preparation than that. If he was to be a pioneer on a voyage of discovery, the fastidious Steve intended to do all he could to ensure the voyage was as Tsunami-free as possible.

Unfortunately, his body had other ideas.

Chapter 31

2007 – MAKING HISTORY

Just as Steve's first granddaughter, Alyssa, was born, so Steve's body rebelled against the extra training miles with a hamstring strain. The further he ran, the worse the pain, forcing him to slow down after five or six miles.

Previously with minor niggles he'd run through them, but as he grew older the less effective that particular tactic seemed to be and, if he was to run 10 marathons in 10 consecutive days, he really ought to at least start off injury-free. Once more he utilised his employer's health insurance, consulting Stow Physiotherapy and being treated by physiotherapist, Lucy Walmsley, who also specialised in acupuncture. Unenthused by the idea of a number of extremely sharp needles being inserted into various body parts, anticipation proved far worse than realisation and, more importantly, had the desired effect.

But then another niggle developed on the same leg, this time behind his knee at the top of the calf. Just like the hamstring, the further he ran, the worse the pain. But still Steve continued to train and race, grinding out

3:21 at Draycote Water in February, 3:24 at the Duchy Marathon and 3:25 at Taunton

In the meantime, Mick McCann, fund raising manager for the Spinal Injuries Association (SIA), invited Steve to represent them at the London Marathon, having been chosen as London's nominated charity that year. A fellow Coventrian and Coventry Godiva Harrier, Mick had followed Steve's progress through the Coventry Telegraph and wanted him as the SIA's 'celebrity face'!

Steve was flattered and delighted to accept: '... it was a great way for me to put something back in return for all the years of enjoyment I'd had from running.'

Prior to race day, Steve visited the SIA's headquarters to talk about his marathon adventures to the charity runners. Butterflies boogied anxiously about his belly as he sat through talks given by Mick and former Olympic marathon runner, Dave Long. And then it was his turn. Ignoring the butterflies that were now positively pogo-ing around in a way Steve himself would have been proud of in his punk days, he talked about his record year, coping with double marathons most weekends, the travelling and logistics, and the Sy Mah record. By the time he got round to his top marathon tips, Steve was chatting like a pro. The butterflies were enjoying a well-deserved nap, and, much to his amazement, the audience were all still awake.

But it was the physio's talk that impressed Steve that day: '...the most informative hour of running information I've ever had the privilege of listening to.'

This was followed by an opportunity for Steve to discuss his current injury. When asked if he could bring on the pain by doing anything specific, Steve cheerily complied. He also complied, somewhat less cheerily, with instructions to lie on his front and grit his teeth. He then endured two 15-second bursts of intense pain as the physio stuck his thumb into the top of his calf, pushing right down into the belly of the muscle, helpfully explaining as he did so that this was the popliteus muscle, which, if not working properly, prevented the knee from bending: '...it was excruciating. I was sweating buckets by the time he'd finished.'

When the physio explained this was a 'trigger point release mechanism', Steve recalled a book he'd been recommended about that very thing. He later bought a copy and has used it with reasonable success ever since.

Training duly resumed and, as the physio promised, the top of Steve's calf pulled painfully with every step, but by the end of the week the pain had all but disappeared. With the 10-in-10 just around the corner, Steve breathed a sigh of relief. With that sigh came the realisation that some injuries can be fairly simply fixed by a therapist who knows what they're doing. Hindsight is a marvellous thing, but it cannot change the past. It can, however, be used to change the future.

Which is exactly what Steve did - not only in his mindset towards seeking professional help if injured, but in trying to prevent injuries in the first place by incorporating all he'd learned into his training and racing routine. All this from a man who only started stretching at the age of 40 and who today firmly believes that stretching after training or racing is a key element of recovery!

Freed of his injury, and despite not having done any speed sessions because of it, Steve was delighted to finish London in 3:12. A week later, conscious that the 10-in-10 was now just 12 short days away, he opted for a more comfortable 3:23 at the Shakespeare Marathon.

Looking back, Steve is painfully aware that his preparation for the inaugural 10-in-10 was: '...woefully lacking.' His mileage wasn't much different to the norm and, thanks to the absence of UK doubles back then, he hadn't run any since the lone one the previous year. Conversely, given his injuries, it may well have been that had he run more, he may have exacerbated the injuries and not made it to Brathay at all!

But make it he did, and on Thursday, 10th May, 2007, he and Teresa came to the end of their 220-mile drive to the Lake District, where they'd started married life eight years earlier, and parked at the end of a long, tree-lined driveway in front of a modestly imposing Georgian mansion known as Brathay Hall.

Situated in the tiny hamlet of Clappersgate near Ambleside, the Hall forms part of a 360-acre estate at the head of Lake Windermere. With breathtaking views across a large, perfectly manicured lawn, surrounded by rolling hills and craggy tors, England's largest lake meanders its glistening way into the distant south. Runners making the finish would run down the tree-lined drive and cross the verdant lawn, the lake shimmering before them, picture-perfect, as they crossed the line.

Taking this in, listening to race director, Scott Umpleby's welcome and introduction to Sir Christopher Ball, Steve felt he was about to embark on something very special. Not just a world first, but something more. He couldn't put it into words, but he felt it just the same. Alongside him, 100 Clubbers, Brent Iddles, John Dawson and Jim Mundy, together with Brian Meakin and Simon Moseley, felt it too.

Scott then drove the runners round the course in a minibus so they could familiarise themselves with the route as, unlike normal marathons, there would be no regular distance markers or drinks stations along the way for the first nine days. In fact, apart from the powdered drink sachets provided to make up their own drinks every day, and Megan, a Brathay employee volunteering to drive behind the last runner and collect any fallers, the runners would be virtually self-sufficient.

Mindful of this, the seven participants boarded the minibus. The course started outside the main gate on the B5286 and followed the road south to Newby Bridge. The bus's occupants noted numerous hilly stretches and a particularly nasty climb at about seven miles, though their mounting fear was fractionally quelled by a definite flattening out over the next few miles.

Fear returned, however, as they headed north along the lake's eastern edge towards Bowness. Here, the course seemed to go either up or down, but mostly up. The occupants grew quiet. Brent threw Steve a nervous glance and nodded at the back window. The hill they'd just driven up in second gear dropped down behind them so sharply the bottom was no longer visible. Steve's stomach knotted; his notion that running round a lake would be flat followed the view out of the window.

From Bowness they continued north before turning towards Troutbeck Bridge. At the 25-mile point, Steve could hardly believe his eyes, they were outside the very restaurant where he and Teresa had enjoyed their wedding day lunch: '…it felt quite surreal.'

The course then continued towards Ambleside, before heading back towards Clappersgate. Despite the final quarter offering some flat and even downhill stretches, there were a couple more nasty uphill surprises including the driveway at mile 26 taking them back to Brathay Hall. Although it did go back down again for the final 75 metres leading on to the lawn and that heavenly finish.

The seven runners left the bus in silence. All Steve could think was: '...10 of these over the next 10 days... nice.' Or not.

Having seen the course and knowing they were going to be pretty much on their own out there, Steve decided to set up his own drink stops. He and Teresa drove straight back round the course armed with chalk and map, marking the road and map at approximately two-mile intervals. They would make up Steve's drinks the night before, put them in a crate and load them into their car. Teresa would then drive to each drink stop in turn, wait for Steve, and then drive on to the next designated stop shown on the map. The 10-in-10 was no longer just a challenge for Steve, it was a challenge for them both; one they would face together as a team. Team Edwards (TE).

Ultimately, it wasn't just Steve who benefited from this plan. Teresa actually took all the runners' drinks round the course in her car (except Brian, who took a Camelback), leaving their individually marked bottles at the pre-planned drink stops chosen by Steve. Those arriving first also benefited from Teresa handing them their drinks, saving them from bending down to pick them up from the ground. Steve's drink stops have since become the official drink stations for today's event – except, of course, today nobody's wife has to slog round the course delivering them, as the race has become one of the best organised and well-supported events on the multi-marathon calendar.

But back at the inaugural event it was a different story. Steve and his crew were mere guinea pigs, but they were guinea pigs who at least enjoyed the hospitality of Brathay Hall, where they each had their own bedroom, some with en-suites, and enjoyed breakfast, lunch and dinner prepared by Brathay's catering staff.

Friday, 11th May – Day 1

The runners met at 9 am on the lawn for the official launch of the first ever 10 marathons in 10 days challenge. Following words of wisdom from fell running legend, Joss Naylor, there was a contrived start from the Hall's lawn with a shotgun fired by the local gamekeeper! This, however, was merely a publicity stunt, after which the runners walked to the official start on the road at the bottom of Brathay's drive. This became a permanent tradition.

Steve's intention was to set off slightly slower than usual and then: '...glide round the rest of the course, hills and all'. He was somewhat shocked then to feel above-normal fatigue and, thanks to the extreme gradients, rock-hard road surface and occasional severe cambers, was forced to continually adjust his pace. If he hadn't, he'd have been exhausted by the finish, and tomorrow he had to get up and do it all again, and every day after that for another eight days. Even with the adjustments, he felt shattered, finishing 10 minutes slower than his anticipated 3:30.

Steve was worried; could he really run a reasonable time every day for the next nine days and remain injury free? There were no physiotherapists (although Lucy had promised to be on the end of the phone should Steve need her), and just one volunteer masseur, Kaz Stuart; a former Brathay employee, offering daily rubdowns. Something Steve jumped at that first day; the only one who did.

Days 2-6:
Steve shared the lead every day with one other runner. The first event of its kind with no precedents to follow, most adopted a cautious approach, running within themselves, taking baby steps uphill and running steadily downwards - all trying to avoid injury and a DNF.

After each run Steve stretched, had a recovery protein drink and ate lunch, before enduring an ice bath in his room followed by a 15-minute massage from Kaz.

His recovery routine served him well. Every morning, extremely tired, he'd get out of bed and apply the litmus test – if he could walk to the dining room for breakfast there was a good chance he could run again that day.

As the days passed, so Kaz's workload increased, with all the runners now utilising her services with an ever-growing list of injuries. Eventually, having already worked in her normal job all day, Kaz was so exhausted she sought additional assistance from a physio friend.

Days 7, 8 & 9:

On day 7, with both Achilles tendons giving him gyp, Steve put homemade cardboard heel inserts inside his shoes to raise the heel and relieve the pressure. He also agreed to the other lead runner's suggestion that they continue running together for the rest of the challenge, including the final day. What better way to demonstrate Brathay's teachings of the importance of camaraderie and teamwork than to cross the finish line as one? And what better way to end a world first? The two men shook hands, a gentleman's agreement.

After nine days, Steve's times were all between 3:40 and 3:54. Sensible rather than exciting, he was just happy to have got through nine days of running a pretty brutal course relatively unscathed. He was also happy to acquiesce to the other lead runner's suggestion that on day 10 he should run off ahead of Steve to make it more exciting for the media. They should then meet up in Bowness, run the remaining few miles and cross the finish line together. Why not? The media loved a bit of drama!

Day 10:

'On day 10 we were joined by almost 1000 other runners arriving for the Brathay Windermere Marathon. A crowd gathered at the start to see us off on what was to be our final lap. I felt like a coiled spring and couldn't wait to get going; my legs felt so good it was as if I hadn't run at all on the previous nine days.

Seven athletes were about to make history if they could just run one more 26.2-mile circuit of Windermere – England's largest lake – and didn't we know it!'

9.30 am – An hour ahead of the main marathon, Steve toed the start line. As agreed, he started out slower than usual letting the other lead runner go ahead. Later, he picked up his pace, and just after halfway, started looking out for the other runner. There was no sign of him. Maybe Steve had misunderstood the plan? But when he caught up with Brent, who'd set off an hour ahead of everyone else due to several bad injuries, Brent said the other runner had mentioned meeting up with Steve at Bowness. There was no misunderstanding.

Steve began to panic and picked up his pace. He was now running at 7 mm pace – after running 257 miles over 10 days. There were just 5 miles to go - and still no sign of the other runner.

At mile 26 he was hit by the sickening realisation that the other runner had reneged on their agreement. He hadn't waited for Steve. He'd finished his race already. They wouldn't be crossing the line together. There was no camaraderie.

After running 262 miles around an incredibly tough course, Steve felt physically drained, and emotionally sick. He couldn't take it in, couldn't believe someone could behave so dishonourably. He crossed the line in numb disbelief, hardly aware of his own incredible achievement. He saw Teresa; she was saying something, instructing him to shake the hand of the winner, let the press have their pictures. Amid the clamour, he only just made out the mumbled apology of the victor.

Steve fell to his knees. People probably assumed it was due to exhaustion. It was not. It was shock and the hurt of betrayal.

Day 11:

TE packed their bags and headed for home. Steve tasted the bitterness of treachery on his tongue. It seeped through his body and into his heart. He welcomed it in. It hardened into resolve. Next year would be different. Next year he would return. Next year he would set the record straight. Next year he would win.

Steve's times for each marathon were: 3:40, 3:47, 3:49, 3:42, 3:51, 3:45, 3:54, 3:54, 3:48 and 3:30, respectively. This gave him a cumulative total of 37 hours 45 minutes 22 seconds, and an average of 3 hours 46 minutes 32 seconds per marathon.

The runners raised £14,000 for Brathay and returned home with a chunk of local slate presented by Joss Naylor commemorating the occasion and knowing they'd achieved a world first, whatever their final finishing places. Their names would be etched forever in Brathay's records; 72-year old Sir Christopher Ball's name heading the list, not only as the instigator of the event but as the oldest man in the world to run 10 marathons in 10 consecutive days at that time.

'We may not have been elite athletes in the Olympic sense, but for a brief moment while we stood on the stage being cheered by the crowds, we had a vague notion of what that might be like as it dawned on us that we had just made history. I thank Brathay for giving me that opportunity.'

Thus inspired and armed with his iron resolve, just a few weeks after returning home, Steve contacted Scott stating his commitment to return in 2008 and offering Teresa's assistance again with the drinks – assuming they would be holding the event a second time of course. Brathay most certainly were hoping to hold the event a second time, improving it from lessons learned at the inaugural one.

Steve felt much the same. He didn't just want to avenge himself, he wanted to run the challenge the way he should perhaps have run it first time round – on his own terms, with the added bonus of having learned so much from the first one in terms of pacing, recovery, and pre-race preparation.

He began straight away, incorporating two new exercises into his training regime – single leg calf raisers on the edge of a step to strengthen the Achilles and single leg squats to strengthen glutes and improve stability, which over 10 days would improve running efficiency, making him less prone to injury. All Steve had learned, not only from Brathay, but previously, was deployed; backed by the childhood determination first spoken of by his parents and further strengthened by his new resolve, plus his meticulous attention to detail. Nothing would be left to chance. Over the next year, everything he knew about running, from training, to nutrition, to physiology, would be utilised. Nothing, absolutely nothing, was going to come between him and his dream of winning outright at Brathay.

He would also try to run more marathons during the year to improve his endurance, although he was wary about overdoing things and risking injury, ultimately jeopardising his long-term goal of breaking Sy Mah's record.

Today, Steve wonders what he was worrying about given the numbers of marathons he and others now run, but back then nobody had ever run 500+ marathons in times averaging sub-3:20 before. In fact, nobody but Steve still has.

He was venturing into unknown territory, and if dangers lurked therein, he would be the one to discover them. Like Neil Armstrong, someone had to take the first step – even if the experts said it wasn't possible, that his knees would give up, his body would burn out and a million other things might happen to prevent him achieving his goal. Steve listened to their concerns and then worked round them, making sure to pace himself throughout the long-term goal and err on the side of caution.

All that said, just a week after the 10-in-10, he ran his second Edinburgh Marathon in 3:12 for his first sub-3:15 of 2007.

A week later came Blackpool in 3:07 – and with it the sweet taste of revenge, not that Steve was looking for it. However, he is unable to deny that overtaking Brathay's 'Judas' at the 20-mile point did feel just a little bit good! It felt good when he beat him on the three other occasions they raced each other after Brathay as well: '...I know what happened wasn't personal, just the irresistible urge to win a world first. He did apologise afterwards and his wife apologised too. I don't blame him anymore. We're all human. It was the betrayal that hurt, I hadn't felt like that since my schooldays.'

And so, with his course firmly set, Steve's sails picked up a favourable wind as his form gradually improved with his new regime of additional strength work and increased mileage. If motivation flagged, he had only to recall day 10 at Brathay and it returned ten-fold.

However, on the evening of the 20th July, it wasn't just motivation Steve needed. He needed the boat that was attached to the sails that had been blowing him along, as two months worth of rain fell in just 14 hours on Gloucestershire causing widespread flooding.

With local roads becoming flooded, Steve left work early. He then detoured to his parents' home for dinner to allow the worst of the rain and busy Friday commuter traffic to abate. At 6.30 pm, he set out on his 35-mile journey home.

His first problem arose on the Warwickshire border, with the Fosse Way road flooded from nearby rivers. Steve sought alternative routes, but each one ended in another flood. He had no alternative but to risk driving through deep water, keeping everything crossed and praying the electrics wouldn't fail or the engine wouldn't stall.

'It was very scary, as I didn't know how deep the water was or, indeed, whether an under-current would sweep the car away into a nearby river. I was phoning Teresa regularly to update her of my progress.'

Three and a half hours after leaving Coventry, Steve arrived at Moreton to find the high street under a metre of water, '…only the roofs of parked cars were visible.'

Forced to abandon his car, Steve waded home through the deep water, first phoning Teresa to check she was okay. He couldn't imagine their house, just a few hundred yards from the high street, could possibly have escaped flooding. However, Teresa, who'd stayed home all day because of the weather and was oblivious to the drama just down the road, reassured him all was well.

When Steve crossed the pedestrian bridge at Moreton railway station, he could see why Teresa was so unaware, and why they'd been so lucky. The railway cutting had been transformed into a canal, with water almost as high as the platform!

Steve finally made it home at 10 pm, utterly drained. The 35-mile journey that normally took 45 minutes, had taken longer than it took for him to run a marathon!

'Although I'd driven for longer and travelled a lot further on some of my marathon trips, that journey felt like one of the longest of my life!

'Of course, I could have just stayed at my parents' house, but I didn't know how bad it was going to be, and, at the time, I just wanted to get home to Teresa, remembering our vow of never spending a night apart!'

Meanwhile, media interest in Steve's running adventures continued, bringing with it some very unexpected moments, such as on the evening after the Dartmoor Vale Marathon in October. TE had just returned home from the marathon weekend where they had also watched England lose to South Africa in the rugby world cup final, when Steve received a phone call from sports commentator and journalist, John Inverdale. John was covering the rugby world cup for The Daily Telegraph and had been told about Steve by someone at the SIA. They'd apparently said that Steve was an exceptional guy and a big rugby fan raising vast sums of money for the SIA and '...you must write about him'. Much to Steve's surprise and delight, John did!

By the end of 2007, Steve had run 26 marathons in an average finish time of 3:28, a downturn on his previous annual average including, as it did, the 10-in-10. Excluding the 10-in-10 reduced the average to 3:16, the same as 2006. Overall, Steve had now run 437 official marathon races in an average finish time of 3:19:39.

Whilst unconcerned by the slippage in the year's annual average time due to the 10-in-10, and confident he could keep the average time below 3:20 until reaching 500, Steve was concerned that, with only 63 races to go, he might achieve his goal prior to 2012. What should he do?

And then it struck him - if he excluded the 10-in-10 from his totals that would delay everything enough to bring it all back into line again.

During 2007, Steve ran just one half-marathon, the Bourton Hilly Half. Starting at 6 pm on a Saturday evening in mid-June, the race is named for good reason, and is: '...a great little scenic event in the heart of the Cotswolds, definitely one for the bucket list'.

But now, as winter approached, the joys of a scenic summer half-marathon were forgotten as he turned his full concentration on the 2008 10-in-10. Not a day passed without him thinking about it. He even began training twice daily, but only when Teresa was at work. He didn't want her worrying he was overdoing it. But Teresa was worrying anyway. All her husband wanted to do when he got into bed these days was sleep. Maybe he'd gone off her? She confronted him. Did he still love her? Of course he still loved her, more than ever! Only then did Steve realise he'd been behaving like a man possessed. Unpleasant memories of a broken marriage flooded his brain. How stupid was he? It was a timely reminder to keep in mind what was most important. For, however much he loved running, he loved his wife far more.

The star stopped its nervous flickering and settled back to its usual steady glow.

1991 - Sunday Times photoshoot, the loneliness of the long distance runner!

1992 - Meeting Sir Roger Bannister CBE and Dr Ron Hill MBE in Malta

*1992 -The finale to a new world
record 87 marathons in one year*

*1992 - Malta marathon, now a
sponsored athlete!*

1993 - Jason finishing the Potteries Marathon with his dad on Father's Day

1996 - Running for Alvis RC

1999 - Just married

2007 - With Teresa on the finish line before the first ever 10-in-10

Chapter 32

2008 – NUTRITION

Despite such timely reminder, Steve's fire burned ever bright and with just eight UK marathons available prior to the 10-in-10 in May, he was delighted when the 100 Club moved their annual race from December to January, giving him the opportunity for an early run. He won the Stevenage race in 3:14, followed by 3:15 at the newly organised Gloucester Marathon later that month.

Race-wise, Steve's plan was to run within himself prior to the 10-in-10, at the same time upping his training mileage by running twice daily on alternate days and training for 10 consecutive days. He believed it was vital for his body to get used to running that number of days without a break. He also increased his strength and exercise routine.

Feeling stronger and more resilient than ever, Steve's January marathons were followed by Draycote Water 3:12, the Duchy 3:13, Dumfries 3:10 and Taunton 3:12.

Astonishingly, it was only now that the analytical, super-organised, and methodical Steve decided to keep a training diary. Previously, he'd never logged any of his training; just run so many days a week, did x amount of miles, some quick, some steady, but all without any real structure. Now he would have a structure, a schedule, and would log every single run. That log shows that from 1st January 2008 to the 10-in-10 in May, Steve ran 1100 training miles, averaging 60 per week, peaking at 85 - the most he'd ever done.

It was also now that Steve finally put aside concerns that his personal goals may prevent him being a loyal and active member of a club and allowed physio, Lucy, to persuade him to join Bourton Roadrunners (BRR). Lucy was a member, alongside husband, Dennis; former world vet masters marathon and 100k champion. Initially unnerved by such prestigious company, Steve was delighted to discover Dennis was as amenable and grounded as he was talented: '...I have huge respect for Dennis's achievements; he's been a great inspiration to me.'

Meantime, Mick McCann asked Steve to represent the SIA at London again. Among the audience at his pre-race talk in Coventry, were fellow Coventrians, Bill Adcocks and David Moorcroft MBE OBE - former international and world record holder. David interrupted Steve in the middle of his talk: 'Steve, I just have to say that before today Bill Adcocks was my hero, but I think you've just replaced him!'

Feet almost back on terra firma by race day, Steve finished in 3:02 – his fastest London for three years, despite running well within himself. As he and Teresa made their way to the SIA's marquee, a breathless

Mick McCann approached them: 'Someone wants to meet you,' he told Steve, mysteriously, as he led him inside the marquee.

With no time to wonder who that might be, Steve found himself face to face with HRH Princess Anne, patron of the SIA. HRH complimented Steve on being such a good ambassador for the SIA and sport generally, and wanted to know exactly how many marathons he'd run. When told 444, her expression said 'gob-smacked', but in a genteel, reserved, royal kind of way. A former Olympian herself, HRH seemed to appreciate just what sort of dedication this might take and fired questions at Steve as to how he'd managed to do that, what training he did, how he stayed injury-free, what races he'd run, which countries he'd been to, and what was his ultimate goal?

'She seemed genuinely interested in everything I said.'

What a weekend for an ordinary bloke – becoming the hero of an athletics legend and being interviewed by royalty! Whatever next?

Well, actually, next came a massage, lunch and the homeward journey, followed a week later by the Shakespeare Marathon where, having begun his tapering for the 10-in-10 just a fortnight away, Steve enjoyed a relaxed, steady run pacing two BRR clubmates, Chris and Ian, and finishing in 3:12.

In the final 12 days leading up to Brathay, Steve ran only relatively short distances. He'd been sleeping, eating and breathing the 10-in-10 for 12 months, as well as raising the £2000 sponsorship money. He felt fit, strong and ready to do battle. A spreadsheet had been prepared by him with his daily regime over the 10 days neatly listed down one side with tick boxes, so he would know exactly what he needed to do each day from getting out of bed to getting back into it, and incorporated time targets, heart rate monitoring, and drink types to be consumed at certain times and at certain mile points. He'd learned from last year that the more tired he grew, the more he forgot essential parts of his recovery, adversely affecting next day's race. It's a lesson that has stayed with him and been applied to all aspects of his running life since. Nothing is left to chance; he believes small margins of gain are vital in sport and can ultimately make the difference between success and failure.

He'd also contacted Guinness to establish the criteria required to break the 10-in-10 record. To his surprise Guinness weren't aware of any such records, including the 2007 Brathay 10-in-10. It seemed nobody had informed them about it and, therefore, so long as Steve won the event and bettered the previous winner's time, he would become the first holder of the Guinness World Record to run the fastest 10 official marathon races in 10 consecutive days.

All that was left was for him to actually run. In this he was confident. Barring injury or ill health, he believed he could not only break the previous year's record, but smash it. He was not being a braggart, he was simply looking at the facts - he'd done the training, run the times, was positive he could average sub-3:30 each day, culminating in a sub-35-hour overall performance for the 10 races. Of course he couldn't account for the other runners and knew from experience not to discount them.

He also couldn't account for the weather and, just a few days before the event, the sun shone and temperatures rose – Steve's most feared running conditions at that time. But there was nothing he could do about that as he and 100 Clubbers - Paul and Sue Adams, Selina Da Silva and Jim Mundy, together with George Russell, Matthew Evans, Ray O'Connor, Michelle Atkins, Phil Roberts and Malcolm Anderson - settled into their rooms at Brathay, home for the next 11 days. This time, the runners stayed in Shackleton Lodge, a few hundred metres from the Hall. Each room had two double bunk beds and most runners shared. There were communal showers, toilets and a kitchen stocked with breakfast fodder. Lunches and dinners were eaten in the Hall's main dining room as previously.

While Teresa sorted out clothing, Steve blue-tacked his time target spreadsheet to the door ready to complete each day to track his progress; arranged supplements, gels and drink powders on the top bunk in day order; and filled a couple of small round bottles with water to be frozen and rolled under his feet each evening to ease soreness or bruising and help prevent plantar fasciitis. He'd also taken bags of frozen peas to reduce any muscle inflammation, but didn't need them, as physio, Amy Bateman from Active Physio, who was there for all 10 days, provided compression ice packs. There was also a masseur and two massage beds set up in Shackleton Lodge. It was a vast improvement on 2007.

Without an en-suite bath this time, Steve found a shallow part of the nearby River Brathay to use for his post-race ice bath instead. He also had three pairs of running shoes to be alternated each day, restoring bounce and giving his legs a better ride.

Among the sponsors that year were Team Nutrition ('TN'), run by Robin Higgins. TN supplied hydration, energy and recovery drinks, plus gels and fruit bars. With the weather forecast to get even hotter, Steve was persuaded to try TN's products, which Robin claimed were lighter on the stomach, not too sweet, and didn't contain artificial ingredients or aspartame.

Spreadsheets at the ready, hydration sorted, it was time to get down to business.

Day 1:
Steve set off at his target pace of 7 minute 45 second miling, quickly establishing a clear lead. As the miles passed and the temperature climbed, Teresa greeted him at each drinks stop with his TN drink. He finished in 3:26; slower than hoped for, but okay given the heat.

However, with the temperature set to rise, Steve was worried. He normally deliberately ran slower in the heat - specifically to avoid ending up like Jim, whose over-exertions had resulted in dehydration and hospitalisation for the night, but if Steve wanted the record he couldn't afford to take it easy. He had to face his demons.

First, though, there was a more immediate problem to solve. As soon as he and the other leading runners finished their race, they enjoyed a cooked lunch courtesy of the Brathay catering staff, but by the time the slower runners finished, the catering staff would have packed up. Perhaps, therefore, their meals could be plated up for later? They could, and they were. Camaraderie.

Days 2, 3 & 4:
As promised, the temperature rose daily and, as Steve set off in the lead on his lonely vigil, it was will power alone that kept him going – plus the TN drinks delivered by Teresa. Hydration wasn't an issue and, although the heat was taking its toll, it was the loneliness that was killing him. With nobody in front or behind, Steve resorted to make-believe, imagining runners ahead to chase down.

Day 5:
By mile 21, Steve was about to catch the imaginary lead group when a car containing a television crew

from Border ITV cruised alongside him and asked if he'd mind being interviewed.

'So long as you don't mind if I keep going.'

A barrage of questions followed. Sweat pouring off him, Steve answered in short bursts of broken sentences, catching a breath every few words, while the camera rolled from the car's open back.

Nearing Brathay, the crew drove ahead to film Steve crossing the line, but took a wrong turn and missed him! Undeterred, they followed him to the river and filmed him taking his ice bath instead, while he explained Teresa's role, all about Brathay and how the runners were raising money. He was somewhat embarrassed then that when the piece aired, all they talked about was him and his record attempt!

Day 6:

Alone once more, Steve returned to chasing invisible runners along steaming tarmac in 80 degrees. Meeting Teresa at the mid-point drinks stop, pace and motivation slipping, he asked her to play his favourite movie soundtrack, 'Gladiator' on the car's cd player – really loudly! It followed him down the road and kept him going to the end.

With four days to go, he still felt confident. His recovery routine - icy dip, TN protein drink, lunch and massage, was working well. Every day he weighed himself to check his hydration. All was good. The biggest plus, though, was that he'd finally overcome what he considered to be his mental weakness with heat. Now all he had to deal with was the loneliness.

Day 7:
He needn't have worried. Somewhat to his chagrin, Teresa shared his aloneness with the other runners, so that on day 7 Ray and George made sure they gave him a race. No more make-believe. Camaraderie.

Ray finished 1st in a PB having already run six consecutive marathons, Steve was 2nd and George, 3rd.

Day 8:
Thankful for the slight drop in temperature, the three musketeers set off ahead of the pack again before Ray pushed on taking George with him. Steve stuck to his tried and tested pace, catching George at 18 miles and Ray at 25. And there he stayed; one good turn deserves another. They crossed the line together in 3:29. Camaraderie.

It was after completing his recovery routine that the habitual Steve realised Teresa was due to give him his regular number one head shave - no matter that he was part way through the 10-in-10! When the others saw what was happening, they all wanted one (the males anyway), '...maybe we'll run quicker if we have our heads shaved!' Soon they were queuing up. 'What'll it be today, Sir?' asked nurse-turned-hairdresser Teresa. 'I'll have a Steve Edwards, please!' they dutifully replied.

Camaraderie!

Day 9:

Sadly, the three musketeers were down to two, with a swollen ankle slowing Ray down to a hobble. As for George, he had his own game plan - to storm round as fast as he could, which he did in 3:22. Steve, meanwhile, bore in mind the morrow and stuck resolutely to his race plan. Even so, he was not alone, as Brian Meakin from 2007's 10-in-10, was cycling round the course supporting the runners.

Crossing the line in 3:29, Steve noticed the Port-a-loos positioned ready for Sunday's main marathon, the day when, all being well, he would claim his fourth world record: '...I never thought the sight of Port-a-loos would make me feel excited!'

Day 10:

Following introductions and explanations to the crowd about the 10-in-10, Steve instinctively drew the other runners into a group huddle: '...all that's left between us and a place on the Brathay 10-in-10 Hall of Fame is a single lap of that lake; a mere 26.2 miles. This is our lap of honour.' That term and the group huddle have since become Brathay traditions.

Steve toed the start line. He wished they'd hurry up so his nervous energy wouldn't explode all over the road! The sooner they got going, the sooner he could cross that finish line - on his own. Company not required. He turned to George, Jim and Phil: '...let's stick together as long as possible and see if we can all finish ahead of the first runner of the main marathon.' Who said that? Oh, he did. Camaraderie.

Steve, Jim, Phil and George ran together to Newby Bridge. Phil dropped off, followed by Jim. Steve and George picked up the pace. Their silent concentration was broken at around 20 miles by a sudden raucous cheer emitting from a man on a motorbike. Brent. He'd made the journey specially to rally Steve along in his record attempt.

The closer they got to Brathay, the denser the crowds. Steve knew Teresa would be waiting for him at the finish line. Making amends for 2007 wasn't just for him.

They reached the driveway leading to Brathay Hall.

'I need to go for a p***,' said George. 'You carry on and finish.'

They were 300 metres from the finish; surely George could wait?

Apparently not.

'Hurry up then, I'm not finishing without you!'

George's ruse to allow Steve to cross the line victoriously alone had failed.

A minute later, they set off again, together. Camaraderie.

Entering the final 50 metres they joined hands, an utterly spent George being practically dragged along by adrenalin-fuelled Steve, who waved happily to the crowds, moving ever faster in his excited haste to cross the line and claim his record.

But George wasn't done yet. One step short of the finish, he released Steve's hand. Steve surged forward across the line, leapt upwards and punched the air in unbridled joy. It was just a pity that his foot landed awkwardly on a pile of tangled PA cables, causing a minor sprain; his only injury of the whole 10 days!

And then he and Teresa moved towards one another, silently, smoothly, like some well-rehearsed piece of seamless choreography. As the world around them erupted into celebration, the two of them took refuge in one another's loving arms, oblivious of anyone or anything else, both desperately trying to stem the tears that threatened to fall. 'We've done it!' Steve whispered jubilantly into Teresa's ear.

Official cameraman, Martin Campbell's years of experience paid off as, sensing something significant was about to happen when Steve entered the final few metres, he set his camera to continuous filming. The intimacy of Steve and Teresa's embrace was perfectly captured forever, as was Steve's victorious finish line leap. Those photos form the cover of this book and have pride of place in Steve and Teresa's home. They were also responsible for a neighbour greeting Steve home from work one day in tears, brandishing a newspaper containing the iconic embrace photo.

Then they faced the noise, the flashing cameras, the joyous confusion, together, the world record holder and his wife. Team Edwards.

Steve wasn't the only record maker at Brathay that year. Michelle Atkins became the first female in the world to complete an official 10-in-10 and also made the Guinness Book of World Records for completing the most official consecutive marathons by a female.

Another notable presence was 22-year old, Adam Holland, who'd finished 4th in the main marathon in 2:53. Adam was intent on taking Steve's world record for the youngest person to run 100 marathons. Now he thought he might like to have a go at the 10-in-10 record too! Steve was thrilled to have inspired such a talented young man.

As hoped, Steve, George, Phil and Jim all finished ahead of the winner of the main marathon and when Joss Naylor presented Steve with his slate saying: 'How the hell you ran like that in that heat, I'll never know!' Steve's happiness was complete: '...coming from such a legend, those are words I'll never forget.'

Aside from believing he'd overcome his mental block of running in extreme heat, Steve also believed his ability to perform so well despite the temperature was largely due to TN's products. He therefore approached Robin about possible sponsorship. Robin immediately agreed and the partnership continues to this day.

Steve's times were: 3:26, 3:36, 3:33, 3:37, 3:35, 3:34, 3:30, 3:29, 3:29 and 3:27, respectively, giving a cumulative total of 35 hours 20 minutes 45 seconds - an average of 3:32:05 per marathon.

As TE drove home, Steve contemplated just how much quicker he might have run had the weather been cooler. The further he drove, the more he thought he should return to Brathay in 2009, just to test out his theory. He glanced across at his wife. She responded with a knowing smile. He had her blessing.

Just three days later, TE returned to Brathay en route to a double marathon in the Outer Hebrides on the islands of Harris and Lewis. Steve had actually forgotten he'd entered the event and considered withdrawing, but his legs didn't feel too bad (he was the only athlete to leave the 10-in-10 without any leg tape), and as it was a one-off event he decided to give it a go. Brathay was conveniently situated on the journey for a welcome break and a chance to mull over that year's 10-in-10 with Scott. Brathay were apparently delighted by all the additional publicity Steve's record had produced and stunned by how many more people now wanted to give the 10-in-10 a go. The Roger Bannister effect all over again. Even Brathay employee, Aly Knowles, had been inspired to give it a go in 2009 – provided Steve would mentor her. He would return for sure, he owed it to himself to try and improve his time and he had a duty to defend his title.

Leaving Brathay behind once more, TE drove on to Skye taking the toll bridge that had opened in 1995, before catching the ferry to Stornoway on the Isle of Lewis and being taken to their B&B. The following day Steve ran the challenging Lewis Marathon, starting from Callanish Stones, in 3:23, followed on Monday by the even more challenging Harris Marathon, in 3:21. The times may not have been spectacular, unlike the scenery, but they were enough for 3rd place overall and 1st vet – not bad a week after the 10-in-10!

It was a further two months before Steve ran another marathon.

In the meantime, his first grandson, Farren, was born, Teresa ran her second official half-marathon at Wycombe in a PB of 2:07, and Steve ran the Bourton Hilly Half in 1:27.

And then came a phone call from Mannatech, a nutritional supplements company who'd read about Steve's record and wondered if he'd be interested in their products, claiming they'd help him become an even better athlete. Initially, Steve was dubious; he'd used his own supplements for years and thought he was doing okay, but when Mannatech offered a free month's trial and potential sponsorship, he couldn't say no.

Researching the company, Steve discovered they developed and produced quality health, weight, fitness and skincare supplements based on real food technology, ie: none of their products contained artificial ingredients or synthetic products. It was something Steve was, and still is, passionate about. Such products may cost more, but because they're developed from real food the body is better able to absorb them.

It didn't take long before Steve was totally hooked on Mannatech products: '...to say I was impressed would be an understatement; they were fantastic.' After just a few weeks, his body started behaving differently. He felt less tired after his lunchtime run and was able to train harder and recover quicker. Even his muscle tone improved. He ditched his own products and Mannatech started sponsoring him. They continue to do so today.

In June, TE were invited to meet the Brathay trustees to discuss the 10-in-10's future development. Steve suggested charging an entry fee, marketing the event as a package, including food and accommodation, and incorporating Teresa's drinks routine. His suggestions were adopted and form the basis of today's 10-in-10.

Eventually, after two months in marathon desert, Steve returned to racing on a hot July day with a 41-lap race at Faversham Park organised by 100 Clubber, Sid Morrison. He finished in 3:18, despite being on antibiotics for a slight infection in his arm. A month later he ran 3:11 on the Isle of Man, and a few weeks after that 3:06 at Wolverhampton.

Unfortunately, Wolverhampton was followed by a minor niggle in his groin. Confident it was just a strain, Steve massaged it through and continued training. He then ran what is recognised as UK's toughest road marathon at Great Langdale – a race he'd run twice before, both times just failing to break 3:30. His groin was still sore, particularly when running downhill, so he took a precautionary pre-race paracetamol and trusted his overall fitness and durability would see him through. He finished in 3:21, 6th overall and 1st MV45, winning a meal for four.

Next day, however, despite having taken a cold soak in a handy river after the race, pain shot through his groin making it almost impossible to walk down the stairs. Enforced rest was inevitable and luckily fell just as TE were due to travel to Hanover for the Mannatech European Convention where Steve was to talk about their products.

Whilst Steve had almost got used to talking to a small room of around 30, this would be to 300 people from a stage using a microphone: '...I was nervous as hell!'

He needn't have worried; the audience loved him: '...I felt like I'd gained an instant fan club!'

On a high, and after four days' rest, Steve tested his groin. It still hurt; he'd see Lucy when he got home.

When Steve failed Lucy's hop test, she recommended he visit Rod Jaques, an experienced sports injury consultant. Rod suspected a stress reaction/fracture injury in Steve's hip and ordered an MRI scan. Meantime, he forbade Steve to run at all. It was the first time in 28 years of running that such a thing had happened: '...I was gutted.'

Fortunately, the scan revealed a less serious injury than Rod's prediction – soft tissue damage to the iliopsoas muscle. Continued rest was advised. But for how long? Was the 10-in-10 in jeopardy and what of his lifetime goal? Nobody could answer his questions. All Steve could do was wait and see. Or not. Why sit around doing nothing when he could be cross-training?

He began cycling for miles in the gym to preserve strength, muscle tone, and aerobic fitness, although it also induced extreme saddle soreness! He also started aqua running [running in deep water without touching the floor whilst wearing a body float], enabling him to replicate long runs, short runs, and even speed work; varying the rate at which he moved his legs through the water and letting the resistance do its job.

Finding something physically demanding and regaining control helped dispel negative thoughts, but the fear that he wouldn't be able to compete in the 10-in-10 with enough fitness to do himself justice and defend his record as best he could, remained. So much so, in fact, that his sleep was disrupted by worries that he'd never run a marathon again or complete his lifetime challenge.

In all, Steve was out of running for six weeks: '... it felt like an eternity.' He distinctly remembers his first run back - Sunday, 12th October. He was at the gym having completed his bike workout and warm down. The treadmill winked at him, dared him. He hesitated. Suppose the pain returned? The treadmill stared at him; was he man or mouse? Sod it! He set it to some ridiculously low pace, took his first strides, and felt ecstatic, even if he was only running at 9 mm pace. The main thing was there was no pain. Come on, urged the treadmill - what you waiting for? Up the ante! Gradually Steve moved the dial to 8:30 mm pace, then 8. Still no pain. He stuck at 8 mm pace for two whole miles and only just managed to stop the tear in his eye from falling on to the cocky treadmill. After six long weeks, he was running pain-free, but he had some seriously hard work to do if he was to get back to his former best.

His first race back came in October at Leicester, a week after the treadmill run. With every mile, Steve felt like he was stepping into the unknown, his mind a myriad of negativity. Would he break down or slow down? Would he have to pull out? Pacing Teresa's brother-in-law to a sub-3:30 at least forced him not to push beyond 8-mm pace and, if things got really bad he could always turn off at the 10-mile cut-off point. Or at least he could have done if he hadn't been so intent on watching his pace that he missed the cut-off point altogether, throwing away his joker in the process. However, by 24 miles, he knew it was in the bag. He felt a little tired of course, but other than that, fine. He finished in 3:28, legs feeling okay and just a tiny ache in his groin. Snowdon the following week then!

'Don't be so daft!' said Lucy.

But Steve wasn't listening. He had faith in his strength and the Mannatech supplements, which helped recovery and renewed cell damage. He arrived at Snowdon in atrocious weather: '...it was the worst I'd ever experienced there.' He finished in 3:34.

After Snowdon came the Cornish Marathon in 3:16, Florence 3:14, and Hastings 3:13 – a race held only once every 100 years since its inception in 1908 – and where, in 2008, Steve's good friend, Rush, fittingly celebrated his 100th.

By the end of the year, Steve had run another 29 marathons, including the 10-in-10, in an average finish time of 3:21. Excluding the 10-in-10, his average finish time for 19 marathons was 3:16, the same as 2007.

Overall, Steve's tally now stood at 466 with an average finish time of 3:19:46, a reduction of seven seconds per marathon. The big question was - should he include the two 10-in-10s? Excluding those 20 marathons would reduce his overall tally to 446 with an average finish time of 3:18:54, but would allow him to reach 500 at the right time - his 50th birthday in 2012. However, popular opinion was that he'd be crazy not to include the 10-in-10s - why do himself out of 20 marathons? Ultimately, it was Mannatech who suggested he get to the 500 sooner than originally planned and find a different goal for 2012. Steve liked the idea, but what could his new goal be?

And then it struck him, it was obvious really – while continuing to chase 500 marathons *averaging* sub-3:30 (or even, hopefully, sub-3:20), why not try for 500 *actual* sub-3:30s? He already had 396, so only another 104 to go. There were 47 months before his 50th birthday.

104 sub-3:30s in 202 weeks - one every 13 days? Piece of (birthday) cake – provided he could find enough marathons to run.

Chapter 33

2009 – TRAINING & TOOLS

By the start of 2009, Steve's training and racing schedule up to the 10-in-10 was all mapped out with 10 marathons, including two doubles, and an average weekly training mileage that would steadily increase from 40-50 peaking at just over 100 around mid-April, before gradually dropping back down during a 2-3 week tapering period. Fortunately, such increase coincided with a further reduction in travelling at work, freeing time for lunchtime runs and a second run in the evening, alone or at the club.

First up race-wise was the 100 Club marathon in early January at Bromley. Steve finished in 3:15.

A week later, TE travelled to Brathay for what is now known as the 'training weekend', giving each year's runners a chance to meet, run some or all of the course, learn about Brathay, fundraising, training and what to expect during the event. Steve gave advice and produced a short guide with tips learned from his own experiences.

In late January, Steve ran Gloucester in 3:07, followed a few weeks later by Draycote Water, finishing

3rd in 3:06. He then ran the Duchy Marathon in early March in 3:11 - his 400th sub-3:30.

Two weeks later, TE travelled to Ireland for Ray O'Connor's (2008 10-in-10), Connemara Marathon double, the first double of Steve's 10-in-10 build up. Teresa would be running the half.

Steve was happy to win Saturday's low-key race, which had limited support and followed the same route as Sunday's main marathon, in 3:17. But it was on Sunday, as he flew up the hill known as the 'Hell of the West' at 23 miles, finishing in 3:11, that he realised just how fit he was.

Teresa too performed well finishing her third half in 2:11 – without Steve's pacing assistance.

For Steve, though, the fitter he became, the more he worried about injury or illness. Taking nothing for granted, his attention to detail never greater, he'd applied an even stricter regime of core work, body strengthening and stretching, as well as continuing the regular sports massages he'd been having since 2008 from Gary Edwards. Today, while still seeing Gary for niggles or a full sports massage, he has regular massages every couple of weeks from BRR's Richard Rasdall: '...I would recommend everyone competing regularly to include massage in their armoury. It's been an important addition to my recovery routine, especially as I've got older.'

Two weeks after Connemara, with training peaking at over 100 miles a week, Steve's second double arrived. Day one was a track marathon at Crawley, organised by 100 Clubber, Pam Storey. Running 106 laps had never excited him, but Steve believed it was good physical and mental preparation for the 10-in-10.

Aiming for sub-3:15 on both days to test his fitness, Steve started cautiously, before gradually speeding up. At 16 miles, he was 2nd with just the leader, friend John Tyler, to chase. John is one of the few UK athletes to run 100 marathons in a sub 3-hour average finish time and has a PB of 2:41. He would be hard to beat.

However, at around 20 miles, Steve sensed he was making ground. With John just two laps ahead and an open view of him across the track, Steve saw John's head drop slightly and knew he was in with a chance. He ramped up his speed to an unplanned sub-7 mm pace and passed John once and then again to take the lead. As he did so, John said: 'You've got this one, Steve, I've had it'.

He was right. Steve took gold and the winner's glass trophy in 3:04, having run the second half of the race six minutes faster than the first. It may have been faster than planned and he may have another marathon to run the next day, but he felt fit and strong right to the finish. Of course John's assertion that Steve wouldn't be able to run sub-3:15 the next day as well may be proved right, but he'd wanted a test…

Next day, Taunton. Steve started at 3:15 pace, intending to maintain it as long as possible. Unlike Crawley's flat track, Taunton's two-lap course was undulating with two distinct climbs on each lap. Steve reached halfway well under his target time and, feeling good, pushed on, anticipating a crash later. The crash never came. Instead, he got faster, finishing in a totally unexpected 3:05.

Steve was delighted. He'd completed two marathons in two days under 6:11, his fastest double since 1992 - when he was 29. He was now 46. John Tyler was dumbfounded. But there was one person who wasn't overawed by Steve's performance, and that was the young pretender, Adam Holland, who beat Steve by over six minutes, having also run a marathon the previous day. If Steve hadn't already considered Adam to be his biggest threat at Brathay, now he was in no doubt. Accepting that at 22, Adam was over half his age, beating him would be an exceedingly tall order.

Two weeks after the double, Steve ran at Lochaber, Fort William, starting at just under 7 mm pace, again wanting to see how long he could maintain it. By halfway he was running 6½ mm. He finished in 2:57, his first sub-3 in 13 years, winning the MV45 trophy and a luxury towel – very useful after a cold soak in Loch Eil!

Confidence booster though this was, Steve was shocked afresh by his fitness. He'd stopped believing he'd ever run sub-3 again, conscious of the longer-term 500 goal and not wanting to risk injury by pushing too hard in training. Had he taken his eye off the bigger picture? His goal was getting closer. He mustn't mess it up now.

The 10-in-10 was 19 days away. With just London before then, Steve started tapering. What a relief! Running 100 miles a week was tiring and had eaten into time normally spent doing household jobs and gardening – things Steve enjoyed as alternative therapy away from running and work.

Then, less than a fortnight before Brathay, Steve learned that his father, who'd been suffering from breathlessness for some time, was to have a heart operation – right in the middle of the 10-in-10. His parents insisted he must carry on regardless, but Steve felt wretched that he wouldn't be there for them and 'what ifs' ran around inside his head as if they were in a track marathon.

London served as a useful distraction with Steve again qualifying with a good for age time. With the 10-in-10 imminent, he should run cautiously, but he couldn't resist attempting another sub-3. He finished in 2:57, his first consecutive sub-3 since 1992.

Again, with the delight came the worry – perhaps he'd peaked too soon? Tapering didn't help, creating fears that he was putting on weight and losing fitness. He fought the temptation to ignore his schedule and do more, reminding himself of the necessity to let his body rest, acknowledging that recovery is as important as training, as it is the recovery window alone that allows muscle tissue to repair and rebuild, providing extra fitness and strength. Without rest, the body just becomes increasingly tired and may never fully repair itself.

By May, Steve had run 1400 training miles in 5 months. Around 40 per cent had been run at 6½-7 mm pace, 40 per cent at 7-7½ mm pace and 20 per cent at 7½ -8 mm pace. It was the furthest and hardest he'd trained in his life. He put his ability to do so down to the nutritional and hydration products he used, plus club training nights where the friendly rivalry urged him to run faster than when training alone. He considered himself fortunate to have access to both. However: '...there is no magic banana when it comes to sport, you can eat and drink all the best products, but you still have to put in the work and preparation.'

Tapering over, bags packed, and tick list complete, TE headed north once more and settled in at Shackleton Lodge. In 2007, there had been 8 runners, in 2008 11. Now, in 2009, there were 15. Three were returning runners, including Steve, and amongst the 12 new faces were Aly Knowles of Brathay, mentored by Steve, David Bayley (Foxy), Adam Thwaites (Adam T - ex-pro footballer inspired by Steve), Tim Charles, Mark Sleeman and Adam Holland (Adam H).

Amy Bateman was again providing physio support along with a masseur and Teresa was distributing drinks around the course.

Day 1:

Intent on putting down his marker but not killing himself, Steve set off at 7½ mm pace. Adam H went with him. As did the rain! At each drinks station, Teresa sprinted alongside Steve and Adam, holding an umbrella with one hand, handing out bottles with the other.

At 10 miles, Adam made a pit stop before catching Steve again, overtaking him and disappearing into the distance. Steve caught him again in the final half mile. They crossed the line together in 3:13. Tim finished in 3:21.

The battle had commenced and the weather, unlike the previous year's heatwave, was forecast to be cold, wet and miserable.

Day 2:

Adam H set off at a similar pace to day 1. Realising they were on sub-3:15 pace again and not wanting to push his luck, Steve held back. Adam finished in 3:16, Steve 3:23, Tim 3:29.

Day 3:

Adam H went off as per days 1 and 2. The younger body was clearly recovering quicker than the older one and Steve had to let him go.

Steve was just picking up his pace when he was struck on the arm by a passing car's wing mirror, forcing him on to the verge and unbalancing him so that he fell over and grazed his leg. The driver stopped a few yards on, but didn't leave his car or apologise. Steve hauled himself back on to jelly legs and began walking slowly to check everything felt okay. Satisfied, he broke into a gentle jog, ran round the parked car, offered the elderly gentleman inside an annoyed glare, and attempted to get back into his stride.

He'd run about 20 metres when he was struck again - by the same car! Once more his elbow felt the force of the wing mirror, once more he was forced on to the verge, although this time he managed to stay on his feet. Once more the driver pulled over, but again remained inside his car. Probably just as well. An irate Steve shouted furiously at him from outside. There was no response whatsoever. Steve had no choice but to run on. Angry and shaken and with a sore arm and leg, he tried to refocus on his race, but it was impossible and he never got properly going again. Somehow he held on to 2nd place, finishing in 3:26. Adam won in 3:11. If it hadn't been for the incident being witnessed by another runner, Steve could have believed he'd imagined the whole thing.

Overall, Adam was now ahead of Steve by 21 minutes.

Day 4:

Sunshine and warmth brought welcome relief as Adam H once more set off ahead with Steve in hot pursuit. However, it seemed Adam had a similar dislike for the heat as Steve had previously, for as Steve reached mile 16 he caught up with a walking Adam. Steve didn't hesitate. Passing Adam, he finished in 3:17, with Tim 3:21 and Adam 3:27.

Adam's lead reduced by 10 minutes.

Steve's three goals coming into the event had been to better his 2008 world record, to run a sub 35-hour cumulative time and to run all 10 marathons under 3:30. He had one further bonus goal - to win the event and set a new world record. Realistically, against a young athlete of Adam's calibre, it was unlikely, but after four days he was only 11 minutes behind. So what if he was the oldest male competitor that year and his wife had taken to calling him, 'The Daddy'?

Day 5:

Steve's previous night's prayers for more sunshine and heat went unanswered. He could only hope that was because whoever was in charge was too busy dealing with his other prayers for his father's op to go okay. Unaware that his worries were etched on his face and he wasn't his usual ebullient self, Steve was touched when Adam T, in an effort to cheer him, reminded him that Steve was the sole reason he was there: '...I'll never forget that.'

Adam H again set off at the front, Steve followed. Adam finished in 3:10, Steve 3:15. Adam's lead extended a further five minutes, but Steve wasn't worried – his father's surgery had gone well and he was now on the road to recovery. That was all that mattered that day.

Day 6:

Adam H and Tim led from the start, Steve followed. At mile 25, Steve caught Tim and was about to steam ahead and chase after Adam when something stopped him. Compassion or camaraderie? Steve wasn't sure, maybe a bit of both? All he knew was he didn't want to leave Tim behind: '...maybe I lack the killer instinct to be a truly great competitor, I don't know, but I can't change who I am.'

Steve and Tim crossed the line together in 3:18, two minutes behind Adam.

With four marathons and 100 miles remaining, Steve was well inside his world record time from the previous year. It was still all to play for.

Day 7:

Adam T looked worried. Steve didn't think it was just down to the returning torrential rain. Having run sub-4 for the first few days, Adam was now finishing beyond 4 hours. Steve remembered his comrade's well-timed words of support two days earlier and returned the favour, encouraging him to believe that his sub-40 hour goal was still possible. Then 'The Daddy' splashed his way round the course to finish in 3:18 to Adam H's 3:14, with Tim 30 seconds behind Steve.

Day 8:

Tim finished joint 1st with Adam in 3:13, pushing Steve into 3rd for a third consecutive 3:18. Not bad for an old man, but with two days left he was starting to hurt. Day 10 couldn't come fast enough, then he could give everything and leave it all out there.

Day 9:

Holding back for day 10, Steve let Tim and Adam H surge ahead giving Tim his first outright victory in 3:16. Adam was 2nd in 3:22, Steve 3rd in 3:25 – his second slowest time so far. He wasn't worried – he'd run sub-3:30 for nine consecutive days, his tank held reserves for the final day, maybe even enough to win.

But this event wasn't so much about the winning as it was about the camaraderie and once more Steve found himself inviting a fellow competitor, Tim, to cross the line with him on the final day. Tim said he'd be honoured. Perhaps Adam H would like to join the party? They could cross the line arm-in-arm as, hopefully, the first trio to record 10 sub-3:30s? Even though Adam H was clearly going to win overall in a new world record time, he thought it was a great idea, although he wanted to set off at his normal pace.

Day 10:

Just the lap of honour remained. Steve led the runners onto the lawn for the pre-race huddle. Dense grey clouds hovered overhead promising to deliver the forecast torrential downpours. As planned, Adam raced off at the start, while Steve and Tim followed, speeding up in the second half. Crossing the little wooden bridge by Ambleside for the final half-mile, they saw Adam slowing down to allow them to catch him. The threesome ran into Clappersgate together. But when they reached Brathay's driveway leading to the finish, they stopped. What was the best way for them to cross the line? Maybe they should have discussed this before they set off?

Eventually, they settled for joining hands at the top of the drive, running down to the finish together, then falling to their knees, spreading their arms aloft and letting out a mighty roar of triumph. If Steve's parents thought their young son liked playing to an audience, they should see him now!

The spectators went wild as the trio crossed the line in 3:20 and, as one, fell to their knees, roared like tigers and spread their uplifted arms – all captured on camera by the indubitable Martin Campbell. The 10 sub-3:30 club was born!

Amidst the media and spectator furore, the three waited for their comrades to cross the line, including Adam T who'd just missed his goal by 2 minutes and Aly Knowles, the first Brathay employee to complete the event. Mark Sleeman also made it to the finish, despite having been in physical bits by day 4: '...he was swathed in so many bandages he looked like an Egyptian mummy!'

That night Steve barely slept as he replayed the previous 10 days' times – 3:13:44, 3:23:09, 3:26:17, 3:17:06, 3:15:23, 3:18:52, 3:18:13, 3:18:44, 3:25:03, 3:20:03. This gave a cumulative total of 33 hours 16 minutes 34 seconds, an average time per marathon of 3 hours 19 minutes 39 seconds and an average mile time for 262 miles of 7 minutes 37 seconds. Steve may have lost his world record to somebody over half his age, but he'd set a new one for the fastest 10-in-10 in the MV45 category. However, Guinness don't recognise age categories so the record has never been formalised. Regardless, Steve's time remains the best vet time for the Brathay 10-in-10.

It probably also remains the best time for a sufferer of thalassemia. Only now did Steve consider just how well his body had adapted to the pressures put upon it over the 10 days, not just this year but also last year in the heat and the previous year. His body may not be in perfect working order, but it was doing a bloody good job!

As for Adam H's performance of 32 hours 47 minutes - that would take some beating.

The following day the press proclaimed Brathay 10-in-10 to be the UK's ultimate endurance running event, heralding Adam H as the new world record holder, while suggesting Steve and Tim's performances were potentially even more remarkable, Steve finishing just 29 minutes behind a man over half his age and setting a new world vet's best while knocking over 2 hours off his 2008 record.

'Those fortunate enough to be present at the finish line were treated to what can only be described as a true master class of endurance running,' was one newspaper's verdict.

Heady stuff indeed, but still it wasn't quite enough for Steve. He believed he could do even better and persuaded Teresa that they should return in 2010.

Steve then took two months off from marathon racing, although he continued training hard, already motivated by the thought of his next 10-in-10. He also ran the Bourton Hilly Half in a pleasing 1:25, while Teresa finished in 2:12.

Just as in 2008, Steve's first marathon after Brathay was Faversham's 41-lap park course in July. Feeling good and getting faster with each lap, Steve won the race in 3:05, setting a new course record. Both were a huge surprise. It was also his 200th sub-3:15. At 47, he'd returned to the sort of form he'd enjoyed in his late 20s. Maybe it really was true that endurance athletes, like fine wines, improve with age?

In August, Steve ran the Isle of Man in 3:03 and Longford, Ireland, a new event for him, in 3 hours 11 seconds.

Pushing aside his disappointment at so narrowly missing a sub-3, Steve tried again at Wolverhampton – 3:04, Robin Hood – 3:01, and Anglesey – 3 hours 55 seconds – thanks to a wasp flying into his mouth and stinging him. Should have stuck to slugs!

After Anglesey, came the New Forest Marathon in 3:02, then a 1000-mile round trip to Inverness for the Loch Ness Marathon in 3:01. It was a long, tiring drive, especially after all the marathons he'd recently run, and by the time he returned home, Steve's back felt uncomfortably stiff.

It was while training with BRR's president, Norm Lane (famed for running John O'Groats to Lands End with two new hips), that Steve's resolve to keep his thalassemia to himself, was tested. Norm suggested that if Steve didn't 'showboat' so much, he was capable of running sub-3s more often. By showboating, he meant Steve always finished looking easy and with a smile on his face. Steve was completely taken aback. He'd never known an easy marathon in his life! If he looked as though he was taking things easy, that was just his style. As for smiling, that was more likely a grimace!

'I can count on my one hand the number of times I've run a marathon without much pain – and I use the word *much* deliberately – there's no such thing as a marathon without *any* pain, it comes with the territory.'

He was still not off the hook, though. About to run the Leicester Marathon, his good friend, Dennis Walmsley, sent him a text that simply said: '2:58'. This time he did pull it out the bag, finishing in 2:59, his 25th sub-3.

He repeated the feat at Abingdon a week later with 2:58, feeling strong all the way to the finish, and then rushed home to take up Moreton FC's invitation to act as official starter for their annual 10k Fun Run that afternoon.

That evening, Steve updated his marathon spreadsheet. In the last 12 weeks, he'd run 10 marathons in an average finish time of 3:01. It was 17 years since he'd run such a sequence.

Confidence fuelled, six days after Abingdon Steve ran the Snowdon Marathon, believing that given his recent form he could well break his own course record of 3:22. In similarly atrocious conditions to the previous year, he finished in 3:18.

Whether it was contentment with his performances or simply the fact that he'd travelled to and run, quite literally, in all four corners of the UK since July, all at once Steve was overcome with tiredness. Luckily, he had four weeks without a race to recover - unlike Teresa, who'd been training hard for the Stroud half-marathon hoping for a sub-2. She succeeded with a determined push in the final 400 metres to cross the line in a shiny new PB of 1:59:27. She was over the moon and Steve was immensely proud of the woman he loved who'd always said she'd never be a runner.

Following Teresa's sub-2, TE travelled to Solihull for Steve to give another talk at Mannatech's European Convention about how their products helped his running. He was keen to do so, believing the secret to successful multi-marathon running and longevity in the sport relies on good recovery, central to which lies good nutrition and hydration. Whilst not advocating replacing good wholesome food with supplements, he does believe good natural supplements help fill the gaps that today's food chain struggles to fill, particularly with fresh produce which, other than organic produce, no longer contains the same level of nutrients as years ago.

During the talk, Steve was presented with his Guinness World Record Certificate for the 10-in-10 - a great advert for the company and something the audience loved. As did Steve, posing for photos and signing autographs, transporting him back to his teenage years waiting patiently at the Coventry Novotel for the away football team's autographs – except, unbelievably, now he was the one wielding the pen!

Suitably refreshed after his month-long marathon vacation, Steve's first return race was the new Town Moor Marathon in Newcastle – an exposed, multi-terrain, five-lap course. Setting off rather harder than usual into a ferocious headwind that saw off many frontrunners, Steve finished 2nd in 3:04. As the rules stated that only runners pre-entering the race would be eligible for prizes and the 1st-placed runner had entered on the day, Steve was, in fact, declared the winner. However, he was asked if he minded the first place trophy going to the other runner anyway. Honestly? He'd rather that than be awarded a prize for a race he hadn't won and was perfectly content to take home instead the Veteran Masters Trophy, which he had properly won.

A week later, TE flew to Lanzarote, an invitation including complimentary race entry and accommodation at the famous Club La Santa complex. The heat was quite a shock to a body grown used to early-winter England and Steve had to work hard on the final loop of a four-loop course around Arrecife to finish in 3:04.

Steve's running year ended in wet and windy Luton; tired legs from a busy season pulling him round in 3:08, contributing to BRR winning the team prize.

Overall in 2009, Steve ran 34 marathons in an average finish time of 3:09, including the 10-in-10. Excluding the 10-in-10, he ran 24 marathons in an average finish time of 3:05. Every marathon had been sub-3:30. Despite being 47 years old, it was one of his best years for marathon performances ever and included four sub-3s.

Technically, he had now reached his 500-marathon target. However, adhering to his own strict standards, 7 of those had not been run from start to finish, so must be discounted. Therefore, his actual total was 493 in an average finish time of 3:18:15. Of the 493, 430 were sub-3:30. Based on races he'd already entered for 2010, Steve was delighted to realise that his 500th would fall at the Connemara Marathon; his friend, Ray O'Connor's event. With Connemara also offering half and ultra marathons, it would be great to turn it into a mini club trip so he could celebrate his 500th with his BRR clubmates, as well as Teresa.

Meanwhile, he took a week off after Luton, during which he celebrated the birth of his third grandchild, Courtney, and started planning his training and racing schedule for 2010. This included upping his mileage to equal that of 2009 and nailing some early marathons in preparation for improving his 10-in-10 performance, plus incorporating some specific sessions targeting areas he thought could still be improved upon, such as steep hill repetitions.

Teresa was also planning. She wanted to run an official road marathon properly, ie: train for it and run the whole way round if she could: '...I wanted to see what my husband puts himself through.' Steve was fully in favour, especially as Teresa was considering doing it at Windermere.

With his week's rest at an end, Steve couldn't wait to start implementing his schedule and upping the mileage. But, five days back into running, disaster struck, as he slipped on a patch of ice just metres from his front door, landing hard on his left hip. Gingerly, he got back up and finished the five-mile run.

A few days later, a pain in the left side of his groin developed, similar to that experienced in 2008 when he'd had to take six weeks off running. He immediately consulted Gary Edwards who mobilised the hip and surrounding muscle structure, but could see nothing that a few days rest wouldn't cure.

Steve took the rest. Just before the end of the year, he put his running shoes back on. The pain was still there, but eased off after a mile or so. That had to be a good sign, didn't it?

Steve stared hard at the night sky as if searching for an affirmative response, but it was a cloudy night and not a single star was visible.

Chapter 34

2010 – LUCK (& LEARN)

Steve's year started with the usual 100 Club marathon at Bromley. Although his groin still hurt when running, he really wanted this to be one of his seven remaining races taking him to his 500th, so he ran it anyway.

The pain started just a few miles in and Steve laboured round in 3:26. His body felt unbalanced, as though one side was compensating for the other. He took a couple of days rest, applied self-massage, then tried again. After just one mile, his hamstring tightened, his lower back and pelvis felt skewed, and his groin ached.

He contacted Lucy. Fully booked herself, she recommended Clare Woodward. Clare thought the tightness was due to running with a crooked posture resulting from the fall and used acupuncture to trigger release Steve's lower back, glutes, groin, hamstrings and stomach, followed by an inconclusive hop test.

Steve then managed four runs totalling 20 miles. The hamstrings felt better, but his groin still ached, especially downhill. He took another week off and returned to aqua running. At least that was pain-free and would help maintain his CV fitness without aggravating the injury.

Mid-January arrived and with it Brathay's 10-in-10 training weekend. The day before leaving, Steve endured further acupuncture from Clare, who advised taking a few weeks off. He heeded her advice, not running at all at Brathay. While there, Graham Theobold of The Body Rehab Clinic, Brathay's physio that year, also examined Steve. He couldn't see much wrong, but without a scan it was hard to be sure. He advised active rest using cross-training – exactly what Steve was already doing.

Once home, however, Steve couldn't resist giving the running another go – three days later the groin pain became unbearable. He returned to Clare who repeated Graham's advice and introduced him to the Swiss Ball for extra core work, which he still uses today.

He then saw consultant, Rod Jaques, for a full assessment and MRI scan. The scan showed signs of stress at the femoral neck, potentially caused by accumulative overload on the skeletal system. In short, Steve had been wearing out bone faster than it could regenerate. Rod didn't think this was due to the fall but to the constant heavy workload Steve's training and racing placed on his body - the fall was the straw on the camel's back. He ordered Steve to stop running for six to eight weeks, threatening him with plastering his leg if he disobeyed and warning him that disobedience may lead to permanent running retirement.

Suitably scared, Steve heeded Rod's advice, ignored his schedule and worked on his aqua running and core routine instead. He missed two marathons, including an invitational package to run at Limassol, and felt very low - at the same time thanking his lucky star that the problem had been discovered early enough to take some action. Then he trained like an Olympic swimmer – he'd forgotten how much it was possible to sweat whilst immersed in water!

Counting down to the day he could run again and desperate to keep Connemara as his 500th race, especially not wanting to let down those who'd already made travel arrangements, Steve started searching out races to replace the ones he'd missed. The 10-in-10 wasn't important, the 500th was. He'd been working towards it for 23 years. He was angry with himself - if he hadn't brought the date forward by two years, he wouldn't be under such pressure. Idiot!

Meantime, Teresa was training like a pro, religiously sticking to the schedule drawn up by Steve, gradually building up her mileage, determined to run from start to finish if she possibly could. Much to his chagrin, Steve hated that Teresa could run when he couldn't. At the same time, he felt immensely proud.

Four long, run-free weeks passed by. Each week took him closer to Connemara, each week his anxiety grew. If he didn't run soon, both 10-in-10 and the 500th could be in jeopardy.

And then he drove over a pothole, which blew a tyre. He stopped at the nearest lay-by. As he crouched down to put on the new wheel he felt a click in his upper leg. When he got up and walked round the car, his body felt different, as if it had realigned itself. He continued to the pool for his aqua session.

His body still felt different the following day so, whilst walking, he risked a little jog. Everything felt fine and there was no pain. He took up Graham Theobold's offer to call him anytime and relayed events. Graham suggested that maybe something had been slightly out and had now gone back.

There were now just 10 weeks till the 10-in-10. Should he pull out? With no chance of improving his 2009 performance, how would he keep going when things got tough?

'When you're in pain you need something to hold on to, some powerful drivers that remind you why you're doing it, they help keep you going mentally.'

Striving for a better performance was always going to be Steve's main driver. Desperately, he sought new ones. He found them – there was the fundraising and not wanting to let his sponsors down; becoming the first person to run four 10-in-10s; hopefully finishing in the top three; and, potentially, adding more sub-3:30s to his 2012 goal. Not to mention personal pride. He couldn't pull out.

Instead, he contacted Rod and explained the latest development. Rod advised against running on the road for at least another week, ideally two. Instead, Steve should run five miles on the treadmill on two consecutive days, then have a rest day, then repeat. Provided everything was okay after that, he should do the same thing over eight miles. Vitally, he must be honest about any pain. If there was no pain, he could start running on the road again. It there was pain he was to stop immediately.

It was a nervous Steve who stood on the treadmill after work the next day. Starting slowly, he gradually built up the pace to 8 mm. It felt okay, no pain other than mild groin ache. An aqua run followed. He did the same thing the following day. Again, everything felt fine. He upped the distance and speed - all fine. Boredom, however, was another matter: '...if I'd run on treadmills all the time, I'd have fallen out of love with the sport very quickly!'

He got the green light from Rod to return to the road – provided he took it easy and built up the miles slowly. Steve fought his instinct that suggested 60-70 miles per week would be about right, and stuck to 30 miles for the first week, building each week by 10 per cent, and using aqua running to make up for the missing miles. By the third week he felt ready to race and ran the Duchy Marathon in a steady 8 mm pace, finishing in 3:28. It was his longest run in over two months by 16 miles and, including the race, gave him a 53-mile, pain-free week.

A week later he ran the Cotswold Marathon, a new event close enough to home to allow him the luxury of a lie in. Maintaining the same cautious approach as Cornwall, he sped up a little in the second half to finish in 3:21 on an undulating course. Again, no adverse reaction and the completion of his first 60+ mile week in a long time. His delight was only equalled by Dennis' race victory.

Still compensating for low mileage with aqua running, Steve continued his search for two replacement marathons. With nothing in the UK, he booked Bratislava at the end of March and Utrecht a week later on Easter Monday, four days before Connemara. On learning of his predicament, both race organisers generously offered invitational packages in return for using his story as race publicity. Steve duly booked flights for Bratislava and the Eurotunnel for Utrecht.

At Bratislava a week after the Cotswolds, keen to test his fitness, Steve started fairly fast and finished in 3:13, while Teresa enjoyed the half-marathon in 2:03. Although running 21.1k instead of 13.1 miles did cause her some confusion – the one thing Steve forgot to mention!

Utrecht followed. It was a long time since Steve had driven abroad to run. Fond memories. Having agreed to pace Ray O'Connor for 3:15, Steve ran comfortably, speeding up at the end to finish in 3:14:49. Ray finished in 3:16.

With 498 marathons run and Connemara just days away, Steve's dream from 1988 would culminate in a double marathon weekend in Ireland. Not quite how he'd have chosen to end his 500 challenge, but chasing times as well as numbers increased the risk of injury and events had conspired against him.

TE arrived in Connemara to glorious weather that was forecast to remain for the whole weekend, and special commemorative t-shirts organised by Ray listing all 500 of Steve's marathons, including locations and finish times: '...you needed a magnifying glass to read them, but they were all there!'

Suitably inspired, Steve rose early Saturday morning for the first day's low-key invitational race. It was a beautiful sunny, azure-sky day, as the runners lined up. George Russell from the 2008 10-in-10 ran with Steve till half way, with Steve taking it steady at just over 3:20 pace before shifting up a gear, leaving George (who was saving himself for next day's 39-mile ultra), behind. Steve overheard George's remark to Dennis, who was recce-ing the ultra course: 'He's a machine!' Dennis replied: 'But machines can break, stick with him!'

Not today, mate! Despite running into a headwind for most of the second half, Steve won the race in 3:19.

499 marathons – tick!

Nervous anticipation and the fire alarm going off in the early hours forcing everyone to vacate the building ensured a restless night. As he boarded the coach taking him to the marathon start, Teresa boarded the coach for the half: '...it seemed strange heading off in different directions.'

The first 10 miles Steve ran with BRR's John Gibson, before picking up his pace. Just after the 13-mile point, he spotted Teresa queuing at the Port-a-loos having already started her race. Satisfying himself that she was okay, he then passed BRR clubmate, Ian Shoemark. That just left the BRR half-marathon ladies to chase! As he passed them, they announced to anyone in earshot who he was and what he was doing – resulting in spontaneous applause! Steve lapped it up and flew round the remainder of the course to finish in 3:22. After 23 long years, he finally had the world record for running 500 marathons in the fastest average finish time – 3:18:18.

Pandemonium broke out. Everyone wanted to shake his hand, take his photo, talk to him. Lucy and Dennis, who'd finished 2nd in the ultra, gave Steve a big hug. Steve burst into tears: '...I don't know what happened. I was just suddenly overwhelmed by emotion.'

But the minute he heard that Teresa was approaching the finish, Steve's tears transformed into a smile as he watched the other half of TE cross the line in 2:06 – despite a six-minute pit stop! The marathon training was paying off.

Back at the hotel, Steve sighed with relief – he'd achieved his dream and recovered from injury. His two sub-3:30 marathons, together with Utrecht, made a 92-mile week - just the boost he needed so close to the 10-in-10. Later, he was presented with a special

'500 Marathons' mug by his BRR clubmates and joined by Dr Ron Hill MBE, whose clothing company was an event sponsor.

That night, as Steve reflected on the Sy Mah record that had driven him all those years, he wondered how much further he could raise the bar. There was his new goal of 500 sub-3:30s in 2012 to aim for initially, and with 437 already acquired that left 'just' another 63 to run in the next two years. In turn, that would improve his overall finish time for 500 marathons - he may as well leave contacting Guinness to register the record until 2012 to see if he could accomplish 500 sub-3:30s first. But could he stay motivated enough to keep driving himself in training for another two years, having already accomplished his long-term goal? And, assuming he could, what would come after that? And when would enough be enough?

He had no answers and raising the questions unsettled him. Ever since returning from Connemara he'd felt low. He couldn't understand it. He'd achieved his dream! So why was he feeling flat instead of euphoric? Dennis, who'd been there himself, explained it was a natural reaction following major success - the anticlimax. 'What did you expect to happen? Flags hung out when you returned to Moreton? Being given the keys to the town? There's only one person your achievement matters to, and that's you.'

He was right, of course. Steve had been working towards his dream for 23 years. It had been the centre of his world, no matter what else was happening it was always there, like a permanent promise of a golden future. But once he'd achieved it, the golden future had disappeared and was now behind him, in the past. In the heart of his achievement, Steve had reached up high enough to actually touch his star, but of course he couldn't stay there, not enough oxygen for one thing. Now he was back down on earth, he had to pick himself up, dust himself down and return to the real world.

For all his down to earth words, though, Dennis wasn't prepared to let the galaxy have all the fun and organised a surprise party for Steve: '...nobody had ever done anything like that for me before. It was a great night. Thanks, Den!'

Steve's first post-record race was the inaugural Brighton Marathon. Not quite back to his usual chirpy self and still tired, he finished in 3:12 to complete a 65-mile training week, while Teresa ran 15 miles of the Brighton course in preparation for Windermere. A few days later she complained of hip pain, and not for the first time. She'd been used to 7-10 mile training runs and a few half-marathons, but she'd never run 15 before. Her main objective at Windermere was to run the whole way if possible under 4:30. She'd been training mainly at 9 mm pace, so allowing for the extra distance, 10 mm pace should be realistic and give her 4:22. Concerned that longer training runs may exacerbate the pain, Steve advised sticking to 7-8 miles on alternate days, with another three 4-5 milers thrown in, giving her close to 40 training miles per week. He believed that would be enough, and Teresa trusted his judgement.

London followed Brighton with Steve qualifying for another good for age place, finishing in 3:09, his fastest that year.

Brathay was now only 12 days away. Steve's level of fitness was well down on previous years. There would be no records broken this time - apart from becoming the first person to run four official 10-in-10 events, assuming he finished of course. He began to taper, allowing his body to recover a little from the previous few busy weeks and hoped the two months of actual proper road running training since injury, plus the aqua running, would see him through. Hopefully, after so many running years, muscle memory would also lend a helping hand.

Spreadsheet updated, bags packed, TE headed to Brathay for Steve's fourth 10-in-10, and Teresa's first marathon.

Eleven others would accompany Steve in the 10-in-10, including Adam Holland.

As usual, apart from day 10 when she'd be running her own race, Teresa was managing drinks support around the course, although this time she had use of a Brathay pool car, while physio Graham was assisted by physio students. One of them, Paul Talbot, on learning of Steve's 500-world record remarked: 'You must be the Godfather of the marathon world!' It reminded Steve of a less-kind, school nickname - 'Fingers'. Back then he'd consoled himself that it sounded like a Mafia name. From Fingers to the Godfather in 40 years! The new nickname stuck.

Less than 100 per cent fit, Steve's only plan for the 2010 10-in-10 was to complete the 10 days in respectable times, although he did harbour a secret hope that he might manage another 10 sub-3:30s, or at least a sub-35-hour cumulative time.

With his first three days all under 3:30, Steve may have made it, but on the fourth day, he started suffering from abdominal pain. He'd had twinges a couple of months earlier, but assumed it had settled. Now, however, it returned with a vengeance, particularly when running downhill. He suspected a hernia and consulted Graham. Graham agreed, and instructed the masseur to give the area a good working over to loosen up the soft tissue. The massage hurt almost as much as the pain, and although it felt slightly better and allowed Steve a couple more sub-3:30s, it wasn't enough for him to realise his goal – despite the welcome support on day nine of the Shoemarks, Speddings and Teagues from BRR, with Neil Teague challenging him to a race – him on his bicycle for two laps, Steve running his one lap!

By the start of day 10, Steve knew the 3:22 he needed for a sub 35-hour cumulative time was unlikely, but hopefully he'd finish ahead of the winner of the main marathon.

As the 10-in-10 runners went into the usual pre-race huddle, Steve suddenly felt very emotional. He had a feeling this would be his last 10-in-10. As the miles passed and the clock reached 10.30 am, Steve's emotions surfaced again, but for a different reason. Teresa would now be lining up at the start of her first ever marathon. He wished he could be with her, but at least her sister Anne and the BRR contingent, including John Gibson, who'd driven from Gloucestershire that day specially, would be there.

One thing he didn't have to worry about this year, though, was his finish line 'act'. Four female members of the physio team would join him on the line, each holding a card labelled with a year from his 10-in-10s. Steve's 'finish line dollies' were Lucy (Miss 2007), Maria (Miss 2008), Katie (Miss 2009) and Roxy (Miss 2010): '...it was a bit cheesy, but gave everyone a laugh!'

Steve crossed the line just 40 seconds outside 3:30, but surrounded by his dollies, he wasn't too bothered! His times for each day were: 3:24, 3:24, 3:27, 3:34, 3:30, 3:34, 3:37, 3:33, 3:29 and 3:30. His cumulative time for the 10 days was 35 hours 06 minutes 18 seconds, giving a daily average for each marathon of 3:30:38 - faster than his 2008 world record. Meanwhile, Dave Wintle successfully joined the prestigious 10 sub-3:30 club and Adam demolished his old record with a cumulative time of 30 hours 20 minutes, averaging 3:02 each day.

Dragging himself away from his dollies, Steve had a massage, got changed and waited for Teresa. The boot was properly on the other foot as he wondered anxiously how she was getting on, glancing at the clock, seeing it was approaching 4:30. And then he saw her, her ponytail had partially escaped leaving auburn trails across her flushed cheeks and he could see the tiredness around her soft blue eyes. His heart flipped and tears welled. There was his girl. And she was running, towards the finish, towards him. Never had he loved her more, never had he felt more proud. She put in one final effort as she neared the line. Steve's eyes met hers, saw his own emotions reflected back at him. Someone handed him a medal to present to her as she crossed the line in 4:26:01.

Teresa Edwards, marathoner, had run just about every step of the way as she'd wanted to, stuck to the 10 mm advised by her husband – even when everyone passed her in the early stages and she was convinced she'd be left behind and finish last. Steve had warned her that might happen and told her to keep the faith. She had, and on reaching 10 miles it was she who was doing the passing, certain then she wouldn't be last after all. In fact she was 559th out of 860 and 100th out of 230 female runners - and all off the back of just one 15-miler, a handful of half-marathons and regular 7-8 milers. She was a natural! When would she be doing her next one?

'Never!'

That's what Steve said after his first one.

'But I mean it - and I've got more willpower than Steve!'

Maybe she had, only time would tell, but for Steve his mind was made up – almost. He wouldn't be running any more 10-in-10s: '...I'm not saying never, but I think it's unlikely.

Overall, of the 12 10-in-10 starters, 11 finished – one having pulled out with a suspected stress fracture.

TE returned home happy. Steve's injury at the start of the year was forgotten and he could return to running some faster marathons. His only real concern was his abdomen, but surely that would settle down again with rest?

However, rest would have to wait a while as the following weekend he'd been asked to run a 10-mile leg for BRR at the Cotswold Hilly Hundred relay race and he wanted to support his club. It was a blisteringly hot day. Despite Steve not running till mid-afternoon on ninth leg, TE were out on the course supporting men's and ladies' teams from the start. Still tired from Brathay and running at the hottest part of the day, Steve finished in 67 minutes, pulling the team up from 3rd to 2nd. Last leg, John Gibson, maintained that position, while the ladies finished 3rd - a good day for BRR with both teams on the podium.

With his next marathon not until Boddington in mid-June, Steve stepped up the training, including some good hard club sessions on Tuesdays, traditionally efforts night, thinking it would sharpen him up ready to attack the 10-lap course.

However, come race day, a communication mix-up meant Steve and several others missed the official start. Realising this was not the runners' fault, the officials allowed them to run, but insisted their time would be the official clock time. Steve set his own watch, starting two minutes down on the official clock.

It didn't take him long to catch the back markers and start working his way through the field. At halfway, he was on for a sub-3 but conscious of the 2-minute deficit, he pushed harder to give himself a buffer.

Approaching 20 miles, he wondered if he'd pushed too much, he felt inordinately tired and his lungs were bursting from oxygen debt. His thoughts drifted to thalassemia. It was impossible to know whether he was working beyond his limits. Just how hard could he push? There was only one way to find out. He carried on pushing, finishing with a sprint. The official clock showed 2:59:31, his 27th sub-3. His own watch showed 2:57:11 – his fastest since Antwerp in 1996. Of course the official time would be the one recorded in his totals, but, either way, he'd now run sub-3 in four different decades, quite an achievement. He also won the MV45 category and a small trophy, plus some Argos vouchers – perfect timing as he needed a new lawnmower, though he'd collect it in his car this time!

Steve continued training hard, encouraged by Dennis' assertions that although Steve was nearly 48, a PB was still possible. The idea of breaking 2:50 certainly appealed. Having achieved his long-term goal, perhaps he could take a few more risks by training harder and attempt a PB before time ran out? He was already back to 60+ mile training weeks including hill reps and speed sessions and felt very fit.

But then, during a lunchtime run – crunch! Something went in his left ankle. It was only mildly uncomfortable so he continued running. The following day he ran another 14 miles including hill reps and although the ankle started off a little sore, it wore off. The day after that, he ran seven miles. Again the ankle started sore, but wore off. It couldn't be anything too serious.

For the next couple of days, Steve stuck to his schedule. Gradually, the pain in his ankle worsened till he could hardly put any weight on it. He rested for a few days, and then tried a steady 3-miler. One mile in, he was forced to stop and walk back home. He consulted Lucy. When his ankle proved too painful to even attempt a hop test, she advised him to stop running and get a scan. A referral to foot specialist, Pete Binfield, followed. The scan revealed a fractured medial malleolus – the lumpy bit on the inside of the ankle forming part of the tibia's base. There was also evidence of extensive hairline fractures - it had been only a matter of time before it went. The only reason he'd been able to continue running immediately after hearing the crunch was because a bone injury bleeds slowly, creating an hiatus between the injury's occurrence and the resultant swelling and pain, which is why bone injuries are rarely spotted before they become a problem.

Fortunately, the fracture hadn't gone all the way through, which would have required pinning, extensive rehab and the possibility of never running another marathon ever again. All Steve had to do was take a 10-12 week break. Steve barely heard the positive news; all he heard was that he'd have to stop running.

It was a massive blow. Assuming he didn't run another marathon in 2010, he'd have 23 months in which to run the remaining 56 sub-3:30s taking him to 500 – provided he could get his fitness back to that level. He'd miss at least nine marathons already entered in the second half of 2010, plus others he'd had his eye on. It wasn't just the wasted entry fees and accommodation bookings that upset Steve, it was missing so many races. By his own admission, he was hell to live with for the next few weeks: '...Teresa had a lot to put up with.'

However, he gradually got his head around his fate and tried to turn it into a positive. A proper break from running after 23 years was a chance to recharge his batteries. He'd been told his muscle memory would stand him in good stead once he started again, although he'd need to be patient and take it steady. At least his ankle didn't need plastering so he could walk around, although he'd had to promise Pete he'd only do so minimally. Luckily, he could still get in the pool, so it was back to aqua running. He also invested in a road bike to complement the aqua running rather than using static gym bikes, which he'd never enjoyed.

Just as he was starting to feel more positive, though, he received notification of redundancy. An alternative post in Derbyshire was offered, but meant a 120-mile round trip, or a move from the Cotswolds.

It felt like his world was imploding; no running and no job. He'd known redundancy was a possibility, but the reality was a shock. Financially, it wasn't a huge problem; he and Teresa had always planned their finances to allow for such an event and knew they could just about manage on a single salary if necessary. As Teresa had recently dropped from five to four days, she could, at worst, return to full-time. What really upset Steve was that after 14 years working for the same company, it should end this way. He understood it was business not personal, but redundancy at 48 after so long struck a bitter blow. It made him feel like a number, not a person, and he'd heard so many stories about people his age being on the scrapheap. He was terrified he'd never find another job.

Meantime, training hard in the pool and on the bike, and doing his usual weights and core work, maintained his fitness levels, but he missed running. However, after about a month, that feeling lessened. It was almost a relief not to have to run and travel somewhere every weekend. Suddenly, he had time to do those long overdue domestic jobs. He also had time to update his CV. He actually started to think his guardian angel had manufactured his injury to coincide with his redundancy just so he'd have time to look for jobs rather than marathons.

Soon he started getting interviews. He'd forgotten how nerve-racking it was to face a panel of people all firing questions at him at once. One good thing, though, they seemed impressed rather than deterred by his level of experience. It seemed age was not the enemy in IT.

Steve began to feel happier, confident a job offer was just around the corner and, after visiting Pete six weeks in, was relieved to hear that the ankle was healing well. Even the news that 23-year old, Adam Holland, had taken another of his records in becoming the youngest man to run 100 marathons, couldn't dampen his rising spirits.

September loomed; seven weeks since Steve's last run and a month before he could start again, the light at the end of the tunnel glimmered tantalisingly close. But then the pain in Steve's abdomen, aggravated by the aqua running, returned with a vengeance. It had never really gone away, Steve had simply ignored it. The glimmer flickered and died. He contacted his employer's health insurers immediately – he might as well squeeze the last bit of juice out of that particular lemon before he left.

The consultant told him it was a sports hernia aggravated only by certain sports. He suggested Steve change sports, perhaps to cycling. The alternative was a hernia repair involving full surgery, but even then there were no guarantees.

Steve was devastated. Could things get any worse? Yes, they could. Driving to a job interview, he hit a loose kerbstone, burst two tyres and was unable to make the interview. Despite phoning to explain, it was obvious they didn't believe him and a replacement interview wasn't even offered.

Desperate to avoid surgery and/or the possible end of his running life, Steve contacted Clare. She suggested seeking a second opinion, recommending Anthony Fox at the Shrewsbury Nuffield Hospital, who'd carried out numerous successful hernia repairs for rugby players. Before you could say bi-lateral inguinal hernia repair, Steve had seen Mr Fox and been booked in for the procedure at the start of October. Mr Fox was confident the procedure could be carried out laparoscopically rather than surgically. Never having had any kind of operation other than on his hand as a baby of which he had no recollection, Steve was naturally apprehensive, although nurse Teresa did her best to reassure him.

Meantime, he continued training as best he could on the bike, went for interviews and then, finally, received two job offers. He chose a temporary 12-month contract with Advance Housing in Witney – a registered charity providing housing and employment opportunities for disabled people - turning down a more lucrative, permanent position from BMW. As a younger man there'd have been no contest, but as an older, wiser and more financially secure man, Steve understood better the choice he was making – quality of life versus money in the bank.

At the end of September, 11 weeks since his last run, Steve saw Pete for one last x-ray and assessment. Reluctantly, he admitted the ankle still throbbed. His honesty paid off – the throbbing was an indication that the bone was healing. Permission was given to start walking again, building up to running.

It was great news and came just days before Steve's hernia procedure. As Steve was required to stay overnight for assessment the following day, and mindful of their vow never to spend a night apart, Steve asked if Teresa could also stay. She was offered a very expensive chair. Consequently, she spent the night in a local Travelodge. It remains the only night the couple have spent apart.

The procedure went well. Steve even managed a short walk around the hospital grounds in the afternoon. He was a little sore, but the painkillers helped, as did Dennis' phone call checking in on his friend, having endured a hernia repair himself some years earlier. The following morning, Steve was given the all clear and advised to return to normal activity as soon as possible. He didn't need telling twice, walking immediately and returning to work just three days later.

Returning to proper running proved a long and frustrating business, starting with just walking for the first two weeks, then running a mile and gradually building up from there to get his confidence and fitness back. He also re-started core exercises, but delayed weights a little longer. Patience was paramount. But he was on his way back and he couldn't thank Anthony Fox enough. It reinforced what he already knew - never believe anyone when they say something's impossible.

In mid-November, Steve started his new job with Advance Housing. With office showering facilities, he sussed out a lunchtime training route, implementing it almost immediately. It felt odd working somewhere new with different people and office politics, but he soon adapted. To his surprise, he actually enjoyed being back in a more junior position with less responsibility. It meant more pure IT support, working 9-5, then leaving it all behind at the end of the day: '...that felt really good.'

Over the next few weeks, Steve gradually increased his running mileage and speed, getting back up to a 48-mile training week before Christmas. He may not be running as fast or as far as before - his longest run was just 12 miles - but he was running again.

Steve ran just 20 marathons in 2010, including the 10-in-10, with an average finish time of 3:23. Excluding the 10-in-10, those other 10 marathons averaged 3:16. After injuring his ankle, he didn't run for nearly 14 weeks and it was 15 weeks before he ran a whole mile. He didn't run a marathon for six months. It was his longest break without running since the mid-1980s.

His overall total now stood at 513 with his average finish time dropping to 3:18:27. Of that total, he'd run 444 sub-3:30s, so needed another 56 for his 500.

But did he have the desire to up his training speed sufficiently to run that kind of pace again? Stats aside, since his injuries, he felt far more cautious about training harder and increasing mileage. His confidence had been severely dented and where once he was a naïve young man who didn't worry about such things, that was no longer the case. He now accepted he was flesh and blood and not an indestructible machine. His father had once said to him that sometimes it seems you have to pay for your successes. Back in 1992, after achieving the 'most marathons in a year' record, his wife left him. Now, years later, he'd achieved his long-term goal and beaten Sy Mah's record, but had lost his job, suffered a stress fracture and undergone a hernia operation. Was success worth it? Or was it all just part of life's rich tapestry? Steve was glad he didn't have a crystal ball. If he did, he might spend his life worrying about what might or might not happen and end up doing nothing at all, just in case.

On the last working day before Christmas, a raffle was held in Steve's office. Unusually, he bought a ticket. He won first prize – a large picnic hamper full of Christmas food. It was the first raffle prize he'd ever won in his life. Maybe, just maybe, his luck was turning?

Hope – friend or foe?

2008 - Meeting HRH Princess Anne after the London Marathon

**2008 - Brathay presentation after
setting the 10-in-10 world record**

*2009 - On the way to a 24th
Sub-3 at London*

*2009 - L to R - Adam Holland, Steve & Tim Charles, the 10 x sub
3:30s club is born!*

2009 - Presentation of the 10-in-10 Guinness WR certificate at Mannatech convention

2010 - After achieving the 500 marathons world record

*2010 - The finale to a fourth
successful 10-in-10*

*2010 - Teresa finishing her first
(and last!) marathon*

Chapter 35

2011 – THE RETURN: TAKE 2

The year started with Steve and Teresa both giving a talk to the Moreton WI. Whilst clearly interested in Steve's talk, which he'd thoughtfully engineered to include facts about female participation in the marathon (only officially allowed since 1972 with the first women's Olympic marathon in 1984), it was perhaps not unnatural that they were just as intrigued by the role Teresa played and her own running experiences.

Talking was fine, but what Steve really wanted was to get a marathon under his belt. Following two 50+-mile training weeks, he did a test run at the Highworth half-marathon, running for BRR. Starting at 7 mm pace, he was up to sub-7 by halfway, slowed for a couple of climbs in the final few miles then picked it up again to finish in 1:30:06. Having decided beforehand that 1:30-1:35 would be great, he now wished he'd dipped below 1:30! Regardless, he'd passed his test and promptly entered January's Gloucester Marathon.

On the start line at Gloucester, his first marathon for seven months, Steve was filled with doubt. Would he be able to run the whole way? If not, how long would he be out there for? It almost felt like he was running his first marathon – except then, ignorance really had been bliss and he hadn't worried at all! He went over his race plan – go out at 7:45 mm pace in the hope of a sub-3:30, maybe a sub-3:25. If okay at 15 miles, pick up pace and try for sub-3:20. He never really thought this possible – more likely he'd slow down. But it was a plan.

As the miles passed, so Steve's confidence grew - until he reached halfway. His longest training run had been 13 miles. Suddenly he felt like he was entering uncharted territory. By 20 miles, however, he knew he was going to make it, even if he slowed. He did, but not as much as feared, finishing in 3:17 - way beyond his hopes - and claiming his 300th sub-3:20 to boot.

He'd come through 26.2 miles unscathed, running all the way. What on earth had he been worrying about? Heartened, he resumed training with a rare 18-miler, rebuilding his endurance with 50-60 mile training weeks and returning to BRR's weekly speed sessions. He could now look forward to the Malta Marathon booked for February, partly as a short winter break and partly to support Naomi Prasad running her 100th marathon at 29; the youngest female in the world to do so at that time.

TE arrived in Malta the day before the race to torrential rain and flooding. At one point during the race, the water was so deep they ran atop a 100-metre-long wall to avoid it. With a sprint finish, Steve finished in 3:04. The machine was back!

His good form continued with 3:10 at the Duchy Marathon, 3:14 at the Cotswolds, 3:09 at Taunton and 3:03 at London (another good for age place). Crossing the finish line with BRR's Ewen Smith, they were filmed by the BBC – whether because he'd just run his 450th sub-3:30 or because they finished alongside retired Olympic rower, James Cracknell, Steve wasn't sure!

During April, Steve paced BRR clubmate, Tony Goodwill, around the Great Welsh Marathon at Llanelli, a new race for Steve. Tony needed sub-3:15 to qualify for a good for age place at London in the MV50 category. They crossed the line in 3:14. Tony got his time – then forgot to enter before London's closing date!

At the end of the month, Steve entered an 'almost double' – 'almost double' because the races were a day apart. First was the Royal Berkshire Marathon on Good Friday, a one-off track race at Greenham & Crookham Common, organised by 100 Clubber, Ian Berry, to coincide with William and Kate's royal wedding. Steve finished in 3:08, mindful of his second race, the North Dorset Marathon, two days' later, which he finished in 3:11. It was a relief to get through two marathons so close together in respectable times. He was beginning to feel much more like the Steve Edwards of old. Maybe his enforced rest had done him good? He certainly felt a renewed zest and vigour for running. Six months ago, he wouldn't have believed he'd be back running such times again.

In May, a week after the North Dorset Marathon, he ran Shakespeare in 3:04, followed by Kildare; another first for Steve, with an invite and a finish time of 3:04.

Confidence soaring and injury a mere memory, Steve returned to Brathay for the Windermere Marathon. It felt strange not being involved in the 10-in-10: '...I really missed it.'

In fact, all week he'd been following the progress of the runners, reading their blogs; sad not to be part of it. He was decidedly cheered, though, by his fastest run on the course in 3:09: '...it was a lot easier not running 10 of them!'

Two weeks later, Steve ran the Wales Marathon at Tenby, an event organised by Matthew Evans (2008 10-in-10). Another first for Steve, he was shocked by the hills, which were: '...as tough as Windermere.' He was therefore delighted to finish in 3:06, while BRR friend, Dennis, won in a course record of 2:41.

It was after Tenby, that a niggle at the top of his hamstring, which he'd first noticed a few days earlier during hill reps, made itself felt. It seemed Tenby's hills and the long drive home had aggravated it. Oh well, he only had one more race then a week off, hopefully that would sort it.

Steve's final June marathon was at Boddington. Things were not looking good - the temperature had rocketed and he'd pulled a back muscle on the same side as the sore hamstring the day before the race whilst on a short training run. By the time the race started at 11.15, the temperature was in the high 70s. Two laps into the 12-lap race, runners started dropping like flies as the temperature soared. Steve kept working hard and at 10 miles felt okay at around 3:10 pace. By 15 miles, back aching, he'd slowed to 3:15 pace. By now, around 30 runners had dropped out and many more were walking or stopping to rest. In all his years of running, Steve had never seen anything like it. The narrow country lanes trapped the heat, Steve felt like he was being slow-roasted. After 20 miles, he was losing his co-ordination and was reduced to a survival shuffle. The final 10k took him 55 minutes: '...it felt like an eternity'. He finished exhausted in 4th place in 3:24:37. In the 90-degree heat, he'd consumed 3 litres of fluid, yet lost 5lbs. With over half the field retiring, the flat-coursed race was won in 3:07, with only four runners, including Steve, breaking 3:30.

Never had a week off looked more appealing. During that week, Steve's back pain disappeared only to reappear with the running, ditto the hamstring pain. He took a few more days off. His hamstring throbbed even when sitting in his office chair, so he took to kneeling on a cushion at his desk instead. Panic set in; surely he couldn't be injured again?

He consulted Clare, who dry-needled the whole area triggering tight spots. This brought some relief, but still hurt when sitting, never mind running. At least he could ride his bike. Hopefully, that would maintain some fitness.

There is never a good time to be injured, but for Steve this fell just as he'd been selected by BT to be a storyteller for the 2012 London Olympics. BT, one of the main sponsors, had launched an initiative for 100 people to tell the story of the Games during the build up. Steve had won a place by entering the pre-selection competition with a written piece about his personal Olympic legacy to run 500 sub-3:30 marathons by 2012: '...I was overjoyed to be selected!'

On July 14th, he travelled to St Pancras to meet The Right Honourable The Lord (Seb) Coe CH KBE (one of the world's greatest ever middle-distance runners), and Daley Thompson CBE (one of the world's greatest decathletes ever), together with the other BT storytellers. After lunch, they were given a tour of the Olympic park. The track may not yet have been laid, but the stadium was awesome and Steve clicked away happily with his camera, chatting to Seb and Daley about his own particular challenge and laughing when Daley referred to him as "Baldy": '...I didn't mind, it was Daley Thompson!'

Two weeks later, Steve saw a consultant at the Birmingham Alexander Hospital about his injury. The consultant could find nothing obviously wrong and an MRI scan also drew a blank. Steve decided to try a Cortisone injection. However, the physio recommended by Clare advised against it, as he didn't think there was anything seriously wrong. Instead, he dry-needled a specific area in Steve's lower glute to relieve the remaining tightness. Painful though this was, he assured Steve it would settle down in a few days and should do the trick.

For the next week, Steve continued cycling and also walked a couple of miles during lunchtimes. It was still uncomfortable, but definitely easing. After five weeks, he attempted short slow runs integrated with walking. Two weeks later, he put in a 30-mile training week. The miles weren't quick, around 7:45-8 mm pace, instead of his usual 6:45-7:30, but it was too uncomfortable to run faster.

His next marathon was an invitation to run in Guernsey at the end of August. In the two weeks prior to the race, Steve upped his training to 40+ miles a week and was able to run below 7:30 mm pace with virtually no discomfort. Just a few days before Guernsey, he managed 5 miles at sub-7 mm pace pain-free.

Even though the fine collection of injuries he'd acquired since 2008 made him wary, and even though after the stress fracture and hernia op he'd decided not to push so hard in training and content himself with slower race times knowing it was more important to stay injury-free and remember the bigger picture of 500 sub-3:30s, Steve still felt the need to chase sub-3:15s. Why? Because he couldn't forget the deal he'd made with himself all those years ago to run as hard as he could at every race, no matter what. Admittedly, he was nearing 49 and all the miles and marathons in reasonable finish times would be catching up with him after 30 years - but a promise was a promise.

Accordingly, a fortnight after returning from his latest injury, Steve ran 3:14 in Guernsey. He'd had to work hard all the way, but he'd maintained his promise. He followed this with 3:13 at both Wolverhampton and Robin Hood, and was a mere 10 seconds outside 3:15 at the New Forest.

And then it was back to the Channel Islands, Jersey this time; another new race for Steve and BRR's annual club trip. One of the warmest October weekends Jersey had ever experienced with temperatures in the high 70s, Steve finished in 3:08.

Steve's good form held with a 3:06 at Abington, followed by 3:12 at his last marathon of the year in Portsmouth.

By the end of 2011, Steve had run 25 marathons in an average finish time of 3:11 and all under 3:30. His total sub-3:30s increased to 469 – 31 short of his 50th birthday goal in 11 months time. He'd also run 237 sub-3:15s – 13 more would take him to 250, another UK first. Meanwhile, his overall total stood at 538 with an average finish time of 3:18:10 – a 17-second improvement per marathon since 2010.

Despite the injury setbacks, Steve was still improving his average finish time, striving for 600 marathons averaging sub-3:18 for every single one.

They'd said 500 would be impossible, his hips and knees would be shot, he'd burn out - they were wrong. Steve felt totally vindicated about taking a leap of faith into the unknown abyss. Along the way, and in tune with the next Olympics, he'd inspired others to set and achieve their own goals. What could be more rewarding than that?

Away from running, his 12-month contract with Advance Housing was ending. He'd applied for several jobs without success, but remained positive. He may be older, but his experience had held him in good stead this past year, there was no reason why that shouldn't continue elsewhere. He was right. He found a permanent IT post at Campden BRI, a food technology company on the outskirts of Chipping Campden just seven miles from home. It would be great working so close to home in a role that used all his expertise and experience. Plus, there were showers, so lunchtime running wouldn't be a problem!

Steve's guardian angel had come up trumps once again.

Chapter 36

2012 – THE FINAL COUNTDOWN

Steve settled into his new job, mapping out lunchtime running routes and planning his race schedule. Unlike before, when he'd struggled to find races in the UK, by 2012 there was no shortage, running having exploded in popularity bringing an increase in trail, multi-day, and mid-week marathons. The only question was: would Steve be able to maintain the times necessary to achieve his goals and stay injury-free?

He ran his first two races in January; the 100 Club Marathon at Bromley in 3:12, followed by Gloucester in 3:11. It was a great start continuing where he'd left off at the end of 2011.

Later in January, TE travelled to Brathay's 10-in-10 training weekend. Steve gave a short presentation and ran his longest-ever training run - 26.2 miles around the Windermere course with some of the new recruits, proffering advice along the way!

Meanwhile, the UK marathon tidal wave brought to shore 'Enigma Running', the brainchild of 10-in-10 and 100 Clubber, David 'Foxy' Bayley. Within his hometown of Milton Keynes, Foxy identified three different lakes with surrounding trail paths that could be utilised for multiple-lap, half, full and ultra marathons. These courses formed several events throughout the year from single marathons to doubles, triples, a quad and even a 7-in-7. Today, Enigma organise around 16 events, facilitating over 30 marathons within Milton Keynes alone.

With Milton Keynes less than 40 miles from home and Enigma's events being official races with official permits, Steve factored some of their events into his 2012 race schedule.

First was the Quadzilla – four marathons in four consecutive days at Caldecotte Lake, each marathon seven and a bit laps. Steve hadn't run any consecutive marathons since the 10-in-10 in 2010. Regardless, he didn't do any extra training miles, relying instead on his residual fitness and accepting slower than normal times – provided they were under 3:30.

All four days were freezing cold with temperatures below zero. With snow and compacted ice underfoot and several twists and turns on each lap, running was difficult. On the first lap of the first day, Steve stuck with a runner who knew the route, then settled into his own rhythm and, mindful of running another three marathons, tried to relax. Easier said than done. The slippery conditions made him tense up and the leggings and long-sleeved top worn for warmth proved inhibiting, making it hard to run naturally. He was therefore satisfied to finish 1st in 3:21. Not quite so satisfying was jumping into his garden water butt back home for his usual 10-minute, post-race recovery ice bath – having first broken the ice with a hammer! Eight minutes later, when he could no longer feel his feet, he got out.

The second day replicated the first, with Steve finishing 1st again in 3:24.

On day three, TE stayed overnight to save a journey. Another good run for Steve in 3:24 gave him a 24-minute lead over nearest rival, Roger Hayes.

On the final day, Roger went out in front. Steve let him go, knowing that to give chase when he felt so tired could jeopardise his overall victory and another sub-3:30: '...blowing up can happen to anyone. The marathon is an event that will always find you out and exploit your weaknesses.'

Steve finished 2nd in 3:25, the overall event winner. Running 30 laps of the same lake over four days had been physically and mentally gruelling. Steve's cumulative time of 13:36:14 gave an average of just over 3:24 for each marathon, not super-fast, but not bad given the arctic conditions.

February closed with the Cotswold Marathon in 3:23, the Heartbreaker Trail Marathon in the New Forest in 3:26 for 3rd place, and, three days later, the Enigma Leap Year Marathon – the first leap year race Steve had heard of and therefore irresistible! Steve won the 17-lap race round Furzton Lake in 3:14.

It was after that race Steve noticed some soreness in his right hamstring, probably due to the twists and turns of the multi-lap course. With the Duchy Marathon approaching at the weekend, he rested for a couple of days and consulted Lucy. She could find nothing wrong other than a little tightness and stuck some needles in. Steve then took a 5-mile test run at 8 mm pace. Despite some throbbing, it was no worse. After discussion with Teresa, and with accommodation already booked, TE drove the 230 miles to Redruth on Saturday. On Sunday, Steve tried a 2-mile jog, but was still unsure whether to run. He rang Lucy. She said that if he was in any doubt, he shouldn't run - better miss one race than several if he exacerbated the injury. She was right; a frustrated Steve drove the 230 miles home again without running – and without receiving a special, Olympic-themed medal.

Steve consulted Lucy again for more acupuncture. She now thought it might be a stress reaction – bone-related rather than soft tissue, and recommended active rest. For the next two weeks, Steve was back on the bike, cycling the 15-mile round trip to work, which at least fitted in easily with his daily life.

Two weeks later, he tried a couple of short runs and felt okay.

After the third week he ran a steady 11 miles, then 13. There was a little discomfort, but a definite improvement. The following week, still cycling to work, he recommenced his lunchtime runs. All felt okay. He would run next weekend's Taunton Marathon.

Steve started cautiously, sped up gingerly and, despite some discomfort, finished in 3:20. What a relief! He'd only missed two races planned for March and would need replacements to fill the gaps in his race schedule, but he was on the mend. However, he would continue cycling to work – it contributed to his fitness without risk of injury and complemented his training schedule.

Five days after Taunton, he was back at Milton Keynes for their Good Friday race. Still not feeling 100 per cent, he won in 3:21.

Next came the first Hull Marathon since the demise of the Humber Bridge race back in the early 1990s, with invitational race entry and accommodation. Steve finished in 3:16, although the course was a little short. Surprisingly, it wasn't something that pedant Steve was worried about – he'd run many more races that measured long, so reckoned they'd cancel each other out.

Besides, he had something far more important on his mind – the tragic death of his old junior school friend, Darren Edwards, who he hadn't seen since a 10k race in Gloucestershire in 2006. Apparently, Darren had an undetected heart issue and had collapsed on a training run. He was 49. Life was too precious to waste on worrying about minor discrepancies; it should be lived to the full while one still had the chance.

And so it was that just three days after Hull, TE were chauffeur-driven to Heathrow for a flight to Dallas. They were heading to Mannatech's US convention in Fort Worth. An all-expenses paid trip in return for Steve giving a presentation at the Fort Worth Conference Centre – to an audience of 3000. He figured the nerves would be worth it! It would also be an opportunity to run The Big D Marathon in nearby Dallas - a replacement race for that weekend's missed, Worcester Marathon.

The minute he stepped outside the airport, the humidity hit Steve and he struggled to breathe. Consequently, next morning, he opted for a 5-mile treadmill run in the hotel's air-conditioned gym, before walking across the road to the convention centre for a rehearsal, allowing him to familiarise himself with the huge auditorium. Exploring Fort Worth afterwards, Steve was far too nervous to take anything in!

After a terrible night's sleep, barely able to eat breakfast, Steve was grateful he was one of the first speakers and could get it over with. Almost before he knew it, he was being introduced to the audience: '… all the way from England, one of the most successful multi-marathon runners in the world today…'

Was that really him?

'Mr Steve Edwards!'

Apparently so. On trembling legs, he approached the stage, walked up to the lectern and bellowed: 'Howdy everyone, how y'all doin'?' in his best Texas drawl! The audience loved it! Not that he could actually see them, the bright lights shining straight into his face ensured virtual blackout, for which he was extremely grateful. He could, however, see Teresa sitting in the front row alongside the Mannatech reps, so when he talked about the importance of an understanding partner, he was able to smile directly at her. The audience loved that too! He left the stage to rapturous applause, photo and autograph requests.

Phew! Now all he had to think about was Sunday's race. He did another run on the treadmill that evening, then the following night he ran outside. Two miles later he was dripping with sweat, but otherwise okay. Hopefully, the storms forecast for later would clear the air ready for tomorrow's 7 am start.

They did and they didn't. Chauffeur-driven to the start at the Cotton Bowl Stadium, former home of Dallas Cowboys American football team, Steve arrived to discover that with thunderstorm activity still in the area, the start was being delayed for safety reasons. Apparently, Dallas storms were potentially life threatening. Eventually the weather system moved away and the race got underway.

Despite the storms and early hour, it was already hot and humid and Steve found it impossible to run quickly. After just a few miles he'd lost a ton of fluid in sweat. Regardless, he finished in 3:18, winning the MV45 trophy.

The following weekend was London and another good for age place. Steve finished in 3:09, his fastest race so far that year. Unfortunately, though, he'd felt a pull in his left calf in the last half-mile.

His calf remained sore over the next few days, slowing him down in training. The same couldn't be said of his car, which had been filmed in London doing 34 mph in a 30 limit. Opting to attend a speed awareness course, even though it meant another journey to London, Steve admits it was worthwhile: '...I was surprised by how much I learned.'

Despite his sore calf, Steve decided to run the Shakespeare Marathon the following weekend. It would be his 20th Shakespeare (the most times he'd run any single annual event at that time), and was only 12 miles from home. Unfortunately, the race was cancelled at the last minute due to heavy rain and flooding.

The following weekend, putting Stratford firmly behind him, Steve ran the North Dorset Village Marathon. His calf was still a little sore, but had survived training, albeit at a slower pace than normal. It would still be a risk running 26.2 miles, but it was already May and although he'd found replacements for the three races he'd missed, he couldn't afford to miss many more, if any.

All went well up to 10 miles. Then the calf flared up and Steve was reduced to a painful limp as he struggled to maintain 8 mm pace. He had to get under 3:30 - otherwise it would be a wasted race. He gritted his teeth and pushed on, finishing in 3:26. He couldn't wait to sit down, take the pressure off the calf and get it iced.

Then he was back to cycling, physio, and missing a fourth planned marathon at Halstead the following weekend.

Thankfully, after a week, the calf improved considerably and running resumed. However, Steve sensibly decided that running his planned double at White Peak and Windermere that weekend might be pushing his luck. He cancelled both, although he still went to Windermere to support the 10-in-10 runners and meet up with Robin from TN.

And it was Robin who, on hearing about Steve's soft tissue injuries, suggested he compare his daily protein intake against the recommended level for male athletes. To Steve's surprise it was lacking. He immediately started taking Mannatech's whey protein supplement every morning before breakfast, as well as before and after training. He already used the protein recovery drinks from TN after racing and hard training sessions, but had never considered using a protein supplement at other times. The science behind putting protein in before exercise rather than just after, is so the muscle-repair process can start more immediately. Steve continues taking whey protein supplements today.

He also invested in a foam roller. Although he had fortnightly massages, he knew a weekly massage would be better – but costly. He'd long since used his trusty cricket ball to free off glutes and hamstrings; a foam roller could be used to massage calves, quads and IT bands. In time, the foam roller was replaced with a heavier duty roller with harder foam and knobbly bits, which worked the soft tissue a treat. Steve continues having fortnightly massages and uses the roller at home most days. He believes both have helped massively to keep injuries at bay.

With the calf still not 100 per cent, Steve cancelled Edinburgh considering it too far to drive if his calf proved problematic. It was his third weekend without a marathon and his seventh missed race since January. It was now June. There were 24 weekends left till his 50th birthday, including the quiet period in July and August with fewer events. What if he didn't make his goal? With an invitation to next run the Cork Marathon on June's Irish bank holiday Monday, Steve decided to risk it, and finished in 3:10; the calf held up, but was replaced by sporadic pain in his left ankle, the same one as the stress fracture.

But the show must continue! He mapped out a revised schedule with seven replacement races taking him up to the second weekend of November, two weekends before his birthday. All being well the big day would be 11th November at Enigma's race, 'The Fox @ 40' - a one-off event celebrating Foxy's 40th birthday. Originally, he'd envisaged completing the record by the start of the Paralympics in August, now he'd be taking it right up to the wire with just one failsafe event on the 18th November at Luton. Still needing 15 sub-3:30s and 8 sub-3:15s, Steve could only hope his guardian angel was paying attention.

Meanwhile, he decided to apply for the 2013 10-in-10. Having run it the first four years, he'd really missed it in 2011 – and, once he'd achieved 500 sub-3:30s, he'd probably need a new goal! Hopefully, by the end of the year he'd be close to 600 – perhaps his 600th could coincide with the 10-in-10, maybe day 10 itself? He'd also like to set a MV50 record for the event. Plus, not having done any fundraising since Brathay 2010, he'd like to redress the balance. There were 400 staff at his new job to tap into, not to mention his new employers. He'd write to them directly!

They responded immediately offering to donate £1000 to Brathay in return for some promotion. Result! That should really help his application. There were three criteria for applying: 1) running experience; 2) having a good story to tell; and 3) fundraising experience and a plan. Steve had the first two in abundance, and with his employer's promised £1000 and their connections to numerous major food and drink manufacturers, he saw no problem in raising at least the requisite £2500 minimum. Moreover, he could offer Teresa's support, and TE's support for future 10-in-10s.

He was stunned then when he was rejected on the grounds that others had better fundraising plans and prospects than him. Equally, he understood they had to select those who could raise the most money. Perhaps it was time to let go? It wasn't easy, but he had to, and did.

Dusting himself down, Steve looked towards his next race, the Wales Marathon in Tenby, doubling as the British Masters Marathon Championship. Steve enjoyed a pain-free run in 3:15, while physio Lucy took the British Masters ladies' title in 3:11.

Tenby was followed by a new 26-lap trail race at Littledown, Bournemouth, in 3:09, followed by the new Lancaster Castle Marathon in 3:18, winning him £50 as 1st male vet. Next came Boddington a week later in 3:06 - his fastest run that year.

July was also unexpectedly busy with Enigma events filling up the normally blank weekends. Steve ran five marathons that month, including the Isle of Man in 3:12 and an Enigma double, winning both races in a cumulative time of 6:34.

August brought with it the London Olympics with Super Saturday, and a single marathon for Steve with another invite to Guernsey. However, while training a week before the race, Steve's left foot suddenly gave way, as it had in Cork, accompanied by an excruciatingly sharp pain running down from his shin. Next day it happened again, twice in succession. He saw his GP, was referred to an orthopaedic foot consultant and secured an appointment that same week. Examination suggested possible bone spurs on the bridge of his foot rubbing on the soft tissue. He was advised to take a couple of days rest, let it settle and everything should be okay. Steve obeyed, then went for a test run. It was a little stiff, but not painful, so he assumed all was okay for Guernsey.

Leaving work as normal late Friday afternoon, anticipating getting home, packing bags and driving to Weymouth for the Saturday morning ferry to the Channel Islands, Steve received a call from the ferry company. Due to high winds and rough seas, the morning's sailing had been cancelled; did he want a refund? No, he did not. He wanted to go to Guernsey. Now, more than ever, he couldn't afford to miss another race. He was told the evening sailing looked likely to go ahead as the wind was forecast to abate, but it would be very busy and going via Jersey first. Following advice to take a refund and then book a Saturday evening crossing on the website, Steve eventually secured two tickets. It wasn't ideal going via Jersey and arriving at Guernsey late evening, but needs must.

The winds remained high and the crossing was very rough: '...people were throwing up everywhere!' TE both felt queasy, but knowing he needed the fuel for next day's race, Steve forced himself to eat: '...I've never taken so long to eat a bowl of pasta!'

The ferry docked well after midnight, leaving TE to walk the short distance to the hotel. Despite knowing the way, having stayed there before, they got slightly lost in the pitch-black night and didn't arrive until 1:30 am, eventually getting into bed at 2. At 7 am Steve ate breakfast, and at 10 am toed the start line feeling decidedly ropey. He was surprised therefore to finish in 3:13, especially as his troublesome ankle had reduced him to a hobble by the end. Ice was immediately applied, and by morning, the pain had almost gone. By the second day, it had disappeared completely and he was back running again without any problems.

In September, Steve ran Wolverhampton in 3:16, then a fortnight later headed south for the New Forest Marathon. It was a dreadful day, gloomy and raining. The rain was forecast to stop, but it would remain overcast. Believing it would warm up, Steve wore his usual club vest and shorts. Reaching the more remote parts of the course, a chill breeze struck and Steve's body grew increasingly cold. By halfway, he'd slowed considerably and his body temperature continued to decrease.

By mile 16, it was becoming increasingly difficult for him to move his legs and he could no longer feel his hands, while his upper body just felt strange. Only then did hypothermia occur to him. But surely that was impossible? He was on the south coast of England, not the Arctic! But why else would his body feel like it was starting to shut down? With 10 miles left, he checked his watch and noted he had 85 minutes to finish under 3:30. Normally no problem, today he was in trouble. He forced himself to focus, to keep putting one foot in front of other, maintain his cadence - easier said than done with his pace having slowed to over 8 mm.

The 20-mile marker was the last mile marker he remembered seeing. He should have sought assistance, got warm, but then he'd miss a sub-3:30 and incur a possible DNF. No chance. He continued and finished in 3:27. With no recollection of miles 21-26, he had no idea how he'd got there. All he knew was that he was now in the St John's Ambulance recovery area covered in blankets being given hot drinks, having his temperature constantly taken – and yes, he was suffering from hypothermia.

Steve, the marathon machine, having run hundreds of marathons over a quarter of a century had made a rookie mistake. He was extremely embarrassed - he hadn't worn the right gear for the conditions and had got hypothermia! Never again would he underestimate the weather and its potential effect. When he was younger he'd rarely run in anything other than a vest on top, but this wasn't about age – hypothermia is not ageist and calories burned to warm a cold body, whatever age, are wasted calories that could be better used to improve athletic performance. For all his knowledge, Steve learned a lot more that day.

With his ego fairly flattened, it was good to have a fortnight off before his next race, time to reflect on his stupidity, accept it, learn from it, and put it behind him. Ironically, it was while he was doing this that sports clothing company, Sub Sports, responded to his sponsorship application. Aware he was about to set a world record for 500 *sub*-3:30s, they were delighted to kit him out with an extensive selection of compression base layer clothing for all weathers. A pity Steve hadn't received the kit prior to the New Forest! Sub Sports still sponsor Steve today.

First time out in his new Sub Sports compression shorts at Chester in October, Steve finished in 3:06 - his second best time of the year: '...I'd long since discovered the recovery benefits of compression-wear, but never raced in them before.'

Confidence restored, and with his local newspaper the Wiltshire & Gloucestershire Standard covering the remaining races in a countdown to the 500th, Steve resolved to finish things in style. A week after Chester he ran 3:10 at Leicester and a week after that 3:13 at Abingdon. Now on 249 sub-3:15s and 498 sub-3:30s, his dream for 2012 and his personal Olympic legacy were in touching distance.

And so to Preston – a marathon held once every 20 years to celebrate becoming a medieval market town with a year-long festival incorporating various running events. It was another one on Steve's bucket list, with the added bonus of an invitation, and meeting marathon legends Liz McColgan MBE and old friend, Dr Ron Hill MBE.

Most important, though, was the race; the one that would bring him the first of his two records. Barely noticing the rain that grew heavier with every mile, Steve was a man on a mission. Then, just two miles from achieving his goal, his right hamstring tightened, forcing him to slow. Did Steve panic? No, he did not. He simply poured cold water down the back of his new shorts! Relief was quick; he picked up his pace again and raced home in 3:14 to become the first British athlete to run 250 sub-3:15s. Sub Sports could not have been a more perfect fit!

But, of course, Steve had even bigger fish to fry. On Friday, 9th November, TE drove to the Blue Raddison Hotel at Stanstead Airport, where Steve was giving a talk the following day for Mannatech. In the dark and early hours of Sunday, 11th November, TE drove to Milton Keynes for the seven-and-a-half-lap race round Caldecotte Lake. By the time they arrived, the sun had risen, the sky was cobalt blue and the air had that pure clear quality that only exists on a perfect autumn day in England. Jason was there with Christine and the children, and friends from the 100 Club and BRR were ready to run and support him. 'The Godfather' was emblazoned across race numbers and Steve's number was 500. There had always been an element of pressure to what Steve did, mostly self-imposed, but today, when people had come specifically to watch him set a new world record, that pressure increased ten-fold. He had to deliver, had to finish inside 3:30, he couldn't fail them: '...I just wanted to get going, get a couple of miles under my belt and then hopefully relax a little in my zone.'

And that's exactly what happened. Two miles in, just under 15 minutes from the start, he was on his way, running at sub-3:15 pace. He needn't run that fast, but, as always, Steve needed a driver, and increasing his 3:15 record provided it. With his focus shifted from the main goal, he was able to relax and the miles flew by.

Meanwhile, Malcolm Hargraves of Running Crazy Limited, specialists in overseas trips for runners, was running round the course popping up at various points taking photos and recording the historic race on his video camera. At the drinks station at the end of each lap, Teresa, Jason, Christine and the children, cheered Steve on, the children passing granddad his drink on the last few laps.

He was still on for a sub-3:15 when he entered the final lap. At about 25 miles, his hamstring tightened just as it had in Preston. Something was definitely wrong. He stopped briefly to stretch it out, then continued for the final half-mile. As he rounded the final bend, Jason told Farren to run in with Grandpa Gump.

'I took Farren's hand and slowed down, intending to run to the finish with him like I used to with Jason at that age. But I was so close to the 3:15 barrier and Farren's little legs just couldn't keep up, so I lost him just before the line.'

It didn't matter. Farren was happy to have been captured on film by Malcolm running along with his world-record setting grandpa!

Steve crossed the line in 3:14, another sub-3:15, just as he'd hoped. But, of course, no world record would be complete without Steve returning to his childhood and playing to the gallery, especially one packed with family and friends, not to mention Malcolm's camera! Crossing the line, Steve looked skywards, spread his arms, and fell to his knees. Only when Teresa gathered him into her arms was the am dram forgotten, replaced by the reality of his achievement and the shedding of a tear.

Twenty-four years ago, Steve Edwards had set out to run 500 marathons in an *average* finish time under 3:30. Today, he'd become the first person in the world to run 500 *under* 3:30, bringing a new world best average finish time for the 500 of 3:15:12. If anyone had told him 24 years ago he'd do that, he'd never have believed them. He'd certainly proved his doubters wrong – those who'd said it was impossible.

'Self-belief is pivotal to success, trying no matter what others might say or think. Never underestimate your potential. Follow your dreams.'

Today, Steve has gone even further and bettered his world best average finish time for the fastest run 500 marathons to 3:12. However much Steve may hope to inspire others to follow in his footsteps, it is probably safe to assume that it will be some time before anyone takes enough steps to overtake this particular landmark.

An achievement of such magnitude must of course be celebrated – with cake, preferably a big one with '500 sub-3:30s' iced on top. There should also be presentations, like a specially engraved pewter plate from Steve's BRR clubmates, an official 100 Club top emblazoned with 'The Godfather' and, almost incidentally, a trophy for the best overall performances of the Enigma Marathon Series during 2012 from Foxy, not to mention a DVD with a compilation of the photos and video recordings made of Steve throughout the race by Malcolm who had, somehow, incredibly put it all together in time for the celebrations. 'I was so grateful to Malcolm for that, having the whole thing captured on film forever is fantastic.'

So, what next? The question raised itself in Steve's mind almost immediately.

A week later, still without an answer, he ran the Luton Marathon in 3:12, followed by a couple more domestic marathons and a small celebration of his 50th birthday, taking him into the next vet age category of 50-55.

By the end of 2012, Steve had run 34 marathons in an average finish time of 3:16. All were sub-3:30 with 16 sub-3:15. His grand total of official marathon races now stood at 572 with an average finish time of 3:18:04, an improvement of 6 seconds per marathon on last year. He'd also set a new world record.

It was while recording his latest stats that Steve found the answer to his question. He needed another 28 marathons to reach 600. Ideally, he'd like to reduce his average finish time to under 3:18. 300 sub-3:15s was, perhaps, also possible.

But why? He'd achieved his original goal, he'd then redefined that goal and achieved that. What else was there to prove? Nothing, other than Steve felt he had more to give. Aside from an increase in minor injuries his fitness was still pretty good, so why not see just how far he could go? Why stop when he was able to continue? Did he want to regret not having tried to keep bettering the stats for as long as possible and then wonder 'what if?' No, what he wanted was to set the best possible benchmarks to make it even harder for anybody else to challenge them in the future: '… it's just something I feel obliged to do for as long as I'm able.'

Steve returned to his stats.

'Statistics have always been my main motivator. They keep me driven, knowing that at some point in the future I'll be able to look back and see that I ran X amount of marathons in an average finish time of Y and know that those stats represent the best multi-marathon performances in the world.'

He then calculated that every race he'd run faster than his slowest races could potentially improve his average finish time for his fastest 300, 400 and 500 marathons. In time, health and fitness permitting, he could do likewise for 600 and maybe even 700. The only thing that might become an issue would be his motivation and desire to continue with the level of training necessary to maintain such consistent finish times. That, and the fact that he wasn't getting any younger and had run marathons pretty much non-stop for the last 24 years.

But, as everyone knows, stars don't just suddenly stop shining.

Chapter 37

2013 – PURPLE PATCH

With the year's mission now clear – to reach 600 marathons in a world best average time, at the same time running as many sub-3:15s as possible to bring the 300 British record closer, Steve immediately began preparing his race schedule for the first six months and entering races in the latter half that were likely to fill up quickly.

The marathon world had changed. The continued increase in the popularity of running had brought not only an increase in the number of races, but also in the number of participants, with many chasing the century. Consequently, smaller events reached their entry limits quickly. If you didn't get in early, you didn't get to run. Old-timer, Steve, wasn't prepared to let the newbies threaten his chances!

First on Steve's 2013 hit list was Enigma's Double Winter Marathon during the first weekend of January. It wasn't that Steve had refreshed his appetite for doubles, it was more a determination to prove that even at 50, he could still knock out some respectable double finish times – at least he hoped he could!

On this occasion, though, hope was the optimist. About six miles into the first day's race at a frosty

Caldecotte Lake he slipped, breaking the fall with his arm to avoid hitting his head but damaging his hip and grazing his limbs. Picking himself up, he started to jog but had already stiffened up. It seemed his aging body was no longer capable of bouncing straight back as his younger body might have done. Shocked by both the fall and the unexpected consequences, he managed to continue, but his leg had tightened up so much he was unable to get back into his normal running stride. Ignoring his heartfelt desire to stop, he finished in 3:18, relieved to escape a DNF.

Next day, however, he was far too stiff and his hip too badly bruised to even contemplate running. No double this time!

All that week he attempted his usual lunchtime runs, but the soft tissue damage in his hip prevented him running properly and after a few miles his hamstring would tighten forcing him to slow down. After three days, he tried resting instead, and then attended Brathay's 10-in-10 training weekend. Despite the rest, his customary training run with the newcomers round Lake Windermere ended after 13 miles.

He knew from experience about the potential impact of injuries on the kinetic chain affecting connecting muscle groups and the importance of keeping the injured area massaged and stretched, applying patience to allow nature time to heal. He therefore knew he wouldn't be running Gloucester

Marathon at the end of the month. It was only January and he'd already missed two races, both paid for, which only added insult to injury. This was not how he'd planned it.

Normal training eventually resumed, albeit his leg was still not 100 per cent. Five weeks after the fall he returned to Milton Keynes for the Enigma Quadzilla – four marathons in four days. Seriously? No. His experience had also given him a modicum of common sense - he would run only one of the four.

Steve finished his one race in 3:17, but his hamstring had played up in the latter stages and two training runs after the race, was even worse. Shorter training runs were manageable, but no way could his leg withstand 26.2 miles. He took the rest of the week off, aside from riding his bike and doing a couple of plyometric sessions, and tried not to dwell on his slow progress towards the 600.

Training resumed again, and although back up to running 13 miles at a reasonable pace, he decided against running the Duchy Marathon at the start of March. It was a long way to go if things went wrong, especially as Paphos was booked for the following weekend as part of a week's holiday.

The extra rest paid off and, despite a bad patch with his hamstring at 15 miles, Steve won the Paphos MV50 race in 3:17, plus a very large trophy that barely fitted inside his hand luggage: '...I thought Ryanair might have to keep it!'

Meantime, Steve had received an invitation to run the Brighton Marathon and Channel 4, who were covering the race, wanted to feature him in their highlights programme. First, they filmed him at home in his 'trophy room' and running around his training circuit at nearby Batsford. Later, they would interview him at the start, during the race and immediately after it.

Away from the cameras, Steve ran Enigma's Good Friday Marathon at the end of March, successfully defending his title from the previous year, in 3:18.

Although relatively happy with his performances given his injury, Steve was concerned by the lack of a sub-3:15, which he needed to qualify for London.

Such concerns were pushed aside, though, as mid-April arrived and with it Brighton. Channel 4 duly interviewed Steve at the start, and reappeared just as he was passing the 3:15 official pacer group at halfway, confident that today could be the day for clearing that barrier - provided he wasn't interrupted by TV interviewers! Maintaining his pace, Steve answered the interviewer's questions as she ran one side of him with the cameraman filming him from the other. He wondered how long the cameraman could continue running carrying all his kit. Not long, as it turned out.

Alone again, hamstring pulling and running into a headwind, Steve battled on. He'd just ramped up his pace another notch for the closing miles when up popped another interviewer who asked how he was feeling! With admirable self-control, Steve, who thought the interviewer seemed familiar, offered a polite response, then upped his pace again. The presenter duly drifted off. Only then did Steve realise it was Dean Macy, former GB Olympic decathlete.

Crossing the line in 3:14 there followed yet another, rather more coherent interview with someone who wasn't Dean Macey, before Steve could finally celebrate guaranteeing his London place for the next two years.

But it was this year's London he needed to concentrate on a week after Brighton. Staying 20 miles from the start with friend, Rush, meant that instead of the usual Saturday morning return drive to London to collect his race number, before driving back again on Sunday for the race, TE enjoyed the luxury of not getting up until 6 am – early enough to allow for road closures and getting to Blackheath, but preferable to the usual 4 am start and 90-mile drive.

Having promised to pace BRR's Claire Harrison, it hadn't occurred to either of them that they'd be starting at different places! By sheer good luck, they met at 3 miles where the starts merged and then ran a consistent 7:25 mm pace. Steve finished in 3:13, Claire in 3:20 – a new PB.

A week later, Steve ran the Marathon of the North – a one-off race in Sunderland. Sadly, his hopes for a third consecutive sub-3:15 were thwarted at 18 miles by his hamstring slowing him down to 3:18.

Another week passed. May, and the Milton Keynes town marathon, arrived. Despite hamstring pain in the latter, undulating, stages, Steve finished in 3:13.

At least Steve's training was going well - 5-7 miles, six days a week, at an average 6:45-7:15 mm pace.

Returning to Windermere a couple of weeks after Milton Keynes brought another 3:18, followed two weeks later by 3:13 at the Kent Roadrunner Marathon – 17 laps of the Cyclopark in North Kent and one of the biggest finish medals in the UK!

Alternate sub-3:15s seemed to be the hamstring's limit. It was time for a bit of acupuncture and back/pelvis straightening from Lucy.

The weekend after Kent brought the Luxembourg Night Marathon, with an invitation in return for some PR. Flying out Friday, TE were transported directly from the airport to the expo and a pasta dinner before going to Luxembourg's TV studios for Steve's appearance on a live chat show. He hoped they'd have a coffee table for him to rest his weary feet upon, like Manchester in 1992! Unlike the early years, a more-worldly, less-anxious Steve was able to enjoy the experience, his English answers being translated into Luxembourgish.

Next day, after exploring the city with Teresa in the morning, Steve spent the afternoon resting and carbo-loading in preparation for the evening race. A live radio interview preceded the start and then Steve was off: '...it felt strange running through a lively town centre on a Saturday night seeing everyone partying while you were slogging your guts out running 26.2 miles!'

Despite Lucy's ministrations, the hamstring played up around 18 miles but settled back down again, enabling Steve to speed up in the closing stages and finish in 3:16. A post-race press conference followed.

Luxembourg was the 33rd country Steve had run in. Capital cities stood at 19.

The following Saturday, Steve ran the Littledown Trail Marathon in 3:18, and back home on Sunday celebrated Teresa's birthday at a local restaurant known as 'the pudding club' - where diners can consume as many puddings as they can manage!

The meal was, in fact, a prize won by Steve for clocking up the most steps in a pedometer challenge during a fitness initiative month at work. Embracing such initiative, Steve introduced a lunchtime running session on Fridays – just a couple of steady miles for anyone interested. Those lunchtime runs continue today with some participants now running 10ks and half-marathons.

As for Steve, one of his biggest challenges of 2013 came a week after Littledown with Enigma's 'Back-to-Front' event at Caldecotte Lake. Two marathons on the same day, one at 9 am, one at 3.30 pm; both run around the same seven and a bit lap-course, albeit in opposite directions. It would be the first time Steve had run two marathons in one day since 1989 when he'd run the Midnight Track Marathon at Bracknell followed by Harlow a few hours later, both sandwiched between two other marathons. But that was a long time ago – when he was considerably younger!

The somewhat older Steve felt decidedly nervous as to how he'd fair, and set himself three objectives to help him get round: 1) to run both races the whole way; 2) to finish both races inside 3:30; 3) to finish in the top three.

His strategy was simple – stick to 7.50 mm pace in the morning (even if he felt he could run faster), to finish around 3:25. Repeat for the afternoon race if possible. Simple theoretically maybe, but not necessarily simple to execute given how his body would feel by the afternoon with the usual DOMS (delayed onset muscle soreness), stiffness and general weariness that accompanies any marathon. The key component for Steve was, of course, the recovery window between the two marathons and what he would do during this period to prepare for marathon number two. To this end, TE had booked a hotel room for Saturday night arranging an early, 1 pm check-in, so Steve would have somewhere to rest and recover as much as possible before the afternoon race.

In total, 30 people elected to run both marathons; others running just the morning or afternoon race. A warm June day, Steve knew good hydration was essential and, with Teresa's usual faultless assistance in ensuring he got the right TN drink at the end of each lap, all went to plan. He also consumed a high protein/ carbohydrate bar on the penultimate lap to kick-start his recovery process. This would, of course, slow him down a little for the last few miles, but he'd factored that into his race plan.

Steve's first race went pretty much to plan as he finished in 3:26:26 in 2nd place from those running both races. In 1st place in 3:21 was 100 Clubber, John Errington, giving him a 5-minute lead over Steve going into the afternoon race.

Now into his three-hour recovery window, Steve immediately downed a TN recovery drink and tucked into a big bowl of cereal and a banana before driving the two miles to the hotel. There he had an ice-bath, a lie down, a warm shower, did some self-massage, and re-hydrated with a litre of TN carbo-loading drink containing vital carbs and salts. He believed it important to emulate what he would normally do before a single marathon.

Just before 3 pm, he donned fresh kit and fresh running shoes, and returned to Caldecotte Lake to discover John had pulled out of the second marathon leaving him in 1st place with a 3-minute advantage over Rik Vercoe – a 100 Clubber who'd won that year's 10-in-10. He would be hard to beat.

Rik set off quickly with Steve chasing him for the first five miles. However, when Rik upped his pace further, Steve let him go. Not just because his stomach felt delicate and his legs heavy, but because he intended sticking to his own race plan.

As the miles passed, so several runners dropped out, leaving Steve with just his GPS and resolve for company. At 23 miles, tummy almost settled, he saw Rik not far ahead, apparently suffering from cramp. Steve's tiredness lifted. With his three-minute advantage, so long as he kept Rik within sight, he'd win.

But that wasn't enough - Steve wanted to win in style! Speeding up two miles from the finish he passed Rik to win in 3:26:19 – seven seconds faster than his morning race, winning the overall event by four minutes.

Thirty runners set out to run both marathons; only 15 succeeded. Steve, meanwhile, achieved all three of his race objectives and, as an added bonus, won the event in a combined time of 6:52:45. Not bad for the oldest finisher in the race: '...I was very tired and sore the next day, though!'

At least his hamstring had held up and his question about what he could do with a true back-to-back aged 50 had been very satisfactorily answered.

'In many ways it would be easier to run the whole 52.4 miles in one hit without the 3-hour gap in between. It's difficult because you have to get the machine started up again just as it's switched itself off and the legs have stiffened up. Your body just doesn't want to know, which makes it mentally as well as physically demanding. But that gap is part of the challenge, so you run two separate marathons.'

Steve has no desire to repeat the exercise, though: '...I ticked that box in 1989 and now I've ticked it again, there won't be a third tick!'

Much as he'd have liked a break after the back-to-back, Steve had committed to run his 600th at Great Langdale on the 21st September, so had to stick to his schedule, which meant running the Coombe Abbey Trail Marathon near Coventry the following weekend. The park brought back fond childhood memories of family visits feeding the ducks and playing on the swings – except back then they were on head-banging tarmac not health and safety-compliant soft bark chippings!

The 12 grassy, undulating laps proved pretty challenging with Steve finishing in 3:15, just 44 seconds short of a sub, but he was happy enough: '...trail races are always tougher than road because muscles have to work harder on the unstable surface and everything aches more.'

With no let-up in the schedule, the next weekend Steve returned to Caldecotte Lake for Enigma's Summer Double, with 3:17 and 3:20 respectively. Steve actually won the first race, taking his victory tally to almost 40. Happy as he was to win, especially at 50, he couldn't help asking, '...where are all the fast youngsters?'

A week later came the Wales Marathon, his third time on the tough course, on one of the hottest weekends of the year. Driving down on Saturday, the temperature reached 30+, and race day was no different. He'd be lucky to run sub-3:30, never mind sub-3:15!

By 20 miles, even a sub-3:30 was questionable, but one thing kept Steve pushing on – a run of 76 consecutive sub-3:30s in the previous 128 weeks – an average of one every 11 days. Tenby would be 77 – how great would 100 be?

Steve finished utterly spent in 8th place in 3:26. The winner finished in 3:09, many runners pulled out and only eight, including Steve, ran under 3:30. It was Steve's hottest running day since Boddington in 2011.

'Extreme temperatures and marathon running are not an ideal match. Marathon running is tough enough on its own. Every step of every mile for 26.2 miles is a real effort and from mile one onwards you're wishing you'd never started because it's so uncomfortable and painful.'

But while Steve was happy with his sequence of sub-3:30s, he remained concerned by his lack of sub-3:15s. However, a week later he ran 3:14 at an Enigma event, followed by 3:13 at the Thames Meander, 3:10 at Wolverhampton and 3:11 at the Highland Perthshire Marathon in Aberfeldy, a new event for Steve. It had all started to click again.

By mid-September, he was on 599 marathons, counting down the days to Great Langdale – as was Teresa, who seemed to have a predilection for the toughest races around and had entered Langdale's half! Staying nearby with Robin of TN who wanted to film and interview Steve for TN's new website, it felt strange on race day to be lining up in the same field as Teresa, even though she was further back to avoid getting swept along with the initial flurry. She would be running one lap to Steve's two and would be waiting for him as usual at the finish.

'Langdale's toughness begins after the first mile with a 1:4 climb, occasionally increasing to 1:3, continuing for almost a mile up to the summit. There are then 24 miles still to run including several other climbs, and, on this two-lapper, a repeat of that awful first climb. Some runners don't even attempt a second lap.'

On such a course, Steve knew a sub-3:15 was unrealistic, but a sub-3:30 would be nice. On such a course too, experience counts, knowing where to take it easy and lose time, confident in the knowledge you can speed up and gain it back later. In the closing miles, a stretch where some of that lost time can be recouped, Steve raced along with the TN guys filming him passing several other runners and finishing in 3:22:26, just 52 seconds short of his course PB, and winning the MV50 prize, presented by Dr Ron Hill MBE, and, of course, setting his new world record.

But even as he crossed the line to the tannoy announcement of his latest feat, all Steve was interested in was finding out how Teresa had fared. She certainly looked happy enough. She was – but crumbs, those hills were tough! At one point on that first climb she really didn't think she'd make it, but then remembered Steve saying about making up time on the flats and downhills and not to worry how long it took to reach the top. She'd carried on and finished in 2:12.

TE were happy, Teresa had completed her toughest half yet and Steve had set a new world record for running 600 marathons in the fastest average finish time of exactly 3:18 per marathon.

But, as usual, Steve was not completely satisfied: '…it would have been nice if my average finish time could have dipped below 3:18.'

Regardless, if his current form continued, he could improve his 600 average finish time.

The more immediate question, however, was did he want to attempt the 700 marathons world record? If he did, he could also try for 600 sub-3:30s. His 500 record still stood, and so long as he was chasing 300 sub-3:15s, there was no reason why he shouldn't extend all or any of his existing records as much as possible, health and fitness permitting. The hamstring was still a concern, and remains so today, but it is just another thing Steve has learned to manage: '… it's all part and parcel of the sport of extreme multi-marathon running.'

It was obvious he was enjoying a purple patch; he should take advantage of the opportunity it offered to improve his average finish time, not only for the year, but also for his overall totals. His training was going well, he'd survived the weekly steep hill reps and interval sessions. His body only had to cope with those sessions at certain times of the year: '…they're hard work, especially when running a marathon most weeks, doing the general weekly mileage and maintaining weights and core work, which is why I don't do them all year round.'

The hard work paid off, though, as, immediately after Langdale, he ran successive times of 3:10 at Robin Hood, 3:04 at Bournemouth's inaugural marathon (his fastest since May 2011 winning him 1st MV50), and 3:09 at Abingdon.

At 50, Steve was regularly winning age group races in similar finish times to those run in his late 20s when first embarking on the 100-marathon trail. The sub-3s may have disappeared, but he was still managing the odd sub-3:05 and sub-3:10 and, somehow, consistent sub-3:15s. Nobody was more surprised than Steve at such form.

Meanwhile, back at the start of the year, no longer able to tolerate the stress of constant understaffing, Teresa had decreased her nursing days to three. Later in the year, however, she joined Kate's Home Nursing, a local charity providing one-on-one palliative nursing care for terminally ill patients in their own homes. She loved it. Forget the admin and paperwork, this was why she'd gone into nursing. At the end of a patient-sit for Kate's, Teresa would recount the experiences of her patients to Steve. Deeply moved, Steve decided he wanted to help. It wasn't hard to decide how. Brathay hadn't happened, but Kate's could. And Enigma had just the event to cater for it – a new seven marathons in seven days challenge being held in March 2014 somewhat prophetically called 'Week At The Knees'!

Steve would obtain sponsorship and every penny would go to Kate's.

As October drew to a close, Steve lined up for Enigma's 'Three Lakes Challenge' – three marathons in three days at three different lake venues in Milton Keynes. Another new event, it hadn't featured on Steve's race schedule at the start of the year, but would be good preparation for next year's 7-in-7. He was also interested to see how he would perform in a triple as a MV50.

Day 1 – Seven laps round Willen Lake – a new lake for Steve and some welcome scenic distraction. His quiet confidence for a sub-3:15 was vindicated with a 3:11:53 finish. Hopefully he wouldn't pay for it tomorrow.

Day 2 – The familiar Furzton Lake - 17 laps of sharp twists and turns: '...very wearing, especially with a tired body and legs making injury more likely.' A sub-3:15 wouldn't happen; he'd pace for sub-3:20. By halfway, he was on course and feeling good. He picked up the pace, felt strong. Sod it! He might never feel this good again or get another opportunity - he'd go for a triple sub-3:15! He finished in 3:12:35 – just 42 seconds slower than day one on a technically more difficult course. He was happy, tired and sore in equal measure. Could he really manage another sub-3:15 tomorrow?

Day 3 – Seven-and-a-bit laps of the familiar Caldecotte Lake followed Steve's usual meticulous overnight recovery routine. As anticipated, the first mile was hard with tired body, stiff legs, and a mind still half in the land of nod. Ignoring all three, Steve set off at a steady 8 mm pace and settled into his rhythm. Fairly soon he upped his pace to 7:45 mm, then 7:30. Digging deeper, he somehow found 7:20. All he had to do now was maintain it. He checked his GPS, he was well on target – but GPS' were notoriously unreliable on multi-lap courses. He put his foot down harder and pushed on: '...sheer hell!' He finished in 3:12:53, 18 seconds slower than day two and just a minute slower than day one.

All three of Steve's finish times were within one minute of each other and his total cumulative time of 9 hours 37 minutes 21 seconds equated to 7:20 mm for each one of the 78.6 miles. He was first MV50 and 2nd overall to Rik.

'I couldn't have done it without Teresa. She always makes sure I get my drinks at the right time. To be honest, most of my races I couldn't do without her.'

Not since 1992 had Steve run a triple sub-3:15: '...I was nearly 51, I really thought those days were over. It just goes to show what can be achieved.'

It was the confirmation he needed that he was still capable of running decent times at 50+ and that 300 sub-3:15s really was possible. One day, age would catch up with him, but today was not that day and he would make the most of it.

Suitably buoyed up, Steve ran another new event for him, the 'Path n Downs', at Hollingbourne – a road marathon with several steep rises. He finished in 3:06 - his second fastest time of the year, and collected another MV50 winner's trophy.

Just after his 51st birthday in November, Steve ran a new double marathon on the south-east coast, the 'Saxon Shore', now one of a series of events entitled the Saxons, Vikings and Normans ('SVN'), organised by current 100 Club chairman, Traviss Wilcox.

A strong headwind over the first half of the four-loop out-and-back course on day one saw Steve finish in 3:20, but on day two, minus headwind, he managed 3:13.

By the start of December, Steve had run another 37 marathons in an average finish time of 3:15:44. All 37 were sub-3:30, with 19 sub-3:15, bringing his total sub-3:30s to 540 and his sub-3:15s to 272. Meanwhile, his overall total had risen to 609 official marathon races run in an average finish time of 3:17:56, an 8-second improvement per marathon since 2012 – for over 600 marathons!

With just a few weeks till the end of the year and the 7-in-7 planned for March, it was time to up the training - always harder through the winter, but with Kate's charity challenge to inspire him, Steve couldn't wait to get started.

Unfortunately, life had other ideas. Two days after Saxon Shore, Steve was cycling home from work speeding downhill when a car came towards him, lights on main beam. Steve was momentarily blinded.

He crashed into the verge, lost control of the bike and flew over the handlebars, bouncing off them with his ribcage and landing awkwardly on the roadside. The driver continued, oblivious.

For a moment Steve lay in agony, unable to move, confused and dazed. He had no idea which side of the road he was on or where the verge was so he might crawl to safety from any other traffic. Fortunately, a kind lady driver stopped, went to his aid and used Steve's phone to ring Teresa. Knowing he'd never be able to lift his bike into the car, Steve convinced Teresa to let him make his own way home.

By some miracle, the bike, though scratched, scuffed and minus its front light, was still rideable – once Steve had reattached the chain and so long as he didn't change gear. However, as he mounted the bike, an agonising pain ripped across his chest making it impossible for him to breathe other than with shallow breaths. He cycled very slowly home, ate dinner, took some painkillers and went to bed, promising Teresa he'd attend the minor injuries clinic for an x-ray first thing in the morning.

A restless night followed, and next morning his chest went into spasm and he felt so dizzy he nearly passed out.

An x-ray showed unbroken but severely damaged and bruised ribs. He was sent home with strong painkillers and strict instructions to rest and do breathing exercises. There was nothing else they could do – it was just a matter of time. Time! He didn't have time! He had 7 marathons in 7 days to run in three months time, he couldn't be sitting around waiting for his ribs to heal!

But he had no choice. The only exercise he could comfortably manage was a slow walk. To add insult to injury, the prescribed painkillers caused constipation resulting in severe stomach cramps. As he shuffled down the road with his wife to buy laxatives and alternative painkillers from the chemist, he knew nobody would believe that only days earlier he'd run a double marathon in 6.33: '...I felt like a wounded old man.' There was one positive side effect to walking slowly, though - when passing the accident site, he found his missing front light!

It was a week before Steve felt able to attempt running again, though body-strength, core and weight training remained firmly on hold. The run was a very slow 6 miles at 9 mm pace; all he could manage with very controlled breathing, the resultant chest pain just about bearable. Not so bearable, was the additional pain caused by the oversized wing mirror of a passing camper van that whacked him right on the back of his damaged ribs near the end of his run.

More rest followed, although he continued walking and doing breathing exercises. Five days later, he managed a 5-mile run at 8 mm pace, though it still hurt to breathe deeply. It wasn't just his ribs that had taken a bashing, his confidence had also been affected. So much so, that he took the unprecedented step of consulting Lucy purely for reassurance that he wasn't causing further damage by running again. Lucy reassured him he wasn't and, by the last week of 2013, Steve managed a 50-mile week and restarted weights, strength and core work.

However, he would never cycle to or from work again in the dark - no matter how bright the stars might shine.

Chapter 38

2014 – BEING HUMAN

Moving into 2014, apart from some mild discomfort when breathing deeply, Steve's ribs were much improved, which was fortunate as the first weekend he was running Enigma's Winter Double as part of his preparation for the 7-in-7 – his priority goal for the early part of the year. His other priority, was to run as many sub-3:15s as possible to get closer to the 300, although with 28 outstanding, it was unlikely to happen this year. The other important goal was to run all marathons under 3:30. He needed another 60 for the 600 - also unlikely this year!

But first, he must plan his training schedule for the 7-in-7. Like the 10-in-10, it would involve some twice-daily weekday runs, running for 7-10 days without a break, plus a handful of marathons, including a couple of doubles. However, at 51, and mindful of his other goals, it wouldn't be sensible to take it up to 100 miles a week; 80 should be adequate for peaking, with 70-80 miles being maintained throughout February. Time was of the essence. He'd ended 2013 on a 50-mile week; he needed to up the miles in January, while sticking to the 'no more than 10 per cent a week' rule.

Meantime, his fundraising got off to a great start with his employers donating £250. Steve then designed a poster and cards advertising his challenge for Kate's, placing them on every notice board and desktop at his work place – some 400 of them! He also set up a Just Giving page and placed a collection tin in the staff canteen for loose change. It was a lot of effort, but donations soon flooded in.

All that was left was to train and deliver a successful 7-in-7. During his heaviest mileage period, he added his second daily run three times a week, covering the 8 miles to and from work or arriving early for a run before starting his day followed by his normal lunchtime run.

His first event, Enigma's Winter Double, had to be moved from the 7-lap Caldecotte Lake course to the 17-lap Furzton Lake course due to severe flooding. The geese populating the lakes had also moved. Steve approached a whole gaggle waddling across the footpath in front of him, forcing him to change direction to avoid them. Unfortunately, a maverick waddled in the opposite direction, straight into Steve's altered path. The goose froze and Steve tumbled head-over-heels over him, smashing his GPS, grazing his limbs and jarring his still-tender ribs.

Gingerly, he got to his feet; already he was stiffening up and the pain in his ribs was torturous. He'd been on for a sub-3:15, now he'd be lucky to get a sub-3:20. Despite an extremely uncomfortable last 6 miles, he finished in 3:17.

Next day, with still-painful ribs and an overnight frost rendering parts of the course treacherous, Steve didn't dare run. Another fall and further damage were too risky. Later, back home, he managed a 5-mile training run, but breathing was painful. Not running the second marathon, he couldn't afford to miss any more training miles if he was to do himself justice at the 7-in-7, so over the next few days he stuck to his mileage plan, but ran only steadily.

The ribs eventually settled, but Steve was now incredibly nervous about any more accidents that might befall him. In the last two months, he'd fallen off his bike, been hit by a moving vehicle and tripped over a goose! Yesteryear's accident-prone kid had returned!

Eleven days after the goose incident, Steve returned to Milton Keynes for a midweek Enigma race around Willen Lake. Once more, flooding caused the race to be moved to Furzton Lake and another 17 laps of the twisting, goose-infested course. This time, though, there were no mishaps and Steve finished in 3:19.

Three days later, Steve ran the Viking Coastal; a SVN race in Birchington, finishing in 3:12, his first sub-3:15 of the year.

The following weekend, TE swapped England's chill for Gran Canaria's warmth, enjoying a week's holiday and another new race for Steve. He finished the two-lapper in a pleasing 3:07, and spent the rest of the week training on nearby undulating trail paths.

By the end of the month, Steve had run four marathons. He hadn't run that many in January since 1992 for the most in a year record, but then most had been overseas. Now, in 2014, he could have run even more, and all in the UK.

In February, training mileage was upped again, alongside another four marathons, including SVN's Martello Marathons in Folkstone; a new double for Steve. Confident of a decent run on both days, he hadn't accounted for battling against raging 60mph coastal winds on the 4 x 10.5k out-and-back course. Slowing to 9 mm with the wind against him, and bowling along at a crazy 6½ mm when it was behind, proved exhausting. He slowed with every mile, eventually finishing in 3:33; the first time he'd failed to break 3:30 since 2010. It ended an unbroken run of 101 sub-3:30s in the previous 159 weeks – one every 11 days! Gutted that it should end in circumstances beyond his control, Steve returned to his hotel room tired, frustrated and downhearted.

Next day, he awoke to a world of sunshine and calm; a perfect, windless, running day. Determined to salvage something, he finished in 3:14. Race-wise, a weekend of mixed fortunes, but great preparation for the 7-in-7.

In total, Steve ran 80 miles that week and was beginning to peak. One more week like that, then he'd start to taper. His last race before the 7-in-7, the tough Heartbreaker Trail Marathon at the end of February, was completed in a new personal course record of 3:23.

In the lead up to the 7-in-7, Steve ran nearly 900 miles in 12 weeks whilst maintaining core, body strength and weight training. He also cycled to and from work several times a week once it was light enough. Drained, he remembered why he'd previously decided against doing any more multi-day events - the training was so demanding; there were days when he'd almost fall asleep at his desk. It was a huge relief to taper and do a few short runs that last week, letting his body recover before the main event.

Booking a hotel for alternate nights and for Friday and Saturday, Steve arranged massages with Richard for the nights he'd be home, in addition to his usual daily ice baths, as part of his recovery routine. As with the 10-in-10, he had a daily plan of everything he needed to do and when.

And, as always, Steve set himself goals: 1) run all seven the whole way; 2) run all seven in sub-3:30 average finish time; and 3) run each one sub-3:30. His fourth secret goal was to win the event outright, although aged 51 he was the oldest of the 20 competitors attempting all seven marathons.

The first two days were at Willen Lake. Steve finished 1st of 29 runners on day one, in 3:18:37. He'd run faster than intended, but felt good. Recovery went well, and although his legs were a little tired on day two and he was chased all the way by 100 Clubber, young Jeremy Isaac, he finished 1st again in 3:18:55.

At the end of day two, Steve led Jeremy by 8 minutes and had nearly 40 minutes over Rik Vercoe in 3rd, who'd recently broken the British record for most marathons in a year and taken Adam Holland's world record for the fastest 10-in-10. With Brit, Sally Ford, holding the women's 10-in-10 world record, it was good to know that GB was home to some of the best multi-marathon runners on the planet.

In such prestigious company, Steve set out on day three around the more familiar Caldecotte Lake. Overnight, he'd nursed a couple of niggles: '...it's almost impossible to avoid them during these events, especially when trying to run competitively every day and you're not so young anymore!'

After a steady start, Steve surprised himself at being able to pick up the pace to finish 2nd in 3:18:51, beaten by 100 Clubber, Matthew Tonks, who was running two of the seven races. Steve's third consecutive 3:18 extended his lead to over 12 minutes and earned him and Teresa lunch courtesy of Robert Barnett, head trustee of Kate's who, with his wife, had come to show their support.

Day four was Steve's least favourite 17-lap Furzton Lake, running into a strong headwind 17 times on tired legs. Battling every step to ensure a sub-3:30, Steve was relieved to finish 1st in 3:24:37, albeit on his knees. Later, after posting his daily report on social media and Just Giving, donations poured in as word spread about his latest charity challenge.

It was also on day four, following his massage with Richard, that Steve slipped on a wet road and, putting out his hand to break the fall, sprained his wrist – he was just grateful that this was one accident that wouldn't affect his running!

Back at Furzton Lake for day 5 and another 17 laps into the still-strong headwind trying to make up lost time when the wind was behind him, Steve finished in 3:25:16, relieved but exhausted, collapsing in a heap over the line.

By the end of day 5, Steve's average time was 3:21:05 - not bad for the conditions, but without the wind he was confident it would have been sub-3:20. Damn wind! Even so, it equated to 131 miles run at 7 minute 40 second pace and increased his lead to over 30 minutes from Jeremy.

Saturday, day 6 – Very tired after his two previous wind-swept races, Steve was nonetheless happy to be facing his favoured Caldecotte Lake and happier still when BRR's Neil and Pauline Teague arrived to support him. As Neil hadn't trained that day, he ran the final three laps with Steve: '...it was good having someone to talk to and distract me from the pain!'

However, about 200 metres from the finish, exhausted and suffering a momentary lapse of concentration, Steve caught his foot on the base of a bench at the edge of the footpath and went flying, smacking his calf on the bench arm. For several seconds he lay stunned and unspeaking as Neil tried to ascertain if he was okay. The clock was ticking, he had to be okay; up he got and jogged to the finish in 3:24:35. Then nurses Teresa and Pauline were on him, checking the damage - a large, painful haematoma already forming on his leg from the impact. Ice was applied to help reduce the swelling. There were other cuts and bruises and another smashed GPS, but it was the calf that worried Steve.

Back at his hotel room, he continued using ice packs and took Paracetamol, hoping the swelling would subside enough for him to get through tomorrow's race. Thank God he had a 45-minute lead as a cushion. Barring (further) disasters and provided he finished in sub-4, he could still win overall.

The following day his calf was sore and stiff, but not as bad as he'd imagined. He could at least walk to the bathroom and, hopefully, once the race started and it loosened up, he'd be able to run. After a slow first lap and despite being unable to run fluidly it did improve, as did his spirits with the arrival of BRR's Susan Hunt and Andy Chapple: '...it's amazing how much of a lift such unexpected support gives you.'

It certainly worked for Steve who, despite everything, finished in 3:24:44 - his seventh consecutive sub-3:30 in seven days, raising £5500 for Kate's. He'd achieved all his pre-race goals, running every step of the way and even winning the event overall in what is still an event record of 23:34:35, with an average finish time per marathon of 3:22:13 - or 183 miles at an average of 7 minutes 43 seconds per mile! It was also a MV50 world best for a 7-in-7.

The day after the 7-in-7, Steve returned to work bruised, battered and sore and voluntarily took four days off running before easing himself back in with a gentle 3-miler. By the weekend, he was back running normal training speed for 5-6 miles.

It was now time for him to catch up on some springtime gardening chores, and happily he took up the shears. Later, less happily, he developed a painful elbow, which he put down to a pulled tendon or a touch of tennis elbow. He thought no more about it, assuming it would disappear in a few days.

At the start of April, he ran the Brighton Marathon in 3:11, followed a week later by London in 3:09, then an Enigma event on Good Friday in 3:14 – all adding to his 300 sub-3:15 and 600 sub-3:30 goals. Meantime, Teresa ran the Enigma half. Although she hadn't specifically trained for the race, she finished 3rd lady in 2:05 - her first podium performance equalling Steve's own finish position that day – and promptly announced her retirement from racing, feeling she had nothing more to prove. A 2:05 for 13.1 miles aged nearly 52, and 1st FV50, would do for the woman who'd said she'd never be a runner.

As April drew to a close, the pain in Steve's elbow worsened, affecting everyday life. As it was his right arm and good hand, he couldn't even transfer those things he found difficult to his other hand, so he consulted his GP and saw a physio. Only then did he recall injuring his wrist in March - it still gave him occasional gyp and was painful if pressed. And only then did it occur to him to connect the two incidents. The physio ordered weekly massage and ultrasound for wrist and elbow.

During May, Steve received an invitation to run as the official sub-3:15 pacer in the Milton Keynes Town Marathon. Delighted to have a chance to help others achieve their goals, Steve took the group to around 20 miles in exactly 3:15 pace before all but two dropped off. Steve finished in 3:14. A fortnight later, he ran Windermere, also in 3:14, and, a week after that, the Stone Marathon in Staffordshire. Known in the 1980s and '90s as the Masters Marathon, being open only to vets, the reintroduced race also accepts seniors and is described by Steve as: '...a good, old-fashioned, single 26.2-mile lap, on quiet, undulating, country roads, with water every three miles.' Steve ran another 3:14 for a sixth consecutive sub-3:15.

Meanwhile, with wrist and elbow remaining painful, Steve saw a consultant, who ordered an x-ray and MRI scan. The x-ray revealed a small fracture in Steve's wrist and a small piece of bone that had broken away. The consultant was happy the fracture would heal by itself in time and the loose bone would just sit there. The MRI scan revealed an inflamed tendon between elbow and wrist. Again, it was just a matter of time, continuing massage, ultrasound, and painkillers if required. Fine by Steve, so long as his running wasn't affected!

At the start of June, Steve was invited to be guest of honour at the Dartmoor Discovery 32-mile ultra marathon by 100 Clubber, Roger Hayes, chairman of Teignbridge Trotters, the race organisers. In return for complimentary race entry, Steve would present the prizes. However, a week before the event, the intermittent pain in his left ankle returned. After a few days rest, he went for a test run and although okay, he reckoned a tough, 32-mile ultra would exacerbate it and decided not to run. Not wanting to let anyone down, though, TE drove to Dartmoor anyway and Steve carried out his 'goh' duties.

The following week his foot caused no difficulties at Littledown's Trail Marathon run in 3:19, nor did it trouble him in his next two marathons, both run in 3:11.

By the end of June, Steve had run 24 marathons, 11 sub-3:15. It was a long time since he'd run so many marathons in the first half of a year. Maybe he could make 50 by the end of it? And maybe, with 'only' 17 sub-3:15s needed for the British 300 record, that too was possible?

July enjoyed a mini-heatwave and at Enigma's Summer Double, Steve finished both races in exactly 3:19:17. Two weeks later, came the 'The Wild One' in Worcester; a new, tough, 12-lap grass and trail marathon in memory of the late Stuart Wild of Black Pear Joggers, which measured half a mile too long and saw Steve finish utterly spent in 3:28. Four days later, he was running again at Enigma's aptly named 'Night Fever' Marathon; a mid-week race round Caldecotte Lake. Despite being an evening race, it was an intense 31 degrees at the start. Anticipating another difficult run, Steve was relieved to finish 1st in 3:27.

Four races in three weeks in a steaming July, with one more still to come. Namely, The Summer Reservoir Marathon in Northampton, organised by 100 Club couple Dave and Linda Major; world record holders for completing the most marathons as husband and wife. If the last two marathons had been difficult, this was worse. From start to finish, Steve could hardly breathe. His lungs were bursting - it was absolute torture. Common sense suggested pulling out, but a DNF was out of the question, no matter how uncomfortable he felt. Again it was hot, but Steve didn't really feel that justified the extent of his difficulties. He finished in 3:29, almost collapsing as he crossed the line trying to catch his breath.

The following week he took a pre-planned five-day break, not training again until the following weekend, and considered his breathing issues. Were they due to running so many successive marathons in the heat? Or was it a combination of the heat and the thalassemia? Or perhaps his low HB blood count had dropped even lower? He would see the doc; have some blood tests.

The blood tests revealed nothing other than his normally low HB count was slightly lower, possibly because he'd stopped taking the desiccated liver supplements thinking he no longer needed them, at the same time decreasing the amount of red meat he ate. He'd start taking the supplements again immediately.

However, his GP was more concerned that Steve's heart may be enlarged and scarred as a result of the marathon running, something that can affect endurance athletes, and referred him to a cardiovascular consultant. Steve was duly monitored whilst running on a treadmill, given a CT scan and an echocardiogram (ECG).

Waiting for the results and still coping with the painful tendon in his arm, Steve's spirits spiralled downwards as he watched his target of 300 sub-3:15s and 600 sub-3:30s fade into an unforeseeable future. It was a huge relief then when the tests came back negative. However, the question about his breathlessness remained unanswered. Ultimately, both he and his GP agreed that it may simply be due to living and running in a rural farming environment during the height of a warm summer while the pollen count was high. Certainly, his difficulties lessened once the temperature cooled.

In mid-August, he ran the Worthing Track Marathon (on grass); his first race in three weeks. Taking it steady in deference to his recent lack of quality training, he was reasonably satisfied to finish the 106 laps in

3:25. The following weekend, better quality training having resumed, he ran 3:14 at the Thames Meander Marathon run by 100 Club couple, Dave and Mel Ross's company, Hermes Running. 'I'd planned a steady run, but felt surprisingly strong. It was a relief to get a sub-3:15 again, though it was hard work!'

Steve followed this with 3:20 and 3:21 at next weekend's Enigma double, finally dispelling any doubts about reaching his targets.

By the start of September, he felt ready to bring steep hill reps back into his training repertoire in preparation for Snowdon. Not having done any since April, it was quite a shock to the system. He then ran his 15th Wolverhampton Marathon in 3:17. Consistency was slowly, but surely, returning.

The following weekend, TE flew to Malmo to stay with Mannatech friend, Tomas Forsberg. Tomas had invited Steve to join him at the inaugural Helsingborg Marathon. The race started well with Steve aiming for a 3:15, but the undulating course combined with still not feeling 100 per cent fit, slowed him to 3:19, his 399th sub-3:20. After running 26.2 miles, Steve spent the evening line dancing!

A week later, Steve ran Hereford's new marathon, a replacement for the defunct 1980s and '90s race, and a 'Festival of Sport' initiative. A challenging course, Steve finished in 3:17, becoming the first European to run 400 sub-3:20s in official marathon distance races – an unanticipated but rewarding milestone.

As the heat of summer made way for autumn's cooler days, so Steve's breathing significantly improved, as did the quality of his training. For the first time since before the 7-in-7 in March, his body, including his arm, was almost completely pain-free. The impact was immediate as Steve ran 3:14 at the Robin Hood Marathon and 3:10 at Bournemouth within a fortnight.

Steve's next challenge to overcome was a cold, his first in years, but luckily, without a marathon that weekend, he could afford an easier training week until the cold subsided. A week later he ran Abingdon in 3:14.

The following day, BRR held their AGM. Steve had joined the committee in 2009, become vice-chairman in 2013 and spent much of 2014 acting as chairman; a position he was now officially voted into. Despite now being used to public speaking, Steve still had to fight the usual nerves to make his acceptance speech and chair the meeting: '...I don't think I'll ever find that sort of thing easy.'

A few days later, BRR travelled to Snowdon for a mini club trip. Steve finished in 3:23, his fourth fastest Snowdon.

Three days after Snowdon came the Enigma Three Lakes Challenge, with Steve running days one and two in 3:17 and 3:24 respectively, but foregoing day three due to Teresa developing a nasty cold: '...it would have been unfair for her to hang around in the cold while I ran, so we went home and stayed in the warm instead!'

By the second weekend of November, TE were back at Milton Keynes for Enigma's Fireworks Double, which Steve ran in 3:18 and 3:22 respectively, followed a week later by the Raceways Shakespeare Autumn Marathon at Long Marston – a new, local event for Steve, which he finished in 3:11.

The following weekend, yet another new race for Steve – the Phoenix Riverside at Walton-on-Thames, organised by Rik Vercoe. With rain falling in Biblical proportions, parts of the course became so waterlogged that runners were forced to wade ankle-deep through the chilling water. Steve's left ankle complained painfully and, by halfway, he also started suffering from extreme stomach cramps, forcing him to make a pit stop. Freezing cold, with sodden feet and legs, he never got properly going again, and wished he'd worn a waterproof jacket. He was horribly reminded of the New Forest race, but this time he was becoming hypothermic despite wearing a long-sleeved base layer. The atrocious conditions saw many runners pull out while Steve completed the four-loop course in what he considered a pathetic 3:41. However, when he posted his performance on social media and people said they'd kill for such a time, he felt considerably better: '...people were so kind and their comments really helped me gain perspective.'

And then he did something totally unexpected. He ran a 5k Park Run: '...they'd become so popular I wanted to see what all the fuss was about!' He did it at Kingsbury Water Park with friend, Jim Maine, bumping into 100 Clubber, John Dawson, 2007 10-in-10 pioneer and oldest man in the world to complete that event in 2011, aged 73.

Steve ran five more marathons that year, including Enigma's Christmas Double, in 3:14 and 3:21 - his fastest double of the year - winning him the men's event, while BRR's Claire Harrison won the ladies event in her first ever double.

Steve's second day race was also his 500th sub-3:25, though he was unaware of it at the time. Perhaps he could run 500 sub-3:20s? It would be some way off and may not be achievable given his age. And, of course, first he must run 300 sub-3:15s, 600 sub-3:30s and 700 marathons in total, but it was an interesting thought.

Among those last five marathons of 2014, a few days after Christmas Day was another Phoenix Riverside event. Teresa was working and unable to accompany him, but Steve was desperate to bury the demons from his 'awful' performance a month earlier, so went alone. The demons didn't stand a chance as he finished in 3:16. And, although he thought he never took Teresa's support at races for granted, he couldn't believe just how much he'd missed her.

By the end of the year, Steve had run 51 marathons in 50 weeks, his busiest running year since 1992. He hadn't planned to run so many, but how could he resist when new races were popping up at the rate of molehills on an untended golf course? The downside to this for someone like Steve, who is as interested in quality as quantity, is that he must continue training hard in between races to maintain his performance level. That grows harder with age, as does the motivation to train regularly; always trying to strike the right balance between achieving peak fitness and avoiding injury. With so many races, the difficulties increase.

Steve's average finish time for 51 marathons in 2014 was 3:19:10, including the 7-in-7 and six doubles. Of those 51, 49 were sub-3:30, 17 were sub-3:15, bringing an overall total of 660 marathons with 589 sub-3:30s and 289 sub-3:15s. His overall average finish time had slipped slightly to 3:18:01. If he wanted to get back below 3:18, he'd have to keep working hard through 2015.

Running-wise, it had been a busy and satisfying year. But for ordinary man, Steve, everyday life also had to be coped with. In 2014, that included spending more time back in Coventry with Teresa whose elderly mother had suffered health problems requiring assistance at home, and, also spending more time with his own ageing parents: '...I feel extremely guilty that Teresa and I neglect our families sometimes because of the running. Teresa always wants to come with me and support me for which I'm very grateful, but it does mean we can't always find time to visit family. I don't see my grandchildren as often as I'd like and I really hope I don't come to regret any of this in later life.'

And Steve, just like the rest of us as the elders in our own families begin to show their frailty, has started to realise that he too is mortal and worries about his own old age.

'It's hard to imagine not being very mobile when at the moment I'm able to churn out a half-decent marathon every week. I'm sure I'll look back and wonder how on earth I was able to do it. Even today, Teresa and I have slowed down in our daily lives. Certain chores seem to take longer and things take longer to organise. And, on those rare occasions we're at home on a weekend, after a training run and a few household chores in the morning, we find ourselves on the couch in the afternoon, feet up, watching TV and dozing!'

The machine is human after all.

Chapter 39

2015 – SHINE ON

2015 was set to be a big year for Steve in terms of attaining targets. He needed just 11 more marathons to achieve 600 sub-3:30s, the same number to achieve 300 sub-3:15s, and another 40 to produce a new world record of 700 marathons run in the fastest average finish time - hopefully under 3:18.

He knew he had to do what he could while he could, for age was catching up with him and, realistically, it was only a matter of time before he might find himself inadvertently running his last race: '...you're only ever one training run or race away from injury and if that happens you never know if it's going to be the end.'

If the worst happened, he'd want to know he'd fulfilled his early promise of running each race to the best of his ability so he would never look back with regrets. That wouldn't change, even if he did feel a lot more tired the day after a marathon than he used to. Especially on a Monday following a Sunday race when he'd struggle to get out of bed and feel below par all day at work. Regardless, he'd continue running approximately six miles at lunchtime or cycling to work, sometimes both: '...it's a good way to loosen the legs and keeps my body used to the workload for doubles.

Maybe once I stop doing doubles, I'll treat myself to a day off after a race.'

Steve had, in fact, already decided that 2015 would be his last year for doubles and multi-day events, conscious that if he wanted to give himself the best chance of running into old age, such events increased risk of injury or physical breakdown: '...I'd never say never, but I won't be chasing after them.'

It was somewhat ironic then, that his first two events of 2015 were doubles! The first was Enigma's Winter Double. After a first day run of 3:18, and following a severe overnight frost leaving lengthy stretches of treacherous ice around the course, sage Steve withdrew from the second day, as he had in 2014, loathe to risk a fall that might compromise him achieving that year's targets.

The following weekend was the Martello Double at Folkstone, where on last year's day one, Steve's sub-3:30 sequence had ended. Once more, the course suffered a strong headwind on the out section, giving Steve a finish time of 3:31. This time, though, he didn't beat himself up about it, just put it behind him and moved on. At least it would count towards his 700 total.

It was another lesson running had taught him – when things happened outside your control, you just had to suck it up! Just as he had to accept that younger runners who he used to beat were now beating him. It was hard to swallow, but a fact of life in the world of sport. It made him appreciate what it must have felt like for the older runners when he'd been younger: '... loss of speed, finding it harder in training to maintain fitness levels – it comes to us all!'

On day two, still tired from day one, but at least with the wind having now dropped to a stiff breeze, Steve was relatively pleased to finish in 3:23.

By the end of January, Steve had run four marathons. Three were sub-3:30, but none were sub-3:15. February, however, was a different story with two sub-3:15s, followed by 3:10 in March at a new road marathon in Wrexham.

After celebrating his father's 80th birthday, Steve ran two more doubles within a week as part of Enigma's 'Week At The Knees' event. Originally contemplating running all seven marathons in seven days to defend his 2014 title, Steve ultimately decided against it. The four he did run, though, were all sub-3:30, bringing his total sub-3:30s to 599.

Steve's anticipated 600th sub-3:30 was run at the Port of Dover Marathon at the end of March. Another double event, Steve had elected to run only Sunday's race. It was a good decision given the atrocious wet and windy weather conditions on both days. One of those was plenty for 52-year old Steve. Even so, if he wanted his 600th on such a day, he would have to fight every inch of the way. On the start line, he glanced across at Teresa who was trying her best to keep her hat on and her brolly from blowing inside-out: '...I knew she was feeling sorry for me, and I was feeling sorry for her.'

The 12-lap course involved running out and back along Dover Pier and it was here, where the pier stretched out into the crashing waves, that the wind was at its worst: '...you had to work hard just to stay upright, never mind run.'

Steve reached halfway in 1:42, exhausted from working so hard, knowing he couldn't maintain that pace. As the race progressed, his time slipped. Every time Teresa handed him a drink, she'd ask if he was still on for 3:30. Each time he had to say he didn't know. It wasn't just the weather that troubled him; Saturday's runners had told him that the course measured slightly long. Consequently, it wasn't until he reached the final 800 metres that he knew he could do it, with the support of the other runners that is: '...it felt like they were willing me on, even though they must have been knackered themselves.'

If Steve hadn't announced his hopes for his 600th sub-3:30 before the race, raising expectations, he might not have made it. As it was, he couldn't bear the idea of failing. Sprinting the final 400 metres, he finished 2nd in 3:28:55; one of only two finishers under 3:30.

Changing afterwards in the dry warmth of the car, Steve was wet, cold and utterly spent, but inside he glowed with satisfaction. Nobody else in the world had run 500 sub-3:30s, and now he'd raised the bar to 600! That night, his stats showed he'd improved his average finish time for 600 marathons (now his fastest 600), to 3:15:35 and his average finish time for 500 marathons to 3:12:52. He could scarcely believe the stats and wondered what Sy Mah would have made of it had he still been alive. Hopefully, he was up there looking down, knowing he'd been Steve's inspiration.

Of course, Steve still had his other two targets to achieve before the year was out, starting with 300 sub-3:15s - he needed 8 more. Now into April, one of the busiest months for big city road marathons, Steve had entered them all. First, though, he ran Enigma's Good Friday Marathon in 3:13. Then it was Brighton in 3:11, followed by a new Manchester Marathon in 3:06, his fastest time since November 2013, and, finally, London. With legs still heavy from Manchester, Steve finished his 20th London, now his most raced annual event, in 3:12. That made four sub-3:15s in 23 days and just four more to go. Maybe he'd make it before the end of May?

He began his assault at the Milton Keynes town marathon, running again as official pacer for the sub-3:15 group on the May Day bank holiday. Steve finished in just over 3:14. Six days later, on a warm day at Halstead on a course he hadn't run for some years causing him to forget how undulating it was, he again finished sub-3:15 with just 27 seconds to spare.

Next came Windermere. Would this be his 299th sub-3:15? In truth, he was feeling weary from his recent exertions and his left ankle was giving him gyp again. On Windermere's demanding course it felt like hard work all the way for a finish time of 3:17, keeping him on 298.

If he was to make 300 sub-3:15s before the end of May, he'd have to run the remaining two on both days of a double - not ideal. Day one was a new SVN event for Steve; the Cakeathon at Fowlmead Country Park near Deal, an undulating 8-lap trail course incorporated within a six-hour event. Cake, as well as drink, was available at the aid station, but Steve declined his first slice saying he'd have all eight slices when he finished! As the race progressed, Steve was 2nd, chasing the leader. Heading into the final lap he took the lead, pushed hard in the final two miles and won in 3:14. 299 down, one to go!

Unfortunately, though, the combination of those final two miles and the uneven course played havoc with his ankle. On the plus side, the medal, featuring a loaded cake stand, was the biggest in his collection to date!

Next day, back at SVN's Summer Martello Marathon at Folkestone run on the same pancake flat course as the Winter Martello race, the combination of a stiff breeze, a sore ankle and general weariness resulted in a disappointing 3:24. It was another sub-3:30, but his 300th sub-3:15 would now have to wait until June – assuming his ankle was better by then.

With two weeks before his next race, Steve consulted his GP, was referred to an orthopaedic consultant and, while awaiting his appointment, relaxed his training and applied ice to his ankle daily.

Now the first weekend in June, TE travelled to SVN's Summer Viking Coastal Marathon at Birchington; a four-loop, out-and-back course. Despite his ankle, Steve was quietly fired up, determined this would be the day. Sunny with a light breeze, the warmth of the day didn't faze him; his TN drinks would take care of his hydration. Setting out at 7:15 mm pace, all was good until his ankle suddenly gave way at halfway. He limped a few painful strides and slowed down a little. At the drinks station he poured cold water down the front of his sock to help soothe the pain. Setting off again, he gradually picked up speed. Once more, he felt good, but would his ankle hold out? After 20 miles, he was in 2nd, chasing the leader. Everyone running back towards him on the looped course urged him on, assuring him the leader was slowing. With his ankle seemingly settled, and knowing this could be his 50th marathon win, Steve sped up and started closing the gap. Sadly, though, the miles ran out and, this time, he had to settle for 2nd. No matter - his time of 3:10 saw him become the first Brit to run 300 sub-3:15 official marathon races. His first had been at Sandwell in 1986 in 3:09. Today, 29 years on, he'd run his 300th just one minute slower. That would do for him.

Just one more target remained for 2015: the world record for running 700 marathons in the fastest average finish time. With 16 to go, Steve checked his race schedule to see when this might happen – October 4th at Bournemouth looked likely. Between now and then, he had a marathon booked virtually every weekend. He couldn't afford any slips ups. He duly announced his intention and prayed his ankle and everything else would be okay.

A week after the Viking Coastal, he ran the new Yeovil Marathon in 3:12, and a week later, another Enigma Marathon at Caldecotte Lake in 3:14. He was on his way, albeit his ankle continued giving spasmodic pain, slowing him down till it eased.

Steve's 50th marathon win eventually came at Coombe Abbey Trail Marathon. Fittingly, his father bore witness to his son's victory at their favourite family park. On the undulating, 12-lap, grass course, Steve moved from 4th to 1st by the start of the final lap and held on to win, despite his throbbing ankle.

July saw the welcome return of the popular Potteries Marathon. Disbanded in 2004, Steve had previously run it 18 times, first in 1986. It was just like old times, with numerous 100 Clubbers re-living the early years. Following much of the original course, it was as tough as Steve remembered. The main difference was the start and finish, which had moved from Trentham Gardens to Stoke City's Britannia Stadium. Unusually, the normally fastidious Steve failed to check the finish prior to the race, so hadn't allowed for the final climb, costing him another sub-3:15 by a mere six seconds. Sadly too, there was no Potteries plate to take home, just a coaster!

2015 - Shine On

As July warmed up, Steve's breathing issues made an unwelcome return, so it felt as though he was working much harder than usual in racing and training. Struggling round the undulating, grassy course at the Wild One Trail Marathon, which had changed from last year's 10-lap course to a different, 20-lap course due to travellers moving in, Steve finished 2nd, just missing a sub-3:30 by 36 seconds.

Steve tried not to worry about his breathing, reminding himself it was simply due to summer's poorer air quality, and would pass. Instead, he turned his mind to getting his overall average finish time for 700 back to sub-3:18.

His first race in August was another new event for Steve, known as the 'Bad Cow', organised by White Star Running, who hold a series of trail marathons in southern England. An undulating, 8-lap course at Holton Lee Country Park near Poole, complete with live cows, it was hard going. Thankfully, his ankle held out, despite the rough terrain. He finished 2nd in 3:23, winning a framed picture of a cow, which now hangs proudly in the cloakroom and is known as, 'the moo in the loo'!

Later that month, Steve ran the Summer Phoenix Marathon at Walton-on-Thames in just under 3:15.

Steve was now racing every weekend to ensure Bournemouth would be number 700. Meanwhile, he saw the orthopaedic consultant. Examination and x-rays indicated bony spurs on the bridge of his foot rubbing on soft tissue, causing inflammation, resulting in pain and discomfort - just as in 2012. Comparing the 2012 and 2015 x-rays indicated no worsening of the problem, but the consultant offered Steve surgery anyway as a day case. However, Steve wouldn't be able to run for a fortnight and would then have to ease himself back in gradually. Surgery for Steve would only ever be a last resort and, with his 700th looming, was a non-starter. Fortunately, the consultant agreed to a six-month open appointment allowing Steve to request the surgery at a later date if he so wished. Meantime, he would try and manage the problem as previously and hope it would settle down.

He then ran his final August marathon, Enigma's 'Shaken Not Stirred' - a Bond-themed race at Caldecotte Lake, in 3:20, adding a particularly nice medal to his collection depicting all things 007, before launching into September's race schedule, with just five marathons required for his 700th.

Steve's first race in September was his 15th Wolverhampton Marathon. Feeling stronger than recently, with his ankle less painful and breathing restored to normal, he finished in 3:16. A week later came Hull, by invitation. Feeling confident and strong, Steve finished in 3:10:09 - his second fastest time of the year, and with only the occasional bout of ankle pain.

Marathon number 698 – Hereford, a week after Hull. An undulating, rural road race reintroduced the previous year. Steve finished in 3:12, placing

7th overall and 1st MV50, a big improvement on last year's performance. His consistent form seemed to be returning, and his ankle felt fine.

Number 699 followed a week later at Barnstaple - another new race introduced last year and a first for Steve. A flat, fast course it was, however, exposed to a strong breeze blowing down River Taw's estuary, slowing Steve in the final few miles to such an extent that the 3:10 he'd been on for at halfway, became a missed sub-3:15 by a frustrating 17 seconds. He should have pushed harder! Teresa reminded him he was only one marathon away from another record and shouldn't be so hard on himself.

Steve's stats now showed his average finish time for 699 marathons as 3:17:56. Assuming he ran sub-3:30 at Bournemouth, that would be his average finish time for the 700 record. It was the sub-3:18 average he'd worked so hard for. Hopefully, he'd run faster future marathons, reducing that average time further. Indeed, after some speedy analyses, he calculated that if he ran 700 sub-3:30s (he was on 622), he could potentially reduce his 700 marathon average finish time to 3:15, just as he had with 600.

But that was for the future. Now, on the eve of his next world record, Steve was just relieved his ankle had settled down and the forecast was reasonable for next day's race. Ideally, England would have won that night's game against Australia in the Rugby World Cup too, but you can't have everything!

Sunday, 4th October, 2015, Bournemouth. A dry, slightly breezy day - initially overcast, due to brighten later. A pre-race announcement about Steve's world record attempt set the crowds and media buzzing, while the man himself fought to remain calm and focussed. It was a relief to start running. Having agreed to pace BRR's Mike Hobbs, Steve set off at 7:20-7:25 mm for a 3:13-3:15 finish. Unfortunately, Mike allowed himself to be carried along with BRR's Tim Hemming instead, who was running at a faster pace, with inevitable consequences.

'Concentration and focus on the race plan is paramount. Looking and planning ahead, watching for obstacles, drinks stations, hazards (geese), keeping an eye on your pace, staying relaxed, especially your upper body, making sure you follow the racing line – all these things you have to be aware of while you're racing. With experience, you can learn to switch off a little while, remaining focussed. That's why running races, especially long races like marathons, can be mentally demanding as well as physically; they are important things to remember. Crucial in fact, if you want to achieve the best you possibly can.'

Meanwhile, Steve switched his focus from pacing Mike to keeping Tim in sight, hoping to chase him down in the closing stages, determined to achieve another sub-3:15. It wouldn't necessarily improve his average finish time for 700. He just didn't want to feel the way he had at Barnstaple.

Turning back along the beach promenade at 23 miles, the strengthening sea breeze blew diagonally across Steve's path. This was where he usually picked up his pace and where he'd planned to catch Tim. Today, though, and despite on-course support from 100 Clubber, Pam Storey, and BRR's Darren Long, Doug Reeve, Claire Harrison, and Dennis, the wind thwarted him.

He crossed the line to the announcement of a new world record and his time of 3:14:59, brushing off the suggestion that he'd run it so close deliberately: '...if only!'

That sub-3:15 improved his overall average finish time by another second, setting the new world record for 700 marathons at 3:17:55.

'So, what next?' asked an interviewer, minutes after Steve had finished. It was a good question, although maybe a little soon to be asking it! However, Steve had his response ready: Perhaps 700 sub-3:30s? Maybe 500 sub-3:20s? The next century landmark – 800 in the fastest average time? A few more sub-3:15s? Plus, trying to improve the record average finish times for his fastest 500, 600 and 700 marathons by replacing slower times with faster ones, making them harder for anyone to beat in the future. For whilst he genuinely hopes somebody will be inspired to go for his records, he's happy to hold on to them for a few years first! Ultimately, he has a deep down desire to reach 1000 marathons - especially if he can run them in fairly respectable finish times.

'To run 1000 averaging sub-3:30 would be fantastic. You could call it the ultimate multi-marathon record, doubling my original ambition, although one day, somebody else will probably go further. It's the human condition to keep pushing beyond what has previously been believed possible. Of course, 1000 is still some way off and all I can do is hope I remain fit, healthy and, indeed, motivated enough to try and go that far.'

According to former international athlete, Martin Yelling, Steve needn't worry. Reporting on Steve's 700 record performance on his 'Marathon Talk' podcast, he commented that Steve was an incredibly fit 53-year old with remarkable buff(!), who made running marathons in respectable times look easy, describing Steve's finishing grimace as: '...a beaming smile'!

Which proves beyond all doubt what a true star Steve Edwards is – for it is only the brightest stars who continue to shine no matter how they feel, so that all others see is their luminosity.

Long may he shine.

2011 - Meeting Daley Thompson CBE for BT Olympic Storytellers

*2012 - With grandson, Farren, becoming first person in the
world to run 500 sub-3:30s*

2012 - With grandchildren Farren, Alyssa & Courtney after running 500th sub-3:30

2013 - Receiving 1st MV50 prize from Langdale race director Rod Berry & Dr Ron Hill MBE after achieving the 600 marathons world record

2014 - Winning Enigma's 7-in-7 in new MV50 world record

2015 - Immediately after running a record 600th sub-3:30

2015 - After becoming the first Brit to run 300 sub-3:15s

2015 - Racing towards the 700 marathons world record at Bournemouth

Chapter 40

IN HIS OWN WORDS

'This book may have come to an end, but that doesn't mean it is the end – at least I hope not! For now, the journey continues. By the end of 2015, I'd managed to run another 46 marathons averaging 3:17, just maintaining an overall sub-3:18 average for all 706 marathons. Looking forward, I'd love to improve the 700 marathons record average to around 3:15 if I can. Running 700 sub-3:30s would achieve this, and, at the same time, may improve my 500 and 600 records.

'I could never have predicted that I'd be running so many marathons at this pace at my current age, given what my body has gone through over the years. Hopefully, that means I've found the right balance of training and the right formula with nutrition and hydration when it comes to recovery.

'Just as unpredictable, is the current interest in the sport of multi-marathon running, which continues to thrive with increasing numbers of marathon events in the UK - another reason I've been able to rack up more marathons than anticipated. It's certainly less stressful being able to run lots of races without having to travel so far. The logistics are simpler and it takes a lot less out of you. It's also less costly, although, unlike yesteryear, these days the race entry fee alone often exceeds the travel costs! When I think of all the travelling I did in 1991/92, going abroad practically every weekend to race, it's impossible to compare what I do today with what I did back then when just getting to a race was often more tiring than actually running it!

'Having talked about the 'what' and the 'how' about my running life, I guess I should now answer the 'why'. In the past, I've always answered this question with the obvious answers: I enjoy running and it keeps me incredibly fit; the camaraderie and social scene through which Teresa and I have made many new friends; the wonderful places we would never have visited had it not been for doing a race there. It's also been rewarding in terms of personal achievement and has provided an opportunity to put something back - supporting and competing in so many races has enabled me to contribute to the sport's grass roots, and raise around £25,000 for various charities.

'I'd also like to think that by setting and realising goals, my achievements as an ordinary runner, not an elite athlete, will give greater inspiration to others. I'm constantly surprised by how many people contact me, not just to acknowledge what I do, but also to tell me that they've been inspired to do something themselves. Reaching into people's hearts like that is both humbling and powerful.

'The body is a remarkable machine, and just like they say the human brain is underused, I also believe that true of the human body. It never ceases to amaze me just how well the body responds when pushed to its absolute limit! It's a fantastic feeling and you could say that I've long since become addicted to the adrenalin/endorphin rush. But more than that, it's a way of life. One that I feel privileged to have been a part of from a relatively early age and one I hope will continue into older age.

'And, while all those reasons are true, they are fairly predictable and understandable. But consider this: why on earth would anybody want to put themselves through the pain of running marathon after marathon, a brutal event that batters your body repeatedly, averaging one every 14 days for over 28 years, and continue to do so?

'Some may think that's exaggerating the effect. So, let me explain further. Assuming a stride rate of just over a metre, running a marathon is the equivalent of nearly 20,000 single semi leg squats on each leg, give or take a couple of thousand depending on your stride length. But that's from a sedentary position. When running, every time your foot lands you put up to four times your body weight through all your joints, depending on speed and gradient. The shock from that varies depending on terrain, concrete being the worst, closely followed by tarmac. That's why it's so important for me to alternate my training routes between road and grass, or compacted soil tracks/footpaths, where the ground is more forgiving. Little wonder then that after running a single marathon it's common for not only the legs to ache and stiffen up, but also back, shoulders, arms - pretty much all of the body has had to work hard to drive it over a distance of 26.2 miles. Which is why I'm convinced that maintaining good overall body strength and fitness has helped me run better, especially over long distances. I'm not just running to keep my body fit, but keeping my body fit to run. There is a difference.

'Someone once asked me if I could define the marathon as an event. This was my answer: "The marathon is widely known as the ultimate test of athletic endurance; 26.2 miles of running. A gruelling and punishing event that tests the limits of one's resolve to overcome fear with sheer guts and determination."

'Of course, running knows no bounds, and with ultra marathon events becoming increasingly popular with distances up to and beyond 100 miles being tackled in extreme events around the world, the marathon distance for some doesn't pose the same challenge anymore. However, as has been reiterated throughout this book, there is no such thing as an easy marathon. Indeed, there is no such thing as an easy race. If you run hard enough and to the best of your ability, whatever distance, it places a gruelling demand on your body. And that one race doesn't take account of all the hours of constant training day after day, week after week and, indeed, year after year, if you want to partake in the sport for a long time. The marathon is also the longest recognised running event in the modern Olympics and, therefore, most people probably consider it the ultimate running distance when measuring fitness. And, returning to the 20,000 or so single semi leg squats on each leg with up to four times body weight of force as each foot lands, the marathon does indeed batter the body, no question.

'So, knowing all that, the question rather than being answered, becomes a bigger, still unanswered question: why on earth would you want to put yourself through all that? Perhaps do it once to tick it off a bucket list, but why do it repeatedly?

'The truth, yes, I enjoy running – as a pastime, but running as fast as I can over a specific distance, it hurts! So no, I don't like that pain, who would? I suspect most other people, including professional athletes, don't like that pain either if they're totally honest. Did I really say that – I don't enjoy running races? Well, it's not quite as simple as that - it's a strange one. In a masochistic sort of way, yes, I do, I enjoy the competition. For me, there are always two separate races going on during an event, the one against others and the one against myself. I also enjoy the after - the euphoria, the endorphin rush, the hot shower; simple things that seem so much better after my body's been through the mill. There's no better cup of tea than the one I have straight after a hard race! After pushing my body to its limits, things normally taken for granted become much more valued, which is, perhaps, no bad thing. But you do have to go through that pain to *really* appreciate them!

'So, running races is a love/hate thing then? Yes, that's exactly it. The other thing I like about running is that it's something that doesn't rely on others. Yes, it's nice to run with others, but you can also do it alone. I remember vividly all through my childhood being ostracised from team sport by my immediate peers and feeling useless. Not because I wasn't capable, but because I was different to everyone else and that hurt because I did enjoy team sports, especially football and cricket. That inevitably led to me having to play sport with younger kids where I was accepted, but when I look back I realise it wasn't the same. For one, I missed out on valuable development in those areas simply because I wasn't playing with my peers. It stands to reason that younger kids weren't as much of a challenge. So, my progression in those sports wasn't as good as it might have been.

'When I became a young adult, I gradually became accepted. However, I will never forget what not being accepted as a kid (family aside), felt like. After running my first marathon and subsequent races, I realised that this simple action of putting one foot in front of the other as fast as possible not only gave me a freedom to enjoy something by myself, but an opportunity to prove to others that I was capable. And although I didn't need to run with others to be able to do it, if there was an opportunity to do that, then that worked too. However, over the course of my life, I would say I've done most of my training on my own. As mentioned in this book, I don't feel particularly comfortable interacting with large groups of people and, unlike most other sports that just happen to be team sports, I feel most comfortable doing something that I can do on my own.

'Looking deeper, running has made me feel good about myself. It has raised my confidence levels to a height that I hadn't experienced in my earlier childhood - and that despite all the good things my parents did to help me grow up as a confident person. After a while I realised not only did it give me more confidence in myself as a person but also, more powerfully, it earned me respect from a wider audience. The respect I didn't have from my peers as a kid growing up. That said, I was raised to believe that respect must be earned, it wasn't an automatic right.

'I often think back to that kid in the school changing room who had little wetting accidents. Having a deformed hand was hard enough, but the weak bladder exacerbated the embarrassment. Children's cruelty knows no bounds and such cruelty made that kid feel just a few inches tall at times. That kid has since grown up and, through achievements in marathon running, now feels 100-foot high; a complete contrast.

'Some might say that what I do is an extreme way of making me feel better about myself and why put myself through so much pain. I guess, ultimately, only other athletes and sports-minded people will truly understand, as they've been there themselves. But for me, personally, I have that added reason; the mental torment I suffered as a kid was, in many ways, far worse than the physical pain I suffer in a marathon. Perhaps that's why my mental strength is so good at overcoming that physical pain?

'So, after 706 marathons and another very successful year, having achieved three more special milestones, this seems like an appropriate place for the book to end. I feel I've achieved my potential, having accomplished everything I ever set out to do, and more, since deciding back in 1988 that I wanted to try and become a successful multi-marathon runner. I also feel that I'm living on borrowed time, trying to maintain this intensity of running, and I don't mind admitting that my body is creaking as a result! Achieving the right balance is getting ever harder and, at times, I get so very tired with it all. Therefore, if I am fortunate enough to achieve further milestones, including the magical 1000 barrier, I will consider them a huge bonus.

'My mum always says that as a kid I did things the hard way rather than choosing the easier alternative. But I always persevered and eventually achieved my goal. I think that applies to my running too. I may have done it the hard way, but it was my way and, hopefully, the right way.'

STEVE'S STATS
(correct at publication):

Previous World Records:

Dec 1990 -   Youngest person to run 100 marathons - 28 years 3days

Mar 1992 -   Most marathons run in a 12-month period - 87, averaging 3:14 for each

May 1992 -   Youngest person to run 200 marathons - 29 years 161 days

May 2008 -   Fastest 10 marathons in 10 consecutive days - 35hrs 20mins, averaging 3:32 for each

Current World Records:

Mar 2009 -   400 marathons in fastest average finish time (see below)

May 2009 -   Fastest 10 marathons in 10 consecutive days in MV45 category - 33hrs 16min. (3:19 average)

Mar 2010 -   500 marathons in fastest average finish time (see below)

Sep 2013 -   600 marathons in fastest average finish time (see below)

Mar 2014 -   Fastest 7 marathons in 7 consecutive days in MV50 category - 23hrs 34mins (3:22 average)

Oct 2015 -   700 marathons in fastest average finish time (see below)

Century Landmark Average Finish Times for fastest:

100 marathons – 3:02:16

200 marathons – 3:06:17

300 marathons – 3:08:45 (British best)

400 marathons – 3:10:45 (World best)

500 marathons – 3:12:42 (World best)

600 marathons – 3:14:49 (World best)

700 marathons – 3:16:59 (World best)

Time Standard Summary:

* Sub 3s - 27
* Sub 3:05s - 72
* Sub 3:10s - 144
* Sub 3:15s - 308 (British best)
* Sub 3:20s - 447 (World best)
* Sub 3:25s - 548 (World best)
* Sub 3:30s - 640 (World best)

Other Stats:

* November 2012 - First person in world to run 500 sub-3:30 marathons
* September 2014 - First person in world to run 600 sub-3:30 marathons
* March 2015 - First Brit to run 400 sub-3:20 marathons
* June 2015 - First Brit to run 300 sub-3:15 marathons
* 53 marathon wins to date
* 100 marathons abroad in 34 different countries and 20 capital cities
* Marathons run in over 60 UK counties, including Scilly Isles and Outer Hebrides

* Official competitive marathon race run on average every 14 days for the last 28 years – and no DNFs – yet!

Half of the marathon medal collection!

STEVE EDWARDS

POWERED BY

Ambrotose®

0800 028 6071
mannatech.com

461